THE BIBLE IN ITS WORLD

David Noel Freedman, *General Editor*
Astrid B. Beck, *Associate Editor*

THE BIBLE IN ITS WORLD series offers an in-depth view of significant aspects of the biblical world. Reflecting current advances in scholarship, these volumes provide insights into the context of the Bible. Individual studies apply up-to-date historical, literary, cultural, and theological methods and techniques to enhance understanding of the biblical texts and their setting. Among the topics addressed are archaeology, geography, anthropology, history, linguistics, music, and religion as they apply to the Hebrew Bible/Old Testament, Apocrypha/Deuterocanonicals, and New Testament.

Contributors to THE BIBLE IN ITS WORLD are among the foremost authorities in their respective fields worldwide and represent a broad range of religious and institutional affiliations. Authors are charged to offer fresh interpretations that are scholarly, responsible, and engaging. Accessible to serious general readers and scholars alike, THE BIBLE IN ITS WORLD series will interest anyone who seeks a deeper understanding of the Bible and its world.

INJUSTICE MADE LEGAL

*Deuteronomic Law and the Plight of Widows,
Strangers, and Orphans in Ancient Israel*

HAROLD V. BENNETT

WILLIAM B. EERDMANS PUBLISHING COMPANY
GRAND RAPIDS, MICHIGAN / CAMBRIDGE, U.K.

Published by Wm. B. Eerdmans Publishing Co.
255 Jefferson Ave. S.E., Grand Rapids, Michigan 49503 /
P.O. Box 163, Cambridge CB3 9PU U.K.

Printed in the United States of America

07 06 05 04 03 02   7 6 5 4 3 2 1

Library of Congress Cataloging-in-Publication Data

Bennett, Harold V., 1962-
Injustice made legal: Deuteronomic law and the plight of widows,
strangers, and orphans in ancient Israel / Harold V. Bennett.
p.   cm.   — (Bible in its world)
Includes bibliographical references.
ISBN 0-8028-3909-6 (cloth: alk. paper)
1. Social legislation — Israel — History — To 1500.
2. Critical legal studies.   3. Social justice — Biblical teaching.
4. Bible. O.T. Deuteronomy — Social scientific criticism.
5 Widows in the Bible.   6. Strangers in the Bible.
7. Orphans in the Bible.   I. Title.   II. Series.

KBM1468.B46   2002
222'.15067 — dc21

2002072197

www.eerdmans.com

CONTENTS

v

PREFACE

This book grew out of my desire to identify and to understand the plight of the oppressed in ancient Israel. This research interest brought the legal codes in the Hebrew Bible into the mainstream of my analyses, for I reasoned that these texts provided windows into the norms and social conventions that governed the treatment of marginalized groups in the biblical communities. I therefore began to examine biblical law and to give particular attention to the rights and protection of minorities, for these social subgroups are often the oppressed in human societies. This examination led to an ambitious program of study that caused me to investigate the structural bases of oppression and to look carefully at the role law played in the bolstering of power and privilege in ancient Israelite society. The present book, then, explores the plight of widows, strangers, and orphans in ancient Israel. I rely heavily upon postmodern hermeneutical theorization and upon the social-scientific study of the Hebrew Bible. These methodological approaches position me to delineate these persons and to identify the institutional phenomena that exacerbated the plight of this social subgroup in ancient Israelite society.

Many of my ideas about oppressed groups and about the interplay between law and society in ancient Israel build upon the research of Douglas A. Knight and Randall C. Bailey. Their scholarship has decisively shaped my thinking about data in the Hebrew Bible, about the social world of ancient Israel, and about theoretical frameworks for reconstructing, discussing, and appreciating aspects of social life in ancient Israel. I owe them an intellectual debt that I am sure I will never be able to repay.

I would like to thank David Noel Freedman for reading and offering suggestions on an earlier draft of this book. The tireless efforts of Allen Myers, Jennifer Hoffman, and Todd Tremlin at Eerdmans Publishing Company did much to bring this book to publication. I am grateful to the faculty of the Department of Philosophy and Religion at Morehouse College in Atlanta, Georgia, for counsel and encouragement that helped me to focus on my research and to finish this book in a timely fashion.

This book would never have reached publication without the sacrifice and support of the five people with whom I share my daily life: Valerie, my wife; Quinton and Imani, my children; and Jacqueline and Lola, my mother and mother-in-law. Thank you for cheering me on and for giving me space to complete this project. Words cannot express my appreciation: just know that I am grateful for the privilege of having you in my life and that I love each of you immensely.

ABBREVIATIONS

ABD	D. N. Freedman, ed., *Anchor Bible Dictionary*
AfO	*Archiv für Orientforschung*
AHW	W. von Soden, *Akkadisches Handwörterbuch*
AnBib	Analecta biblica
ANE	ancient Near East
ANET	J. B. Pritchard, ed., *Ancient Near Eastern Texts*
ATR	*Anglican Theological Review*
BA	*Biblical Archaeologist*
BASOR	*Bulletin of the American Schools of Oriental Research*
BC	Book of the Covenant
BDB	F. Brown, S. R. Driver, and C. A. Briggs, *Hebrew and English Lexicon of the Old Testament*
Bib	*Biblica*
BN	*Biblische Notizen*
BR	*Biblical Research*
BSac	*Bibliotheca Sacra*
BTB	*Biblical Theology Bulletin*
BZAW	Beihefte zur ZAW
CA	*Current Anthropology*
CAD	*The Assyrian Dictionary of the Oriental Institute of the University of Chicago*
CBQ	*Catholic Biblical Quarterly*
DC	Deuteronomic Code

DtrH	Deuteronomistic History
EncJud	*Encyclopaedia Judaica* (1971)
ETL	*Ephemerides theologicae lovanienses*
EvQ	*Evangelical Quarterly*
EvT	*Evangelische Theologie*
GTJ	*Grace Theological Journal*
H	Holiness Code
HB	Hebrew Bible
ICC	International Critical Commentary
IDB	G. A. Buttrick, ed., *Interpreter's Dictionary of the Bible*
IEJ	*Israel Exploration Journal*
Int	*Interpretation*
JAAR	*Journal of the American Academy of Religion*
JAOS	*Journal of the American Oriental Society*
JBL	*Journal of Biblical Literature*
JBS	*Journal of Black Studies*
JETS	*Journal of the Evangelical Theological Society*
JNES	*Journal of Near Eastern Studies*
JNWSL	*Journal of Northwestern Semitic Literature*
JSOT	*Journal for the Study of the Old Testament*
JSOTSup	Journal for the Study of the Old Testament–Supplement Series
JSS	*Journal of Semitic Studies*
LH	Laws of Hammurabi
LXX	Septuagint
MAL	Middle Assyrian laws
MT	Masoretic Text
OBT	Overtures to Biblical Theology
OTL	Old Testament Library
PEQ	*Palestine Exploration Quarterly*
RSV	Revised Standard Version
SBLDS	Society of Biblical Literature Dissertation Series
SBLSP	Society of Biblical Literature Seminar Papers
SJOT	*Scandinavian Journal of the Old Testament*
TDOT	G. J. Botterweck and H. Ringgren, eds., *Theological Dictionary of the Old Testament*
TS	*Theological Studies*
TWAT	G. J. Botterweck and H. Ringgren, eds., *Theologische Wörterbuch zum Alten Testament*
TynBul	*Tyndale Bulletin*

VT	*Vetus Testamentum*
VTSup	Vetus Testamentum, Supplements
WW	*Word and World*
ZAW	*Zeitschrift für die alttestamentliche Wissenschaft*
ZEE	*Zeitschrift für evangelische Ethik*
ZTK	*Zeitschrift für Theologie und Kirche*

Chapter 1

PROLEGOMENON

Deut 14:22-29; 16:9-12, 13-15; 24:17-18, 19-22; and 26:12-15 purport to improve the circumstances of widows, strangers, and orphans in ancient Israelite society. These laws, on the one hand, treat the presentation, consumption, and allocation of wheat, fruits, wine, and meat (14:22-29 and 26:12-15); the celebration of major agricultural festivals (16:9-12 and 13-15); security for loans (24:17-18); and entitlement with respect to gleanings in the biblical communities (24:19-22). On the other hand, they treat widows, strangers, and orphans as a social group. This literary feature suggests that points of contact were present among the social conditions of these types of people. Since these codes treat these types of persons as a category of people and claim to offer public relief to them, it is plausible that these persons were a category of socially weak, vulnerable human beings in ancient Israel. Four interesting research questions about these legal prescriptions, then, suggest themselves: What social characteristic did the widow, stranger, and orphan in these regulations share? What socio-historical issues provoked the drafting of these codes? Were these legal injunctions part of a larger political-economic program? What role did these laws play in the circumstances of these sorts of persons in the biblical communities?

History of Scholarship

F. C. Fensham, H. von Waldow, P. C. Craigie, A. D. H. Mayes, B. Malchow, L. Epsztein, and F. Crüsemann produced important secondary literature on the DC. These scholars try to answer questions about the Deuteronomic regulations governing behavior toward widows, strangers, and orphans and about the relationship of these codes to the dilemma of these persons.[1] Fensham places these laws into a comparative framework. He gathers and surveys texts from Mesopotamia, Egypt, and Ugarit and shows that the protection of vulnerable subgroups and the needy is a common theme in literature throughout the ANE; consequently, he argues that the concern for ameliorating the predicaments of widows, orphans, and other vulnerable subgroups was a feature of communities throughout the ANE. Fensham suggests also that this custom of providing welfare services and safety nets for vulnerable social subgroups — categories of people without means of socioeconomic support and legal protection in the ANE — contributed to the drafting of the legal injunctions in Deuteronomy that treat widows, strangers, and orphans, and to efforts to allocate scarce resources to socially weak persons in ancient Israelite society. Fensham writes about social welfare programs in the ANE:

> The protection of widow, orphan, and the poor was the common policy of the ancient Near East. It was not started by the spirit of Israelite propheticism or by the spirit of propheticism as such. From the earliest times on a strong king promulgated stipulations in connection with protection of this group. Such protection was seen as a virtue of god,

---

1. F. C. Fensham, "Widow, Orphan, and the Poor in Ancient Near Eastern Legal and Wisdom Literature," *JNES* 21 (April 1962): 129-39; H. Eberhard von Waldow, "Social Responsibility and Social Structure in Early Israel," *CBQ* 32 (1970): 182-204; P. C. Craigie, *The Book of Deuteronomy* (Grand Rapids: Eerdmans, 1976), pp. 233-34, 244-47, 310-24; A. D. H. Mayes, *Deuteronomy* (Grand Rapids: Eerdmans, 1991), pp. 245-46, 259-61, 326-27, and 335-37; Bruce V. Malchow, *Social Justice in the Hebrew Bible* (Collegeville, Minn.: Liturgical Press, 1996), pp. 8-30; Léon Epsztein, *Social Justice in the Ancient Near East and the People of the Bible*, trans. John Bowden (London: SCM Press, 1986), pp. 113-18; and Frank Crüsemann, *The Torah: Theology and Social History of Old Testament Law*, trans. Allan W. Mahnke (Minneapolis: Fortress, 1996), pp. 215-34. A major publication that identifies issues that are at the heart of elucidating the relationship between Deut 14:22-29; 16:9-12, 13-15; 24:17-18, 19-22; and 26:12-15 and the plight of widows, strangers, and orphans in the DC is Gerhard von Rad, *Deuteronomy*, trans. Doretha Barton, OTL (Philadelphia: Westminster, 1966).

kings, and judges. It was a policy of virtue, a policy which proved the piety and virtue of a ruler. Great Mesopotamian kings like Urukagina, Ur-Nammu and Hammurapi boast in their legal inscriptions that they have accomplished this principle. Success was not possible if this principle was not carried out. It is also obvious that this policy was closely connected to social reform or a new legal promulgation.[2]

Von Waldow suggests that priests drafted Deut 14:22-29; 16:9-12, 13-15; 24:17-18, 19-22; and 26:12-15 in response to fresh socioeconomic dynamics in the North. He argues that the Israelite monarchy created a new socioeconomic milieu in the biblical communities, and that this development exacerbated the plight of widows, strangers, and orphans, *personae miserabiles,* in ancient Israel; consequently, he declares that priests reinterpreted extant regulations regarding the presentation and distribution of tithes or produce, the celebration of agricultural festivals, and the allocation of grains, fruits, and other produce that remained in the fields, and reformulated these laws in order to ameliorate the plight of socially weak human beings in ancient Israelite society. Regarding laws in the DC that treat the defense of vulnerable people in ancient Israel, von Waldow states: "Here we have the results of the attempt to actualize and reinterpret the ancient law traditions so that they may better meet the needs of a new time. Now it is acknowledged that there will always be 'poor and needy brothers' (Dt 15,11). What the ancient order tried by all means to avert is now a matter of course. The question is not any longer, how to prevent people from being impoverished, but, rather, how to ease the fate of the poor fellow citizen. Following this tendency, ancient regulations are given a new meaning."[3]

Points of contact exist among Craigie, Mayes, and Epsztein on the relationship of Deut 14:22-29; 16:9-12, 13-15; 24:17-18, 19-22; and 26:12-15 to the plight of widows, strangers, and orphans in the biblical communities. These scholars acknowledge that these laws sought to rectify economic disproportion among these types of persons and inveighed against taking advantage of them; consequently, they contend that these codes supplied resources and provided services that ameliorated the quality of life for these types of people in the biblical communities. Furthermore, these critics link

2. Fensham, p. 129.
3. Von Waldow, p. 197.

the formulation of these codes to a widespread socioethical consciousness in the biblical communities, namely, to a special interest among a politico-economic subgroup that committed itself to caring for those who were without a steady means of support and legal defense. Craigie, Mayes, and Epsztein, therefore, maintain that a philanthropic disposition among a collectivity of social actors provoked the drafting of these legal injunctions.[4]

Malchow follows the lead of Fensham by contending that these legal prescriptions reflect the ancient Near Eastern custom of providing basic services to persons who were without means for economic and legal support. He discloses that a special interest in the plight of vulnerable social subgroups was a dominant theme in the African literature.[5] Although Malchow concedes that these regulations echo notions about the treatment of vulnerable people that are present in literature from Mesopotamia and Egypt, he raises questions about the sociohistoric dynamics in the biblical communities that contributed to the formulation of these laws. He argues that centralization and urbanization altered greatly the socioeconomic infrastructure of the tribal confederacy, and that the appearance of an elite ruling class and an impoverished underclass was concomitant with the formation of the state in ancient Israel. Malchow declares regarding socioeconomic asymmetry in areas in the North during periods in ancient Israelite history: "In Samaria, the eighth-century capital of the North, the luxurious homes of the rich, decorated with imported ivory, have been uncovered. Thus, archaeology shows Israel's class divisions. This, then, is the way in which the class structure of Israel developed and the setting of its appeals for social justice."[6]

Malchow, therefore, argues that socioeconomic conflict was widespread in the biblical communities after the appearance of the monarchy, and that this phenomenon increased the buying and selling of commodities on the societal and individual level. Consequently, he proposes that this shift in milieu contributed to widespread injustices and to the drafting of laws that called for the redistribution of wealth, for impartial court proceedings, and for charitable morality toward widows, strangers, and or-

---

4. See Craigie, pp. 233-34, 310-11; Mayes, *Deuteronomy*, pp. 246, 261, and 335-36; and Epsztein, pp. 113-18.

5. Malchow, pp. 2-3.

6. Malchow, p. 12.

phans in ancient Israelite society. He particularly declares that severe economic disparity was widespread in the North, and that by the eighth century B.C.E. this phenomenon contributed to the mistreatment of vulnerable groups. Thus he provides a context for arguing that these regulations circulated first in the North, and that subgroups in the North formulated them to suppress actions that impoverished widows, strangers, and orphans in ancient Israelite society.[7]

Crüsemann places these statutes into a sociohistoric framework. He identifies a faction, and he provides insight into the dynamics that incited this camp to place these moral injunctions into a legal corpus. He particularly argues that the people of the land (ʿam hāʾāreṣ) incorporated these laws into the DC during the reign of Josiah. He argues that these laws are adaptations or expansions of extant regulations. He contends that the DC is a composite: it is a reworking of the BC and a reformulation of older subgroups of laws that were present in ancient Israelite society. Several conclusions therefore become plausible: (a) Deut 14:22-29 and 26:12-15 are expansions of Deut 12:15-19, for Deut 12:15-19 is a distinct, older regulation that treats the presentation and distribution of tithes in the biblical communities; (b) Deut 16:9-12, 13-15 is a reworking of Exod 23:14-17, for Exod 23:14-17 is an older subgroup of regulations about the observance of cultic festivals in ancient Israelite society; (c) Deut 24:17-18 is a later version of Exod 22:21-24; 23:9, for these codes in the BC protect the rights of vulnerable groups; and (d) Deut 24:19-22 builds upon Exod 23:10-11, for this code provides insight into the distribution of gleanings in early Israel.[8] The most distinctive point about the position Crüsemann takes regarding the widow/stranger/orphan regulations in Deut 12–26, however, is the significance he assigns to Deut 14:22-29 and 26:12-15. According to Crüsemann, this law is a window on the theological and political underpinnings of Deuteronomy, for it shows that the local farmers owe no one but the deity. He therefore suggests that the freedom from paying tithes of crops, wine, oil, and meat to the monarchy and the privilege of sharing these items with Yahweh induced the formulation of Deut 14:22-29 and 26:12-15.[9]

Crüsemann argues elsewhere that a subgroup which championed a

---

7. Malchow, pp. 20-29.

8. "Early Israel" in this chapter denotes the biblical communities from 1200 to 1000 B.C.E. For treatment on the relationship of the Covenant Code to this period, see Dale Patrick, Old Testament Law (Atlanta: John Knox, 1985), p. 65; and Crüsemann, p. 197.

9. Crüsemann, p. 221.

philanthropic social theory was present in ancient Israelite society.[10] He posits also that ideas among this faction, e.g., notions about munificence, shaped a public welfare system for widows, strangers, and orphans. He accordingly links laws in Deuteronomy that prescribe morality toward these persons to this camp, and he implies that the relief program of this politico-economic subgroup was an altruistic effort to ameliorate the plight of the underclass. He asserts that

> The laws regarding tithing and the regular forgiveness of debts are the most innovative and radical prescription, but they should be understood as part of a broader legislation whose structure must be examined. All of the laws are intended to provide materially and socially for the problem groups of the society of the period. The laws seek to prevent or at least to make it more difficult for the free, landowning Israelites, the stratum distinguished by the exodus and the gift of (the) land, from falling into the whirlpool of social decline. The context of these laws demonstrates a well-thought-out social safety net. It reveals itself best when viewed from the perspective of an Israelite farmer.[11]

Critique and Thesis

The scholars cited in this chapter help to answer questions about the circumstances that provoked the drafting of the widow, stranger, and orphan regulations in Deut 12–26 and about the role these laws played in the biblical communities. One claim is that these injunctions are reworkings of earlier regulations on the presentation and consumption of tithes, the celebration of cultic festivals, loans to the vulnerable, and the allocation of gleanings in the biblical communities. These scholars propose that older laws on these issues are present in the BC, and that this body of law is a literary basis for the DC. These scholars therefore suggest that Deut 12:15-19 informs Deut 14:22-29 and 26:12-15. Also, these commentators proffer Exod 23:14-17 as the basis of Deut 16:9-12, 13-15. Further, they contend that Exod 22:21-24; 23:9-11 is the textual basis of Deut 24:17-18 and 19-22.

A second proposition is that the dilemma of widows, strangers, and

---

10. Crüsemann, pp. 225-34.
11. Crüsemann, p. 231.

orphans was a social problem in ancient Israel prior to the drafting of these codes.[12] Fensham, von Waldow, Craigie, Mayes, Malchow, Epsztein, and Crüsemann note that texts that deal with the plight of this class of people were present elsewhere in the HB, and that regulations that deal with the conditions of widows, strangers, and orphans are present in the BC, the oldest legal corpus in the Pentateuch. These assumptions compel these critics to argue that the plight of these types of persons attracted the attention of subgroups in the biblical communities prior to the formation of the state in ancient Israel. But these critics argue that the dilemma of widows, strangers, and orphans became a significant problematic after the appearance of the state, for the concomitants of the monarchy, e.g., urbanization, social stratification, bureaucracy, and the ascendancy of a mercantile economy, spawned the formulation of Deut 14:22-29; 16:9-12, 13-15; 24:17-18, 19-22; and 26:12-15.

A third claim is the effect of these legal injunctions in the lives of widows, strangers, and orphans in the biblical communities. The commentators cited in this chapter posit that these codes prescribed public assistance and protective services for this category of socially weak, vulnerable persons, and that these types of moral injunctions established and legitimized a new public relief system that ameliorated their circumstances in ancient Israelite society. Craigie, for example, states that the system for the relief of these types of persons — the welfare program that stemmed from these laws — improved their circumstances. "Those without regular means of subsistence, such as aliens, widows, and orphans, were thrown onto God, the Lord of the community, for provision. In receiving it from the tithe, which properly belonged to God, their needs were met."[13] Traditional scholarship, therefore, argues that the widow, stranger, and orphan laws in the DC ameliorated the circumstances of this class of people, and that they enabled these types of persons to be self-supporting and to live with a degree of independence in the biblical communities. Conventional scholarship, then, advocates the position that these laws were part of an efficient social welfare system — or in the words of Crüsemann, a well-thought-out social safety net — for widows, strangers, and orphans in the biblical communities.[14]

---

12. In this study "social problem" means a major socioeconomic dilemma in a human community that warrants improvement or elimination.

13. Craigie, p. 234.

14. Crüsemann, p. 231.

A fourth claim is that the drafting of these laws was a conscious, politico-economic activity in ancient Israel. This bolsters the probability that a camp served as a major source of ideas for social programs and laws in the biblical communities — social phenomena that influenced morality toward widows, strangers, and orphans. Perhaps this subgroup adopted its ideas about proper morality from local customs. If this is the case, it is possible to argue that legislators in the biblical communities simply reinstitutionalized norms and social conventions.[15] Thus scholarship on these codes suggests that regulations governing public assistance to widows, strangers, and orphans in the DC stemmed from a camp with a humanitarian ethos. For instance, Crüsemann avers: "The provisions of deuteronomic social law are often described as 'laws of humanity.' The sympathetic character indicated in this way might be typical of ancient legislation for the poor, but the label doesn't really express the radicality of the law nor its theological role in deuteronomic thinking."[16] Traditional scholarship, then, advocates the position that a revolutionary social idea about intervening into the lives of an element among the peasantry, out of a humanitarian concern, circulated among legislators, and that this consciousness was a precipitating factor for the drafting of laws in the DC that prescribe morality toward widows, strangers, and orphans in ancient Israel.

While the commentators cited in this chapter bring into play ideas that help to identify the sociohistoric issues that provoked the drafting of Deut 14:22-29; 16:9-12, 13-15; 24:17-18, 19-22; and 26:12-15, and that throw light on the role these regulations played in the situation of a category of vulnerable, socially powerless persons in the biblical communities, several key questions suggest themselves. A group of issues centers in the claim that these laws are a reworking of extant cultic and social regulations from social subgroups and institutions in the biblical communities. These scholars work from the position that the Deuteronomic widow/stranger/orphan texts are adaptations of earlier laws that circulated among social groups in ancient Israel, and that a political-economic subgroup incorporated them into a body of law by the seventh century B.C.E. This point of view suggests that the date of these codes might be different from the date of the DC, and it leaves questions unanswered about the date they were

---

15. See Peter J. Haas, "'Die He Shall Surely Die': The Structure of Homicide in Biblical Law," in *Thinking Biblical Law,* ed. Dale Patrick, Semeia 45 (Atlanta: Scholars, 1989), p. 74.

16. Crüsemann, p. 224.

drafted. While the earlier commentators on these laws provide insight into the complex of historical factors that converged to prompt a camp in the biblical community to place miscellaneous regulations into a single legal corpus in Jerusalem during the seventh century B.C.E., these scholars do not examine the historical factors that account for the drafting of these laws in the first place.

A second issue stems from the fact that widows, strangers, and orphans appear as a collectivity in these codes. Yet these critics are silent about the identity of these persons and the rationale for their appearance here as a social group. On the one hand they simply presuppose that the social identification of widows, strangers, and orphans in ancient Israel is a self-evident phenomenon. On the other hand they assume that these types of people shared an everyday social feature, but they do not delineate the common thread among them in the legal injunctions. None of these critics provides insight into the sociohistoric feature(s) that caused the listing of these types of people together in these legal prescriptions. The absence of treatment on this issue obfuscates the common, everyday social characteristics that distinguished these persons from the other poor in ancient Israel and placed them at a distinct disadvantage in the biblical societies.

A third constellation of issues arises from the positions of the mentioned scholars on the conceptual paradigm for reading and discussing the interplay between law and society in ancient Israel. These scholars state that the laws under consideration rectified the conditions of widows, strangers, and orphans in the biblical communities, but they never identify the sociolegal framework that informs their investigation. The fact that they do not delineate a theoretical framework for discussing the role that these legal injunctions played in Israelite society is a critical flaw in the research of Fensham, von Waldow, Craigie, Mayes, Malchow, Epsztein, and Crüsemann into the widow, stranger, and orphan regulations in the DC. At the center of my critique is the claim that it is unsafe to work from the position that a consensus is present among legal scholars on the function of law in human societies generally.

A fourth problem proceeds from the fact that the earlier commentators on these passages indicate that the creation of legal prescriptions was a deliberate phenomenon in ancient Israel. Thus the enactment of moral ideas into authoritative guidelines for human behavior might be a response to social unrest or to other dilemmas critical enough to threaten the interests of powerful social subgroups in the biblical communities.

What is more, the formulation of law provided significant opportunity for legislators in the biblical communities to make significant innovations in extant legal prescriptions. The scholars whose work is discussed in this chapter, however, leave this issue unexplored: they examine these laws independent of a concern about the relationship between these codes and economic and political interests in ancient Israel. While they state that the plight of widows, strangers, and orphans was a social problem, they disregard the fact that opportunities to advance self-interests accompanied the opportunity to compose regulations regarding the public assistance of vulnerable social subgroups in the biblical communities. Consequently, Fensham, von Waldow, Craigie, Mayes, Malchow, Epsztein, and Crüsemann examine those codes that are at the center of the present investigation without giving attention to the possibility that these laws were more beneficial to the formulators than to widows, strangers, and orphans: the destitute, vulnerable subgroup that is present in these regulations. In fact, it is possible that these moral injunctions protected the interests of power elites instead of diminishing the suffering and misery of these types of persons at moments in ancient Israelite history.

The absence of discussion about the perennial implications of Deut 14:22-29; 16:9-12, 13-15; 24:17-18, 19-22; and 26:12-15 for the predicament of widows, strangers, and orphans in the biblical communities from a perspective analogous to the vantage point of these types of people is a fifth problematic in the studies of the aforementioned scholars. At the heart of this problem is that these scholars do not discuss the consequences of these codes or the effects of this welfare system from the vantage point of a major social subgroup that is immediately affected by these laws, namely, widows, strangers, and orphans in the biblical societies. This book avers that variance of opinion might have existed among destitute, vulnerable social subgroups in biblical Israel on the same moral problems and issues with which they struggled. This research project, however, argues that dominant and subordinate social subgroups in human societies often hold competing loyalties and different bases for judging law and other social phenomena. Thus underclass persons — especially those who are socially and politically weak — might view law and public policy decisions differently from those socioeconomic elites who formulate social policy regarding public programs in a human community. Thus, scholars on law in the HB risk misunderstanding the role of law in ancient Israel, for they position themselves neither to raise questions about the role law played in the establishment of power and privilege nor to examine legal sanctions with a sensitivity to the ways individual legislations worked to the disadvantage of subgroups in the biblical communities.

Therefore this study builds upon the work of those scholars cited earlier in the project. In what follows I argue that widows, strangers, and orphans were part of a strategy to regulate the behavior and to shape the ideas of local peasant farmers regarding the distribution of goods in ancient Israel.[17] Specifically this project argues that Deut 14:22-29; 16:9-12, 13-15; 24:17-18, 19-22; and 26:12-15 exacerbated the plight of widows, strangers, and orphans — a category of socially weak but politically useful persons in the biblical communities — positioning intellectual elites to stave off potential uprisings by local peasant farmers in the North during the ninth century B.C.E.[18]

Thus this project examines legal injunctions in the DC that treat widows, strangers, and orphans with a concern for inequality and concealed sociopolitical interests. Launching an investigation into these types of moral injunctions with a consciousness about these social issues places the present project on social-scientific terrain.[19] Social-scientific methodology is an amalgamation of approaches, where angles of vision from the social sciences and humanities intertwine to form fresh methodological constructs. The aim of this perspective is to introduce paradigms for interpreting data in the HB, and for producing detailed representations of social history in ancient Israel. Social-scientific angles of vision on the biblical communities, therefore, help to develop possibilities on the inter-

17. Points of contact are present between the thesis in this book and a study on public relief programs in capitalistic societies. See Frances F. Piven and Richard A. Cloward, eds., *Regulating the Poor: The Functions of Public Welfare* (New York: Vintage Books, 1993).

18. The reasons for situating these codes in the North during the ninth century B.C.E. appear in chapter 5 of this project.

19. For examples of and discussion on social-scientific study of the HB and the biblical communities, see A. D. H. Mayes, *The Old Testament in Sociological Perspective* (London: Marshall Pickering, 1989); Frank Frick and Norman Gottwald, "The Social World of Ancient Israel," in *The Bible and Liberation,* ed. Norman K. Gottwald (Maryknoll, N.Y.: Orbis, 1989), pp. 149-65; J. W. Rogerson, "Anthropology and the Old Testament," in *The World of Ancient Israel: Sociological, Anthropological, and Political Approaches,* ed. R. E. Clements (Cambridge: Cambridge University Press, 1989); Norman Gottwald, ed., *Social Scientific Criticism of the Hebrew Bible and Its Social World: The Israelite Monarchy,* Semeia 37 (Decatur: Scholars, 1986); and Cyril S. Rodd, "On Applying a Sociological Theory to Biblical Studies," *JSOT* 19 (1981): 95-106.

nal dynamics of biblical Israel, an otherwise inaccessible community. Thus the next section identifies the legal paradigm for answering questions about the precipitating factors for the widow, stranger, and orphan codes in Deuteronomy and about the role these legal prescriptions could have played in the biblical communities.

Methodological Considerations

Deut 14:22-29; 16:9-12, 13-15; 24:17-18, 19-22; and 26:12-15 are facts, raw data only. It is important to add immediately that the HB nowhere tells the reader how to interpret the data it contains. Facts and the interpretation of facts are separate elements in academic inquiry; this issue is at the center of the complex relationship between historical consciousness and biblical scholarship and influences reading strategies among critics of the HB. Regarding the complex relationship between historical consciousness, biblical scholarship, and hermeneutical approaches to the HB, R. Weems states:

> Within recent years, there has been growing attention to the influence that readers themselves exert in interpreting texts. Meaning is no longer seen, as it has been in formalist circles, as the sole property of the text, and the reader is no longer viewed simply as one who is to perform certain technical operations (literary analysis, lexical studies, etc.) upon the text in order to extricate its carefully guarded, unadulterated message. Rather, meaning in contemporary discussions is viewed as emerging in the interaction between reader and text; that is, the stimulus of the text (language, metaphors, literary form, historical background, etc.) interacts or enters into exchange with the stimulus of the reader (background, education, cultural values, cosmology, biases, etc.). . . . In fact, one's socio-cultural and economic context exerts enormous influence upon not only how one reads, but what one reads, why one reads, and what one reads for.[20]

The present study on these Deuteronomic texts therefore brings into play the intellectual and the existential: it draws from contemporary theo-

20. Renita J. Weems, "Reading *Her Way* through the Struggle: African American Women and the Bible," in *Stony the Road We Trod: African American Biblical Interpretation,* ed. Cain H. Felder (Minneapolis: Fortress, 1991), p. 64.

ries of law and society and from the life experience of the scholar. It is important to mention that the academic framework for examining these regulations proceeds from critical theory.[21] This approach evaluates social phenomena with a special sensitivity to class, socioeconomic inequality, ideology, interests, and the consequences of issues for the everyday, practical affairs of social subgroups in human communities.[22]

Since 1970 critical theory has spawned three major legal trajectories: critical legal studies (CLS), feminist legal theory, and critical race theory (CRT). These movements use critical theory to discuss the role that law plays in human communities. CLS advocates the position that the formulation of legal prescriptions is indissociable from political and economic considerations. Feminist legal theory draws from the experience of women, and it argues that legal injunctions, if they do not in fact guarantee, at least contribute to the subordination and exploitation of women in American society. Critical race theory draws from the histories of Korean Americans, Chinese Americans, Japanese Americans, Hispanic Americans, and African Americans, and it cites evidence to support the claim that law protects the interests of social subgroups and impedes the progress of others in human societies.[23] Critical theorizing about law embraces a move-

21. About ten years ago Haas raised the question about social-scientific paradigms for analyzing subgroups of moral injunctions in the HB. In short, he argues also that one should analyze biblical law much in the same manner that one would examine laws in other human societies. See Haas, p. 68.

22. For a concise and insightful article on critical theory, see Göran Therborn, "Critical Theory and the Legacy of Twentieth-Century Marxism," in *The Blackwell Companion to Social Theory*, ed. Bryan S. Turner (Cambridge, Mass.: Blackwell, 1996), pp. 53-82. For detailed treatment in major ideas and writings that work from a critical perspective, see Roger S. Gottlieb, ed., *Key Concepts in Critical Theory* (Atlantic Highlands, N.J.: Humanities Press International, 1997); and Andrew Arato and Eike Gebhardt, eds., *The Frankfurt School Reader* (New York: Continuum, 1997).

23. For examples of and discussion on these critical perspectives, see Surya Prakash Sinha, *Jurisprudence: Legal Philosophy* (Saint Paul: West Publishing Co., 1993), pp. 296-346; Andrew Altman, *Critical Legal Studies: A Liberal Critique* (Princeton: Princeton University Press, 1990); Raymond Belliotti, *Justifying Law* (Philadelphia: Temple University Press, 1992), pp. 162-89; Kim Lane Scheppele, "Legal Theory and Social Contract," *Annual Review of Sociology*, Annual 20 (1994): 383-407; William Chambliss and Robert Seidman, *Law, Order, and Power* (Reading, Mass.: Addison-Wesley, 1982), pp. 72-73; Allan C. Hutchinson, *Critical Legal Studies* (Lanham, Md.: Rowman and Littlefield, 1989); David Trubek, "Where the Action Is: CLS and Empiricism," *Stanford Law Review* 36, nos. 1-2 (January 1984): 575-622; Charles Sampford, *The Disorder of Law: A Critique of Critical Legal Theory* (Oxford: Oxford Univer-

ment of sociologists, legal scholars, political scientists, and philosophers, whose research and professional work analyzes the role that laws play in maintaining relations of domination and subordination in American societies. This study cites Quinney, West, and Crenshaw, and it extrapolates the major program ideas of critical theorizing about the role of legislations in American societies from these scholars. R. Quinney, a sociologist whose work allows critical theory to shape his research into the social origins and function of legislations in the United States, provides a window on the main tenets of critical theorizing about law: "Society is characterized by diversity, conflict, coercion, and change, rather than by consensus and stability. Second, law is a *result* of the operation of interests, rather than an instrument that functions outside of particular interests. Though law may control interests, it is in the first place *created* by interests of specific persons and groups; it is seldom the product of the whole society. Law is made by men [*sic*], representing special interests, who have the power to translate their interests into public policy."[24]

---

sity Press, 1989); Roberto Unger, "The Critical Legal Studies Movement," *Harvard Law Review* 96, no. 3 (January 1983): 561-675; Cornel West, *Keeping Faith: Race and Philosophy in America* (New York: Routledge, 1994); Abraham L. Davis and Barbara Luck Graham, *The Supreme Court, Race, and Civil Rights* (Thousand Oaks, Calif.: Sage Publications, 1995); Mary Frances Berry, *Black Resistance–White Law: A History of Constitutional Racism in America* (New York: Viking Penguin Press, 1995); Derrick A. Bell, "Racial Realism," in *Critical Race Theory*, ed. Kimberlé Crenshaw et al. (New York: New Press, 1995), pp. 302-12; Harlon Dalton, "The Clouded Prism: Minority Critique of the Critical Legal Studies Movement," in *Critical Race Theory*, ed. Crenshaw, pp. 80-84; Angela P. Harris, "Forward: The Jurisprudence of Reconstruction. Symposium: Critical Race Theory," *California Law Review* 82, no. 4 (July 1994): 741-85; Robert Hayman, "The Color of Tradition: Critical Race Theory and Postmodern Constitutional Traditionalism," *Harvard Civil Rights–Civil Liberties Law Review* 30, no. 1 (winter 1995): 57-108; Robert Chang, "Toward an Asian American Legal Scholarship: Critical Race Theory, Post-structuralism, and Narrative Space," *California Law Review* 81, no. 5 (October 1993): 1241-1323; Gerald Torres and Kathryn Milun, "Translating 'Yonnondio' by Precedent and Evidence: The Mashpee Indian Case," in *Critical Race Theory*, ed. Crenshaw, pp. 177-90; bell hooks, *Feminist Theory: From Margin to Center* (Boston: South End Press, 1984); Mary Joe Frug, *Postmodern Legal Feminism* (New York: Routledge, 1992); Deborah L. Rhode, "Feminist Critical Theories," in *Feminist Legal Theory*, ed. Katherine T. Bartlett and Rosanne Kennedy (Boulder, Colo.: Westview Press, 1991), pp. 333-50; and Angela P. Harris, "Race and Essentialism in Feminist Legal Theory," in *Critical Race Theory: The Cutting Edge*, ed. Richard Delgado (Philadelphia: Temple University Press, 1995), pp. 253-66.

24. Richard Quinney, *The Social Reality of Crime* (Boston: Little, Brown, 1970), p. 35.

C. West states:

CLS helps us perceive legal systems as complicated structures of power which both shape and are shaped by weighty historical legacies of class exploitation, racial subjugation and gender subordination. The type of historical consciousness promoted by CLS is inseparable from theoretical reflection because attention to structures of power over time and space requires description and explanation of the dynamics of these structures. Such a requirement pushes one into the frightening wilderness of social, political and cultural theory.[25]

K. Crenshaw, a black feminist legal scholar, writes:

Although society's structures of thought have been constructed by elites out of a universe of possibilities, people reify these structures and clothe them with the illusion of necessity. Law is an essential feature in the illusion of necessity because it embodies and reinforces ideological assumptions about human relations which people accept as natural or even immutable. People act out their lives, mediate conflicts, and even perceive themselves with reference to the law. By accepting the bounds of law and ordering their lives according to its categories and relations, people think that they are confirming reality — the way things must be. Yet, by accepting the worldview implicit in the law, people are bound by its conceptual limitations. Thus, conflict and antagonism are contained: the legitimacy of the entire order is never seriously questioned.[26]

As was said above, Quinney, West, and Crenshaw reflect major perspectives among critical theorists about law. While these scholars draw from different sources of knowledge and explore distinct research questions, five shared ideas about law appear in their literature.

1. Critical theorizing about legal sanctions argues that law is a powerful institutional tool for social control. Law induces conformity by compelling members of human societies to keep their actions within well-defined limits. That is to say, legal sanctions advocate the position that certain acts are undesirable by imposing penalties on the perpetrators. Commendation and criticism are also informal types of social control, and each

25. Cornel West, "CLS and Liberal Critic," in his *Keeping Faith*, p. 220.

26. Kimberlé Williams Crenshaw, "Race, Reform and Retrenchment: Transformation and Legitimation in Antidiscrimination Law," in *Critical Race Theory*, ed. Crenshaw, pp. 108-9.

can influence proper behavior and encourage people to abide by cultural rules. Law, however, differs from these types of social control in that legal injunctions involve the enforcement of moral injunctions by a socially authorized third party. The role that legal sanctions play in society, then, is the major "object" for investigation, the salient point of interest, for critical theorizing about the intricacies of legal sanctions and society.

2. Critical theorizing about law contends that legal sanctions are often the result of special interests in human communities. Underpinning this claim is the idea that laws reflect the ethos of powerful subgroups in societies. Critical theorizing about legal injunctions contends that elitist socioeconomic subdivisions in human communities hold common beliefs about such issues as superiority, property, human rights, and the distribution of goods, and that this subgroup has the resources to enact laws that establish and justify their ideas about these issues and about their positions of privilege. This shared consciousness and economic status not only provoked the drafting of legal sanctions that advantaged certain elitist subgroups in human societies but also provided the bases for the ascendancy of subgroups of moral injunctions in human communities.

3. Critical theory about law argues that legal sanctions often focus on categories of persons in human societies. These angles of vision contend that social criteria over which people have little or no control, e.g., race, gender, and class, become the basis for social subgrouping, and that membership in this subgroup is key in patterning social relations with people in this social subdivision. What is more, critical perspectives propose that a link is present between common social features and socioeconomic location in America; thus critical theorizing about law and legal sanctions posits that people who share the same social characteristics that differ from the norm often constitute the lower socioeconomic strata in the United States.

4. Critical theory about law claims that legal sanctions reflect conflict in human societies. These angles of vision work from the assumption that struggle is a recurrent feature of social life. Points of contact are present between this idea and Marxist readings of law, but critical theorizing about law posits that proponents of economic determinism, i.e., Marxist approaches to studying law and human societies, should pay equal attention to other features of social life. Critical legal scholarship, therefore, breaks with Marxist theorizing about law by introducing the subjective into the conversation on struggle in human societies. Critical theorizing about law

advocates the position that gender, race, class, culture, and other issues provoke the drafting of laws in human societies; consequently, critical theory regarding law emphasizes the role that overt struggle between competing subgroups plays in the formulation of legal sanctions.

5. Critical theorizing about law rests upon the premise that any framework that aids in understanding legal injunctions that deal with subordinate, vulnerable social subgroups in a human society should include the perspective of those vulnerable social subgroupings. Critical theory about law does not defend an essentialist position; this way of analyzing legal sanctions argues that competing ideas regarding social phenomena are present among persons in vulnerable social subgroups. Two beliefs in critical theory about law inform the proposition that the vantage point of vulnerable persons should shape paradigms that govern analyses of legal sanctions in human societies. Critical theory on legal injunctions, on the one hand, advocates the position that socioeconomically subordinate people view social phenomena differently than do dominant powerful people. Thus a different angle of vision on reality might be present between socioeconomic subgroups in human societies. On the other hand, critical theory argues that those socioeconomically subordinate people whose lives are affected by a layer of law have a valuable opinion regarding the function of laws and legal sanctions that purport to govern morality toward them. In a word, critical theory about law is pragmatic: it examines the effects of these legal injunctions in the everyday, common affairs of subgroups. Thus critical theory recognizes that the personal experience of vulnerable underclass persons provides important insight into the effects of laws and other social conventions in human societies.

This book borrows assumptions and analytical strategies from critical theory about legal injunctions in human societies, and it allows these phenomena to inform, not to control, the conceptual framework for explaining the drafting of Deut 14:22-29; 16:9-12, 13-15; 24:17-18, 19-22; and 26:12-15, and for identifying the effects of these codes among subgroups in the biblical communities. The usage of a legal framework that draws from critical theory, therefore, allows the present investigator to look out from his own center and to bring into play a point of view on the study of biblical law that stems from membership in a vulnerable underclass subgroup in a human society. Grounding the present legal framework in critical legal theory prevents a purely arbitrary approach to discussing the sociohistoric origins and effects of the legal injunctions in the biblical communities.

What is more, it links the legal framework in this book to a sociolegal tradition that has the support of philosophers and current legal scholars in this country.

First, the academic study of biblical law and features of ancient Israelite society justifies the usage of critical theory about law to inform the present investigation into these laws in the DC. As was said above, a number of the scholars whose work is discussed in this project propose that the BC is a literary basis for the DC, and that laws in the DC that treat widows, strangers, and orphans came into being after the appearance of the state in the biblical communities. M. Chaney postulates that the formation of the state in ancient Israel spawned a network of sociohistoric issues. He suggests that urbanization and political and economic centralization were concomitants of the Israelite monarchy, and that these phenomena contributed to the development of a tiered community where one group controlled large percentages of the means of production.[27] With the appearance of the Israelite monarchy, the construction of the first temple, and the foreign and domestic policy of Solomon and Omri, the social composition of the Israelite communities became more diverse and stratified. Prophetic circles, levels in cultic leadership, owners of large amounts of land, monarchic officials, sages, and other social groups became more apparent. Concomitant with political and economic centralization and urbanization in ancient Israel, the socioeconomic infrastructure was present for the emergence of an elite ruling class whose bases of social standing and economic affluence were not dependent upon land ownership completely. Critical theory about law presupposes the presence of competing socioeconomic subgroups in human communities, and it argues that it is problematic to explore laws and legal sanctions without regard for these entities and for the antagonisms that proceed from the presence of these social elements in human societies.[28]

Second, D. Knight and J. Barton aver that ideas about morality in the Hebrew Bible might not be conterminous with ideas about morality among the masses in ancient Israel.[29] Working from the position that

27. See Marvin L. Chaney, "Systemic Study of the Israelite Monarchy," in *Social Scientific Criticism of the Hebrew Bible and Its Social World*, pp. 53-76.

28. Chapter 2 of the present study identifies the major socioeconomic subgroups that were present in the biblical communities from which Deut 14:22-29; 16:9-12, 13-15; 24:17-18, 19-22; and 26:12-15 emerged.

29. Douglas A. Knight, "Introduction: Ethics, Ancient Israel, and the Hebrew Bible," in

Knight and Barton are correct, this study is led by their research into the ethics of ancient Israel to the conclusion that subgroups in the biblical communities separated acceptable moral ideas from unacceptable ones. What becomes clear, then, is that the moral points of view in the DC identify those ethical positions that were crucial to a substratum of people in the biblical community, and that the ethical positions in these laws were responses to issues that the drafters of these codes sought to prevent or restrain. As was said above, critical theory about law and legal sanctions rejects the idea that laws are above political-economic considerations, and it posits that legal codes often reflect the values of elitist subgroups in human societies.

Third, Deut 14:22-29; 16:9-12, 13-15; 24:17-18, 19-22; and 26:12-15 are human creations — a person or a subgroup in the biblical community produced these codes. This phenomenon justifies attentiveness to the overwhelmingly important role that self-interest plays in moral conduct. This book advocates the position that a plethora of motives informs moral action, but that it is a grave error to neglect the fact that human beings often behave in ways that proceed from their own self-regard. Since these legal prescriptions are human creations, this justifies raising questions about self-interests while exploring the function of these regulations in ancient Israel. These laws, then, become windows on the morality of a single person or camp. Competing notions on behavior toward vulnerable groups were present among persons in ancient Israel, and the moral points of view on the widow, stranger, and orphan regulations in Deut 12–26 identify those ethical issues that were crucial to a substratum of the biblical community. It is therefore probable that the ethical positions represented in these laws contain the ideas of a politico-economic entity regarding morality toward widows, strangers, and orphans, a major category of vulnerable persons in ancient Israel. Furthermore, Deut 14:22-29; 16:9-12, 13-15; 24:17-18, 19-22; and 26:12-15 regulate the dispensing of commodities in the biblical communities, and this phenomenon justifies suspicion concerning economic proclivity in these codes. Critical theory about law focuses on the human element in the drafting of laws and legal sanctions. It probes statutes and all legal data with a special interest in the contribution of legal

---

Ethics and Politics in the Hebrew Bible, ed. Douglas A. Knight, Semeia 66 (Atlanta: Scholars, 1986), pp. 1-8; and John Barton, *Ethics and the Old Testament* (Harrisburg, Pa.: Trinity Press International, 1998), pp. 5-6.

injunctions to the advantage of the overprivileged and to the disadvantage of the underprivileged in human societies.

Fourth, the scholars whose work informs the present study posit that the current Deuteronomic regulations that this book examines shape social conventions regarding the dispensing of goods and favors to widows, strangers, and orphans in the biblical communities. It, however, is reasonable to study these regulations from the perspective of these persons, for these codes immediately affected their lives. What is more, widows, strangers, and orphans were among the economically and politically powerless in ancient Israel. Critical theorizing about legal injunctions examines laws with a concern for the economically and politically powerless in a human society, and it allows the historical consciousness of these types of people to elucidate discussion on the effects of law in human societies. A theoretical framework informed by critical theory about law honors the perspective of a category of vulnerable persons in ancient Israelite society by treating these types of persons as the central subjects in the investigative process. By exploring these texts from a perspective that might be analogous to the perspective of vulnerable underclass persons in societies, scholars permit unheard voices in these codes to speak. What is more, this methodological approach introduces a different center from which to discuss law in the DC, and from which to reconstruct social history in ancient Israel.

Finally, Fensham, von Waldow, Craigie, Mayes, Malchow, Epsztein, and Crüsemann indicate that widows, strangers, and orphans appear as a social subgroup in Deut 14:22-29; 16:9-15; 24:17-18, 19-22; and 26:12-15. This innovation in these codes implies that these types of people shared a social feature, and that this socially relevant characteristic distinguished them from other vulnerable groups in the biblical communities and designated them for public relief. Critical theorizing about legal sanctions looks at categories of people and contends that social features over which people have little or no control connect these persons and become the criteria for their social grouping. Critical theorizing also proffers that membership in this social category positions people to become the victims of injustice and to experience socioeconomic disadvantage.

A conceptual framework that draws from critical theory about law, therefore, provides an analytic perspective that uses class, power, socioeconomic interest, pragmatism, and institutionalization to discuss texts in the DC. What is more, the adoption of this perspective positions scholars to examine aspects of these legal injunctions from a vantage point that is analogous to perspectives among widows, strangers, and orphans in the biblical communities: a viewpoint that is not present in contemporary scholarly discussions about the effects of these laws in this subgroup in the biblical communities.

Arrangement

Critical theory about law proposes that legal sanctions disadvantage categories of vulnerable underclass people in human societies. In this book I argue that widows, strangers, and orphans constitute a social group in the biblical community. Chapter 2 therefore delineates this social subgroup: (a) it identifies the terms in biblical Hebrew that appear as widow, stranger, and orphan in English translations of these laws; (b) it brings into play terms in literature from elsewhere in the ANE that might help delineate these persons in Deut 14:22-29; 16:9-12, 13-15; 24:17-18, 19-22; and 26:12-15; (c) it delineates the concepts of the widow, stranger, and orphan that emerge from the contexts in which these terms appear; (d) it suggests a possibility regarding the common social feature among this category of persons in these laws; and (e) it posits a possibility on the socioeconomic location of these persons in the biblical communities.

Critical theory also contends that laws and legal sanctions work to the advantage of ruling subgroups in human societies. This book argues that the contents of codes offer suggestions about the identity of those persons or subgroups whose interests are protected by layers of law, and about the effects of these laws in the lives of those people or subgroups whose interests these legal sanctions undermine. It becomes probable that the innovations in these legal prescriptions are clues to the identity of the drafters, the ultimate beneficiaries of these codes, and that the fresh additions to these regulations elucidate the part these codes played in the oppression of widows, strangers, and orphans, a group of vulnerable persons in the biblical societies. In Chapter 3 I examine the literary features of these laws by discussing the distinctive pedagogy, literary formulas, and grammatical features of these codes. Chapter 3 has five objectives: (a) to introduce my translation of these texts;[30] (b) to provide a textual analysis of these legal

---

30. Unless indicated otherwise, the translations of the biblical evidence in this book are mine.

injunctions; (c) to distinguish the prominent literary features and ideologies of these laws; (d) to provide a scholarly context for understanding the prominent aspects of these legal prescriptions; and (e) to examine the data that help to identify the drafters of these regulations.

Critical theory posits that law contributes to the oppression of vulnerable underclass social subgroups. In Chapter 4 I explore this phenomenon regarding the widow, stranger, and orphan regulations in the DC by working toward an understanding of oppression with respect to this class of persons. The present writer argues that the oppression of this class of people was more than an instance of suffering or an act of injustice, and points out how the innovations in these legal injunctions contributed to the oppression of this vulnerable social subgroup.

Critical theory proposes that social problems in human societies provide the opportunity for subgroups to draft laws that oppress vulnerable subgroups and protect their self-interests. As was said above, I argue that the concern of cultic officials to co-opt local peasant farmers in the North during the ninth century B.C.E. is a plausible backdrop against which to understand the drafting of the laws. In Chapter 5 I explore how a major social problem in the North, i.e., the taxation of local peasant farmers by the Omride administration, created a unique political-economic opportunity for cultic officials to incorporate extant ideas about charity toward widows, strangers, and orphans into their political-economic program. In this chapter I show also how this safety net could regulate the behavior of local peasant farmers in the North.

In Chapter 6 I summarize my argument and discuss the importance of critical theory for examining and interpreting biblical law, and for reconstructing social history in ancient Israel.

Chapter 2

TEXTS AND TERMS

Delineating the Widow, Stranger, and Orphan
and Identifying Their Socioeconomic Location

Introduction

Deut 14:22-29; 16:9-12, 13-15; 24:17-18, 19-22; and 26:12-15 represent widows, strangers, and orphans as a social subgroup, and these legal injunctions imply that these types of individuals were a category of underclass, socially weak persons in ancient Israel. Proposing that they were a subgroup of oppressed underclass persons brings into play two main questions: What was the common social feature of this category of human beings? What was the social location of this subgrouping in the biblical communities? Thus the objectives of this chapter are to depict the widow *('almānâ)*, stranger *(gēr)*, and orphan *(yātôm)*, and to identify a sociohistoric criterion that might account for the linking of these persons together in these codes. This chapter uses a fourfold approach to accomplish these aims: (1) it identifies and evaluates recent scholarship on the meanings of these terms in the HB; (2) it isolates texts and Semitic cognates that appear in literature from elsewhere in the ANE that might provide more insight into the identities of these types of persons; (3) it introduces a distinct sociological perspective that helps to delineate notions about the *gēr* in Deuteronomy; and (4) it delineates the prominent socioeconomic problem that might have been common among the *'almānâ, gēr,* and *yātôm.*[1]

---

1. With great caution this chapter introduces Semitic cognates for *'almānâ, gēr,* and *yātôm.* Several issues warrant this hesitancy: (1) Words may share the same radicals or an et-

The Widow in the Deuteronomic Code

History of Scholarship

Harry Hoffner, Léon Epsztein, and Paula Hiebert launch different investigations into the meaning of *'almānâ* in the HB.[2] These authors focus primarily on lexical, anthropological, textual, and comparative data, and are consequently helpful for delineating this type of person in ancient Israelite society. Hoffner surveys ancient Egyptian, Mesopotamian, and Ugaritic texts for lexical configurations that have points of contact with the consonantal pattern present in *'almānâ*. He points out that *'lmn* underlies *'almānâ*, and that this consonantal pattern was widespread in ancient Semitic languages: (a) *almattum ('almantum)* appears in Akkadian texts; (b) *'lmt ('almanatu)* is present in the Ugaritic literature; and (c) *'lmt ('almant)* appears in Phoenician. Hoffner declares that the *'lmt* consonantal pattern often described nouns with which it appeared. Regarding the socioeconomic predicament of the *'almānâ* in ancient Israel, he says this woman was bereft of a husband, masculine protector, living relatives, money, and influence.[3]

Epsztein implies that *'almānâ* denotes a woman whose husband is dead. He indicates that this type of person in ancient Israel was without legal protection and was liable for the economic debts left by her husband.

---

ymological connection and may not have the same meaning. (2) Attestation of *'almānâ, gēr,* and *yātôm* in the HB is widespread. Thus sufficient evidence is present in the HB for inferring possible meanings of some of these terms in ancient Israel. (3) It is probable that other words or expressions appear in the HB and in the ANE that have the same referents as *'almānâ, gēr,* and *yātôm.* (4) Words arranged in sense units are a key piece of evidence on the possible meaning of a word in a passage. Thus the context of a word, i.e., literary or historical, becomes an important issue for determining the meaning of a word. Moreover, selective exegesis of texts in the HB and in the ANE where these words are present positions this study to undertake a task that is manageable and to bring provisional closure to the present argument on the identities of these types of persons. For treatment on the capabilities and limitations of word studies and on clues for determining the meaning of words, see James Barr, *The Semantics of Biblical Language* (London: SCM Press, 1983).

2. Harry A. Hoffner, "אלמנה," in *TDOT* 1 (Grand Rapids: Wm. B. Eerdmans, 1977), pp. 287-91; Léon Epsztein, *Social Justice in the Ancient Near East and the People of the Bible,* trans. John Bowden (London: SCM Press, 1986); and Paula S. Hiebert, "'Whence Shall Help Come to Me?' The Biblical Widow," in *Gender and Difference in Ancient Israel,* ed. Peggy L. Day (Minneapolis: Fortress, 1989), pp. 125-41.

3. Hoffner, pp. 289-90.

Epsztein compares the dilemma of this type of individual in ancient Israel with the predicament of widows in societies in Mesopotamia, and he argues that her plight was more severe than that of widows in Assyria and Babylon. He therefore suggests that a concern with ameliorating her plight was present in Israel, and that this concern found expression particularly in subgroups of law in the Pentateuch which attempted to regulate morality toward this type of individual.[4]

Hiebert adduces evidence from the Middle Assyrian Laws (MAL), Priestly law, Gen 38, and the Psalter to support her position. She infers from these data that 'almānâ in the HB refers to a woman who was bereft of her husband and was without kinship ties. Num 30:10 is a chief piece of evidence in her argument on the social characteristics of this type of person, for it states that vows made by this individual and the gĕrûšâ (divorcée) were binding. It is noteworthy that Num 30:1-17 implies that vows made by women were subject to the approval of their fathers or husbands.[5] Num 30:10 suggests that no male in the biblical communities passed judgment on or authorized vows made by the 'almānâ. Hiebert argues that this type of person was without a male authority figure and without family ties. "The Hebrew 'almānâ then, like the gēr, existed on the fringes of society. In a society where kinship ties gave one identity, meaning, and protection, both the 'almānâ and the gēr had no such ties. Unlike the gēr, however, the 'almānâ lived in this liminal zone as a woman. Not only was she bereft of kin, but she was also without a male who ordinarily provided a woman with access to the public sphere."[6]

The idea that the 'almānâ was without kinship ties, then, motivates Hiebert to raise questions about her material endowment. She therefore suggests that bride wealth and the dowry were possible sources from which the 'almānâ drew sustenance. The focus on the Psalter and the degree to which she develops her argument on the economic support system of this type of person differentiate Hiebert's treatment of the 'almānâ from the analyses of Hoffner and Epsztein on the socioeconomic characteristics of this type of person in ancient Israelite society.

Thus the scholars cited in this chapter invite conversation about the sociological features of the 'almānâ in ancient Israel. On the one hand,

4. Epsztein, pp. 113-15.
5. More will be said about Num 30:1-17 shortly.
6. Hiebert, p. 130.

these scholars give sparse attention to the narrative material in DtrH. This issue is conspicuous in Hiebert's position on the social characteristics of the *'almānâ*, for she cites extensively from the Psalter and Gen 38. On the other hand, Hoffner and Hiebert state that this type of person was bereft of her husband and was without family ties.[7] These critics therefore raise as many issues as they settle. Is the *'almānâ* a woman without a living father-in-law? Is she without living natal brothers? Is she without living mature sons? Is she without living uncles? Is she without living nephews? Or is she without living mature daughters?

The next section, accordingly, begins the inquiry into the social characteristics of the *'almānâ*.[8] The strategy is to pose the aforementioned questions to the Mesopotamian and Syria-Palestinian literature that contains words that share the *'lmn* consonantal pattern, narratives in DtrH that contain *'almānâ*, and narratives in the HB where this word is not present but that provide insight into the predicament of this type of person in the biblical communities.

Widows in the Mesopotamian Literature

As Hoffner shows, points of contact are present between the term for widow in biblical Hebrew *('lmnh)* and terms for this type of individual in the Laws of Hammurabi (LH) and MAL. This study cites LH 177 and MAL 28, 33, and 34. This is the rationale for introducing these texts: (1) LH 177 and MAL 28, 33, and 34 contain terms that have points of contact with the HB; (2) LH 177 and MAL 28, 33, and 34 contain guidelines on behavior toward the individual denoted by the *'lmn* consonantal pattern in Mesopotamian societies; (3) the date for the codification of MAL 28, 33, and 34 is the eleventh century B.C.E., which is not far in time from the appearance of the BC, the oldest body of law in the HB that prescribes morality toward the *'almānâ* in ancient Israel; and (4) LH 177 and MAL 28, 33, and 34 provide insight into the social features of widows in Babylon and Assyria.

---

7. Epsztein is silent as to whether the *'almānâ* was without any living relatives.

8. Within this chapter the "social characteristics" refer to the presence of living adult males who are part of either her consanguineous family or larger network of relations.

Widows in the Laws of Hammurabi

LH 177 says:

> If a widow (*almattum*) whose children are still young should decide to enter another's house [remarry], she will not enter without (the prior approval of) the judges. When she enters another's house, the judges shall investigate the estate of her former husband, and they shall entrust the estate of her former husband to her later husband and that woman, and they shall have them record a tablet (inventorying the estate). They shall safeguard the estate and they shall raise the young children; they will not sell the household goods. Any buyer who buys the household goods of the children of a widow (*almattum*) shall forfeit his silver; the property shall revert to its owner.[9]

LH 177 treats the remarriage of widows and the distribution of the estate of the previous husband, and it is a window on the social characteristics of widows in Babylon during the eighteenth century B.C.E. While this law implies that the *almattum* has young children, it is silent on a larger kinship association. That is to say, LH 177 does not state if the *almattum* has any living natal brothers, nephews, uncles, mature daughters, or a father-in-law.

Widows in the Middle Assyrian Laws

MAL 28 says: "If a widow (*almattu*) should enter a man's house [remarry] and she is carrying her dead husband's surviving son with her (in her womb), he grows up in the house of the man who married her but no tablet of his adoption is written, he will not take an inheritance share from the estate of the one who raised him, and he will not be responsible for its debts; he shall take an inheritance share from the estate of his begetter in accordance with his portion."[10]

MAL 28 treats the remarriage of pregnant widows. What is more, information in this regulation implies that the inheritance rights of unborn children were at the center of controversy among subgroups in Assyria.

9. See Martha T. Roth, *Law Collections from Mesopotamia and Asia Minor* (Atlanta: Scholars, 1995), p. 116.
10. Roth, p. 163.

MAL 28 shows that unborn children of widows have no entitlement to the estate of the new husband. It also implies that the adoption of the unborn child by his/her stepfather entitles him/her to the estate of the stepfather. If the stepfather does not adopt the child, the child does not become liable for the economic debts of his/her stepfather.

MAL 33 provides insight into a plethora of issues, namely, circumstances that surround a woman who has no husband. It says: "If a woman is residing in her own father's house, her husband is dead, and she has sons, [. . .] or [if he so pleases], he shall give her into the protection of the household of her father-in-law. If her husband and her father-in-law are both dead and she has no son, she is indeed a widow *(almattu);* she shall go where she pleases."[11]

MAL 33 is a major piece of evidence for the social characteristics of the *almattu* in Mesopotamia. This law suggests that *almattu* delineates a woman who has neither husband nor male offspring. Moreover, it leaves open the possibility that she may remarry or enter a new conjugal relationship. It also states that if her father-in-law is not present, she can make her own decision concerning remarriage or entering another socioeconomic relationship.

MAL 34 treats the remarriage of a widow: "If a man should marry a widow *(almattu)* without her formal binding agreement and she resides in his house for two years, she is a wife; she shall not leave."[12]

While MAL 34 provides insight into the remarriage of the *almattu*, it is a window on conditions that prohibited this individual from leaving a new husband. This legal injunction indicates that if she remarried against her will and remains with her new husband for a stated period, she forfeits the right to terminate the relationship. MAL 34 raises questions about marriage in certain Mesopotamian communities and about the social characteristics of the *almattu* that would allow a man to marry her without her consent.

Information on the social characteristics of the *almattu* in Mesopotamian communities emerges from LH 177, MAL 28, 33, and 34. These injunctions are silent on a biological father, father-in-law, natal brothers, mature sons and daughters, nephews, uncles, and brothers-in-law, but they provide insight into the legal and economic problems that concern

11. Roth, p. 165.
12. Roth, p. 165.

widows and children of widows. They therefore are inconclusive for determining the social characteristics of widows, for they do not indicate if the absence of living adult male relatives was an existential problem of this type of person in Mesopotamian communities.

On the other hand, MAL 33 provides evidence upon which to base an answer about the social characteristics of widows elsewhere in the ANE. It suggests the satisfaction of three requirements before a woman became a widow. First, her husband must be dead. Second, her father-in-law must not be alive. Third, she must have no living sons.

To summarize, in the Mesopotamian legal data, husbands and minor children are present with widows in the code of Hammurabi, and fathers, sons, and new husbands are present with this person in the Middle Assyrian Laws (MAL 28 also mentions a fetus). MAL 33 is a basis for arguing that widows in Assyria had relatives, for it suggests that the father of this person is alive. The next section examines texts in the Ugaritic literature that contain the *'lmn* consonantal pattern.

Widows in the Ugaritic Literature

The Keret legend contains several citations of *'almnt*. In one place it says:

Let the widowed *('almnt)* (mother) indeed hire herself out,
the sick man take up (his) bed (and go),
the blind man indeed stumble along behind,
and let the newlywed husband go forth,
let him make away with his wife to another,
with his beloved to a stranger.[13]

This text is part of a larger story that recounts the preparation for a military campaign by Keret. He assembles an army that includes newlywed husbands and the sick. While this text recommends that the *'almnt* should enter a contractual agreement, it is silent on the motivation for this proposition. Perhaps Keret deployed her adult masculine family members and no more adult male relatives were available to protect her. This text therefore suggests that the *'almnt* was bereft of adult male relatives. Also, it

13. The Keret Legend, tablet 14, col. ii, ll. 97-102. See J. C. L. Gibson, *Canaanite Myths and Legends* (Edinburgh: T. & T. Clark, 1977), p. 84.

lends weight to the claim that this type of person had the right to enter legal agreements without the consent of an adult male relative.

A text that is present elsewhere in the Keret legend declares:

The lad *Yaṣṣib* departed,
he entered into (the presence of) his father,
(and) he lifted up his voice and cried:
"Hear, I beseech you, o noble Keret,
hearken and let (your) ear be attentive.
While bandits raid you turn (your) back,
and you entertain feuding rivals.
You have been brought down by your failing power.
You do not judge the cause of the widow ( ),
you do not try the case of the importunate,
you do not banish the extortioners of the poor,
you do not feed the orphan before your face
nor the widow *('almnt)* behind your back."[14]

Yaṣṣib complains about either the negligence or impropriety of Keret. Yet *Yaṣṣib* accuses him of malfeasance by pointing out that he allowed wickedness to run rampant in the community. This datum lists the *'almnt* with other oppressed persons, and it suggests that her protection was the duty of the king.

The Aqhat legend contains one citation of *'almnt:*

And behold! on the seventh day,
thereupon Daniel, man of Rapiu,
thereat the hero, man of He-of-Harnam,
raised himself up (and) sat at the entrance of the gate,
beneath the trees which were by the threshing-floor;
he judged the cause of the widow *('almnt),*
tried the case of the orphan.[15]

This passage implies that Daniel, the king, administered justice in the gate. While it declares that he paid attention to the case of the *'almnt,* it is silent about the familial situation of this type of person.

---

14. The Keret Legend, tablet 16, col. vi, ll. 39-50. See Gibson, p. 102.
15. The Aqhat Legend, tablet 17, col. v, ll. 4-8. See Gibson, p. 107.

The Ugaritic literature is silent on the social characteristics of the *'almnt*. These data do not mention biological fathers, natal brothers, uncles, fathers-in-law, or any other relation of the *'almnt*. This is a major discrepancy between the Ugaritic literature and the Mesopotamian literature. The Ugaritic data, therefore, become a basis for arguing that the onus for protecting the *'almnt* was on other individuals in the community. Perhaps this is a clue that this person had no adult male relatives who could function as an advocate for her. The next section examines data in the HB that contain the *'lmnh* consonantal pattern, and that provide information on social characteristics of this type of person in ancient Israelite society.

Widows in the HB

A common current runs through Hiebert and Hoffner, and it is agreement on the social characteristics of the *'lmnh* in the biblical communities. These scholars concur that she is bereft of living adult male relatives and is without kinship ties and protection. Hoffner says: "In Biblical Hebrew, the word *'almanah* has a completely negative nuance. It means a woman who has been divested of her male protector (husband, sons, often also brothers)."[16]

This study therefore reevaluates this angle of vision on the sociological characteristics of the *'lmnh* in ancient Israel, particularly the idea that she has living adult male relatives and family ties. Thus the next section delineates the *'lmnh* in the legal material in the HB.

Widows in the Legal Corpora of the HB

The *'lmnh* consonantal pattern is present in Exod 22:22 (= Hebr. 22:21) and Exod 22:24 (= Hebr. 22:23). Exod 22:22 is a prohibition against the mistreatment of her. This regulation contains no information on the social characteristics of this individual. Yet the passage lists the *yātôm* with the *'almānâ*. This text suggests that injustice toward both persons is unacceptable. In so doing, Exod 22:24 provides a window on possible social characteristics of the *'almānâ* during a certain period in the history of the biblical communities. Exod 22:24 says: "My anger will be aroused, and I will slay you with the sword; your wives will become widows, and your children

16. Hoffner, p. 288.

will become orphans." This passage therefore implies that a woman whose husband is dead is an *'almānâ*.

The *'almānâ* appears twice in the Holiness Code and once in the Priestly Code. These texts are Lev 21:14; 22:13; and Num 30:9 (= Hebr. 30:10). Lev 21:14 deals with the marriage of priests, and it states that a priest could not marry an *'almānâ*. What is more, this passage states that priests could marry neither a *gĕrûšâ* nor a prostitute *(ḥălālâ zōnâ)*. Maybe Lev 21:14 is a counterattack to marriages between priests and such women in the biblical communities. Yet it undermines the *'almānâ* acquiring a major source of economic support, for it is probable that subgroups of cultic officials in the biblical communities were among the affluent in ancient Israel, and that such women sought liaisons and even marriages with them.

Lev 22:13 deals with a subgroup of widows in the biblical communities. This text, however, considers the *'almānâ* who is the daughter of a priest. It indicates that if she has no children, she may return to her natal home. Yet the presence of the phrase "if she has no children" attracts attention. At the center of this issue is why the presence of children precludes her from returning to the house of her father. Perhaps the age and gender of the children are factors. Young children might create an economic hardship on the biological father of the *'almānâ*, for he might be unable to feed and clothe her and her dependent children. Since Lev 22:13 allows the daughter of a priest who is an *'almānâ* to return to her natal home after the death of her husband, it confirms that this type of woman was not without living adult male relatives in the biblical communities.

As was mentioned earlier in this chapter, Num 30:10 deals with pledges made by the *'almānâ*. This text implies that her vows were not subject to invalidation. This issue neither left room for the invalidation of vows made under duress nor provided opportunity for the negation of vows that exacerbated her predicament. The fact that vows made by her were binding might be a window on her social characteristics, for it implies that she had no adult male relative to whom she was accountable. Thus it is probable that the *'almānâ* was the object of exploitation in the biblical communities. Most texts in the legal corpora in the Pentateuch are silent about the social characteristics of the *'almānâ*. A text in the BC, however, indicates that this type of person has dependent children.

Widows in Narrative Texts in the HB

Gen 38:1-30 is a major piece of evidence on the 'almānâ in the biblical communities. In this pericope this consonantal pattern refers to Tamar, a woman who survives her husband. This literary unit also provides a window on sociological features of Tamar. Er, her husband, is dead. Yet neither the Hebrew nor the Greek of Gen 38 provides sociohistoric clues on reasons for his death. The syntax in Gen 38:7, however, leaves open the possibility that flaws in his personality account for his death, for Gen 38:7 implies that the wickedness of Er was the reason for his death.[17]

Gen 38:11 indicates that Tamar had living adult male relatives. It says: "And Judah said to Tamar his daughter-in-law, 'Return as a widow ('almānâ) in the house of your father until Shelah my son grows up.' Judah said this for he thought that Shelah would die like his brothers did, and Tamar returned to the house of her father." Gen 38:11 states that Shelah, the brother-in-law of Tamar; Judah, the father-in-law of Tamar; and some masculine members of the natal family of Tamar were alive. The probability that Judah relinquished responsibility for Tamar, and that she returned home to live out her life as a husbandless woman, is to what Gen 38:11 attests.

Second, Gen 38:8 leaves open the possibility that Tamar was sonless, not childless. In this text Judah tells Onan, the brother of Er, to perform the duty of the brother-in-law (yābām), for it was the responsibility of the living brothers of the deceased to impregnate their sister-in-law if their brother died childless. Consequently, it became Onan's obligation to have sex with Tamar, his sister-in-law, and to produce a descendant (zerā') for Er, his dead brother.[18] While this term could refer to male offspring or a

---

17. The fact that "evil" is a predicate adjective in the MT and LXX introduces the possibility that flaws were present in the personality of Er.

18. An inconsistency is present in the Greek version of Gen 38:8. In contrast to the MT, the LXX links marriage to the duty of the brother-in-law. It is possible that the custom in the biblical communities regarding the duty of the brother-in-law shapes moral action in the Tamar narrative also. This custom finds legal expression in Deut 25:5-10. Yet the legal formulation of this custom says nothing about which brother should perform the duty of the brother-in-law. What is more, evidence is lacking in Deut 25:5-10 on whether the one performing the duty of the brother-in-law was the choice of the wife of the dead man. In short, the levirate legislation implies that brothers of the dead man had the legal obligation to have intercourse with their dead brother's wife. The regulation does not mention that the brother of the dead man had to marry his sister-in-law; his option was to impregnate her. Perhaps

descendant in general, it is probable that in Gen 38:8 it denotes a male descendant. But Gen 38:8 does not exclude the possibility that Er fathered daughters by Tamar. Thus the Tamar story challenges the idea that the 'almānâ lacked family ties, for Gen 38:1-30 shows that she was not bereft of living adult male relatives. This text provides a basis for arguing that her husband is dead, and that she has no adult male relative who is willing to assume responsibility for her.

Second, 2 Sam 14:5-7 provides insight into the social characteristics of the 'almānâ in the biblical communities. It shows that Joab persuaded a woman from Tekoa to assume the identity of an 'almānâ and to recount a supposed event between her two sons.

> And the king said to her, "Who are you?" She said, "I am truly a widow, and my husband is dead. Your maidservant bore two sons, and they were wrestling with one another in the field and there was no one present to separate them; one struck the other and killed him. Behold, all my relatives arose against your maidservant, and they said, 'Hand over to us your son who struck his brother, and we will kill him in exchange for the life of his brother and exterminate the heir also.' If they kill my only son,[19] they will destroy the name of my husband and leave him no descendant on the earth."

The manner in which the woman describes herself attracts attention. She tells David that she is a widow ('iššâ 'almānā). She also indicates that she had two sons, and that one remains. Moreover, she states that her family sought to administer justice. 2 Sam 14:5-7, therefore, depicts an 'almānā, and it suggests that she had living adult male relatives, for it is probable that the adult male relatives administered justice.

2 Sam 20:3 is a report on the activity of David: "And David returned to his house in Jerusalem, and he took ten of his wives, his concubines, whom he left to watch the house, and he put them in the house under a guard. David provided provisions for them, but did not have sex with them. They were bound until they died, living like widows." This passage recounts that David returned to Jerusalem and sequestered ten of his concubines. He provides food, shelter, and physical protection for them but discontinues

---

the introduction of marriage in Gen 38:8 in the LXX is an attempt to make the custom of brothers having sex with their dead brothers' wives seem humane.

19. The text reads literally, If they "extinguish the only burning coal that remains."

his conjugal visits. His actions toward these women warrant the suggestion of the Deuteronomistic historian, namely, the insinuation that their predicament was analogous to, if not the same as, that of the ʾalmānâ in ancient Israelite society. It is conspicuous that an adult male protector is alive, namely, David, and that these women have sustenance and shelter. Yet 2 Sam 20:3 contends that points of contact are present between the dilemma of these women and the plight of widows in ancient Israel.

The Ruth legend provides more evidence on the social characteristics of widows in ancient Israel. It is striking that this story uses ʾēšet-hammēt and not ʾalmānâ to refer to Ruth, the heroine of the story.[20] The usage of the former term for Ruth and the latter term for Tamar in Gen 38:1-30 and for other husbandless women in the HB suggests that competing terms for women whose husbands were not alive were present in the biblical communities. It is possible that the usage of different terms in the HB to denote women who were bereft of their husbands is stylistic, and that it is an example of how different words may refer to the same reality.[21] Yet the Ruth narrative introduces Boaz, a kinsman of Ruth's dead husband, and it asserts that he was wealthy and influential in the community.[22] This description of Boaz shows that Ruth was not without a living adult male relative.

More evidence for identifying the social characteristics of the ʾalmānâ is present in 1 Kgs 7:13-14; 11:26; and 17:8-16. The former passage identifies Hiram, an adept artisan who adorns Solomon's temple: "King Solomon sent and took Hiram from Tyre. Hiram was the son of a widow from the tribe of Naphtali, and his father was from Tyre. Hiram was a craftsman of bronze, and he was filled with wisdom, understanding, and knowledge about all kinds of work with bronze, and he came to King Solomon and did all of his work." Furthermore, 1 Kgs 7:13-14 states that Hiram's mother was a widow. The text implies that Hiram worked deftly with metal, and it is probable that this expertise developed after many years of working with metals. It, then, is probable that Hiram was not a minor child. This text therefore identifies a woman with an adult son, and it states that she was a widow (ʾiššâ ʾalmānâ).

The mother of Jeroboam I was a widow. In fact, 1 Kgs 11:26 declares: Jeroboam son of Nebat, an Ephraimite from Zeredah, rebelled against

---

20. Ruth 4:5.
21. See Barr, pp. 116-17.
22. Ruth 2:1-23.

King Solomon. The name of his mother was Zeruah, and she was an *'iššâ* *'almānâ* and a servant of King Solomon. This text points out that she was bereft of her husband. It shows also that Jeroboam conspired against Solomon. Elsewhere in the pericope in which this text appears, information is present concerning Jeroboam. Paramount is the datum concerning his royal responsibilities, for 1 Kgs 11:27 shows that he was an influential member of the community and was an administrator in the regime of Solomon. This passage therefore becomes a basis for arguing that widows in the biblical communities were not without family ties, for Jeroboam's mother was a widow and she had living adult male relatives.

The passages we have examined contain evidence on the social characteristics of the *'almānâ*. These data are bases for arguing that she had living adult male relatives and was not without kinship relations. These living adult male relatives might have been biological family, for not all members in an extended family unit were blood relatives. Tamar's father-in-law was alive, but Gen 38:1-30 suggests that Tamar was an *'almānâ*. The unnamed woman in 2 Sam 14:5-7 had an extended family, for it is probable that her adult male relatives sought retribution for the murder of her son. David was a source of protection for his concubines, but his absence in their lives caused the writer of 2 Sam 20:3 to contend that points of contact were present between their predicament and the plight of the *'almānâ*. Furthermore, 1 Kgs 7:14 and 11:26 show that women who were bereft of husbands had living adult sons.

Widows in the Prophetic Literature in the HB

The prophetic literature groups the *'almānâ* with other vulnerable persons in ancient Israel. This literary feature implies that a relationship was present between her economic predicament and that of other subgroups. The passages in Isaiah link her plight to the dilemma of the *yātôm* and the poor (*dal*). Jer 7:6 and 22:3 link her predicament to the condition of the *yātôm*, innocent person (*nāqî*), and *gēr*. Ezek 22:7 and 44:22 link her predicament to the plights of the *yātôm* and the *gĕrûšâ*. Zech 7:10 implies that her situation was analogous to, if not the same as, the dilemma of the *yātôm*, *gēr*, and the humbled individual (*'ānî*). The fact that no adult male family member appears with her in these texts is a window on how the prophets understood the dilemma of this woman.

Widows in Job, Psalms, Proverbs, and Lamentations

The *'lmnh* consonantal pattern is present in Job 24:21; 29:13; Pss 68:5; 78:64; 94:6; 109:9; 146:9; Prov 15:25; and Lam 5:3. These data also group her with other vulnerable individuals in ancient Israelite society (*yātôm* and *dal*). Job 24:21 and 29:13 associate the plight of the *'almānâ* with the predicaments of the barren woman (*'ăqārâ*) and the individual who is in deep misery (*'ōbēd*). None of the male family members of a kinship group appears in texts with the *'almānâ* in Job, Psalms, Proverbs, and Lamentations.

Summary

Data in the HB bring into play two possibilities concerning the social characteristics of the *'almānâ*: (1) she had living adult male relatives and received economic and legal protection from them; and (2) she had living adult male relatives but received neither economic nor legal protection from them. This study argues for the second view. It advocates the position that this person had living adult male family members, but that none of them would provide economic or legal support for her. Gen 38:1-30; 2 Sam 14:5-7; and 20:1-3 inform this claim. While these texts imply that women called widows were without the support and protection of living adult male relatives, they also suggest that this absence of support was voluntary. It is important to notice the following features of these texts: (a) Judah refused to care for Tamar in Gen 38:1-30; (b) no males in the clan offered economic help to the unnamed *'almānâ* (2 Sam 14:5-7); and (c) David deserted his concubines (2 Sam 20:1-3). The possibility that the *'almānâ* had living adult male relatives, and that these men were reluctant to protect and provide economic support for her, is critical, for this point of view elucidates the stigma associated with widowhood in ancient Israel. It suggests that the *'almānâ* was a woman whose adult male relatives, if any were still living, were either too poor to help her or wanted nothing to do with her. This social feature of her predicament invites suspicion and denigration of this person. It breaks ground for the exploitation of this individual by other social actors in the biblical communities also.[23]

---

23. The phenomena that contributed to the absence of support and protection from adult male relatives of the *'almānâ* will be treated in chapter 4 of this study.

The Stranger in the Deuteronomic Code

History of Scholarship

William Robertson-Smith, Johannes Pedersen, Max Weber, Roland de Vaux, Diether Kellermann, Frank A. Spina, Léon Epsztein, Christiana van Houten, and Christoph Bultmann wrote major treatments on the *gēr* in the biblical communities.[24] Robertson-Smith studied Arab Bedouin communities, and he noticed that these socioeconomic subgroups contained a category of individuals who were free but had no political rights. This individual was the *jār*. Robertson-Smith perceived that this type of person lived permanently in a tribal area where he/she had no consanguine relations, no blood kin, and thus was bereft of socioeconomic and legal protection. He argues that the *jār* placed himself/herself under the care and protection of a powerful chieftain or clan in order to stave off crises that might develop as a result of his/her social condition. Robertson-Smith drew attention to the etymological points of contact between *jār* in Arabic and *gēr* in biblical Hebrew, and he argued that points of contact were present between the circumstances of these individuals.[25]

Johannes Pedersen takes the discussion on the identification of the *gēr* in the biblical communities in a different direction. While Robertson-Smith examines the philological underpinnings of this term and explores the identity of this type of person in ancient Bedouin communities, Pedersen studies this person within the framework of ancient Israelite history. He indicates that the *gēr* resided in an area where he/she had no kin, and he elucidates the geographic origins of this type of individual.

---

24. William Robertson-Smith, *Lectures on the Religion of the Semites* (London: A. & C. Black, 1927); Johannes Pedersen, *Ancient Israel: Its Life and Culture*, vol. 1 (London: Oxford University Press, 1927 [1973]), pp. 39-46; Max Weber, *Ancient Judaism*, trans. Hans Gerth and Don Martindale (New York: Free Press, 1952); Roland de Vaux, *Ancient Israel: Social and Religious Institutions*, vols. 1 and 2 (New York: McGraw-Hill, 1961); Diether Kellermann, "גּוּר," in *TDOT* 2:439-49; Frank A. Spina, "Israelites as *gērîm*, 'Sojourners,' in Social and Historical Context," in *The Word of the Lord Shall Go Forth*, ed. Carol L. Meyers and M. O'Connor (Winona Lake, Ind.: Eisenbrauns, 1983), pp. 321-35; Christiana van Houten, *The Alien in Israelite Law* (Sheffield: JSOT Press, 1991); Christoph Bultmann, *Der Fremde im Antiken Juda* (Göttingen: Vandenhoeck & Ruprecht, 1992); and Epsztein, *Social Justice in the Ancient Near East and the People of the Bible*.

25. Robertson-Smith, pp. 75-83.

It is true that a fairly large number of foreigners lived in Canaan. David's guard consisted of hired foreigners, and we learn that in Samaria certain bazaars were inhabited by Aramean merchants (1 Kgs 20:34). But the *gērîm* alluded to in the laws cannot be identical with these foreigners. They form a limited social class, closely allied with the Israelites, and making an important part of their most intimate institutions. They can only be the conquered, not wholly but nearly assimilated early population.[26]

Pedersen suggests that the conquered inhabitants of Syria-Palestine, who did not fully become part of the Israelite social order, were the *gērîm* in the biblical communities. This explanation proceeds from a line of thinking about the Israelite appearance in Syria-Palestine. In a word, Pedersen assumed that a unified, swift, and violent conquest of Syria-Palestine by the Israelites transpired.

Max Weber argues that the *gēr* was of *foreign* stock. That is, this type of individual was from elsewhere in the biblical community and was not a full member of the host community that she/he inhabited. According to Weber, this person was normally landless; consequently, the *gēr* became a protégé. The belief that this person placed himself/herself under the guardianship of a household or a patron led Weber to argue that his/her predicament differed from the plight of the total foreigner *(nŏkrî)*. In short, the *gēr* enjoyed legal and religious rights, and the *nŏkrî* was without protection in the host community.

> The norm (Lev. 25:35) [*sic*] probably transmitted from pre-exilic times decrees that "impoverished," i.e., landless, Israelites are *gēr* [*sic*]. Hence, and quite understandably, landlessness was a normal though perhaps not universal criterion of the *gēr*. Whatever his position with respect to the ownership of land, the sources regularly mean by *"gēr"* a denizen who was not only under the private protection of an individual with the religious protection of guest right, but a man [*sic*] whose rights were regulated and protected by the political organization.[27]

Weber therefore argues that before the exile, landlessness, residence in an area without blood relations, and the lack of full membership in the reli-

---

26. Pedersen, pp. 40-41.
27. Weber, p. 33.

gious assembly were features of the predicament of the *gēr*. Moreover, he maintains that landlessness was a point of contact between the economic dilemma of the *gēr* and subgroups of other landless people, i.e., artisans, merchants, and musicians. Weber stands in the tradition of Robertson-Smith by advocating the position that the *gēr* was not born in the land he/she inhabited and that this person solicited the services of a patron in the host community.[28]

De Vaux states that *gēr* represents the *foreigner* who lived permanently in the midst of subgroups in ancient Israel. According to de Vaux, the *gērîm* were among the two main subgroups of foreigners who constituted the biblical communities: the traveling foreigners, who had no legal rights in the biblical communities where they lived, and the *tôšāb* who lived among the Israelites but had a different legal status from that of the *gēr*. De Vaux declares that the indigenous Canaanite population that "Israel" found upon her arrival in the land and refugees from the North constituted the *gērîm*. Moreover, he advocates the position that these persons were poor and did not have full protection under the law. "From the social point of view these resident aliens were free men, not slaves, but they did not have full civic rights, and so differed from the Israelite citizens. They may be compared with the *perioikoi* of Sparta, the original inhabitants of the Peloponnese, who retained their freedom and could own property, but had no political rights."[29]

Kellermann represents the textual and comparative approaches to studying the *gēr* in the HB and in ancient Israel. He surveys ancient Egyptian, Mesopotamian, and Ugaritic texts for occurrences of terms that have etymological points of contact with the Hebrew term *gēr*.[30] Points of contact are present between Kellermann and de Vaux, for Kellermann argues that the legal position of these persons prior to the razing of Jerusalem by

---

28. Weber states that after the exile, *gērîm* denoted converts to early forms of Judaism and full members of the religious community. Weber therefore implies that the date of the text in the HB in which *gēr* appears is a window on the referent of this term. For a critique of Weber and his approach to studying ancient Israelite society, see S. Talmon, "The Emergence of Jewish Sectarianism in the Early Second Temple Period," in his *King, Cult, and Calendar in Ancient Israel* (Jerusalem: Magnes Press, 1986), pp. 165-201.

29. De Vaux, 1:74-76.

30. Kellermann explores the philology of *gēr*, for it is possible to link this term to three verbal roots in biblical Hebrew: (a) *gûr* (sojourned); (b) *gûr* (stirred up strife); and (c) *gûr* (dread/be afraid).

the Babylonians was neither native Israelite nor complete foreigner. "In the Old Testament the *gēr* occupies an intermediate position between a native and a foreigner. He lives among people who are not his blood relatives, and thus he lacks the protection and the privileges which usually come through through blood relationship and place of birth."[31]

Moreover, Kellermann implies that the population of foreigners in the South increased during the seventh century B.C.E. While he contends that these people came from different places in Syria-Palestine, he indicates that a major element emigrated from the North. "When Deut 14:29; 16:11, 14; 24:17-18, 19, 20, 21; 26:13; 27:19 mention the *gēr* alongside orphans and widows, presumably they have in mind fugitives from the northern kingdom, who had settled in the southern kingdom from the fall of Samaria in 722 B.C. on."[32]

Kellermann therefore argues that the proliferation of vulnerable individuals became a social problem in Judah that spawned the codification of regulations that provided guidelines on behavior toward this socioeconomic subgroup. Consequently, he contends that the *gēr* in the DC fled from the North to the South because of famine, war, or other phenomena that proceeded from the destruction of Samaria by the Assyrians.

Frank A. Spina suggests that the *gēr* immigrated into a new region and was without sociopolitical protection or privilege in the different host community he/she inhabited. Spina elucidates the range of phenomena that contributed to the displacement of an individual or a people, i.e., famine, war, the failure to incite revolution or to secure pasturage, or the seeking of asylum. Consequently, he introduces a translation of *gēr* that reflects these socioeconomic problems. He proposes that "immigrant," not "resident alien" or "sojourner," is a better translation of *gēr*, for "immigrant" conveys the store of ideas that are concomitants of emigration.

> In this light "immigrant" may be proposed as an acceptable translation for *gēr*. This term is richer in nuance and less awkward than "resident alien." Likewise, it seems preferable to the somewhat archaic "sojourner," which also has the disadvantage of reflecting only one social feature involved in being a *gēr*, namely, the roles, functions and relationships in the new host society. Not only does "immigrant" contain the nuances inherent in "resident alien" and "sojourner," but it also calls at-

31. Kellermann, p. 443.
32. Kellermann, p. 445.

tention to the original circumstances of social conflict which are inevitably responsible for large-scale withdrawal of people. It is my contention that *gēr* should be translated by a word that underscores not simply the outsider status in the adopted social setting, but in addition those factors and conditions related to the emigration in the first place.[33]

The main contribution of Spina to the discussion on the *gēr* is the insight he provides into the phenomena that might have triggered the departure of this person from his/her homeland in the first place.

Christiana van Houten gives detailed attention to the legal status of the *gēr* in ancient Israel; thus the major bodies of law in the Pentateuch inform her discussion on the identity and rights of this type of individual. Van Houten groups the legal materials in the Pentateuch into three major categories: (a) pre-Deuteronomic laws, (b) Deuteronomic laws, and (c) Priestly laws. She translates *gēr* as "alien," and states that this translation takes into consideration the social and political turbulence that caused the emigration. Moreover, she argues that the alien did not settle completely in the host community.

Van Houten, however, contends that the identity of the alien changed throughout the history of the biblical communities. She contends that a clan ethos shaped notions about the *gēr* in the oldest subgroups of law in the Pentateuch. She therefore argues that in the BC, the alien immigrated into a new tribal area from a tribal area elsewhere in Syria-Palestine. In short, this person was from a different clan, whether Israelite or non-Israelite, and was an unequal member of the Israelite community where he/she lived; consequently this person placed himself/herself under the protection of a patron. Van Houten argues that in the DC, alien is a religio-political designation, namely, a non-Israelite who lived among the Israelites. This type of person might have been an Edomite, a Moabite, or an Ammonite, and it was impossible for him/her to become a part of the Israelite society. She writes: "In this body of material aliens are consistently characterized as people who are needy and who are non-Israelites. They are defined according to their socio-economic status and ethnic identity. This, as I have shown, is related to the Israelites' definition of themselves. Israelites defined themselves in terms of their past history, i.e. in terms of what God had done for them."[34]

---

33. Spina, p. 323.
34. Van Houten, p. 108.

Van Houten maintains that the heritage of the alien was different from that of the Israelite in the DC, but she is silent on what this heritage is. She alludes to the intervention of the deity in the history of the Israelites; perhaps she means the deliverance from bondage in Egypt, guidance through the wilderness, and the gift of the land. Consequently, being an Israelite showed that one affirmed a particular religio-political position. This feature of the DC suggests that a social subgroup which defended Yahwism was a major political camp in ancient Israelite society, and that this faction drafted legal injunctions in the DC. Thus the Yahweh-alone community was the *in-group*, and those persons who worshiped other deities the *out-group* — they were the aliens in the DC.

Van Houten therefore provides insight into the identity of the *gēr* in the DC by suggesting that this type of individual was a person from a different political group who immigrated into Israelite territory. The *gēr* was not a full member of the Israelite community where he/she lived.

Christoph Bultmann offers the most recent treatment on the *gēr* in the DC. While he explores the meanings of this term in different layers of literature in the HB, he gives detailed attention to its meaning in Deuteronomy and in the literature that proceeds from this tradition in the HB. Regarding this type of person in the DC, Bultmann declares: "It is determined for the meaning of the figure of the *gēr* in the deuteronomic law that it was described nowhere as a stranger in Israel — therefore not as strangeness in regards to the monarchy in whose political borders he lives comes the expression — but as a stranger in local milieu, as stranger in relation to an individual respective village of his residence *('šr bš 'ryk)*. It is incorrect to translate the word *gēr* as immigrant for the evidence in the deuteronomic law."[35]

Bultmann argues that *foreign origin* is a sociohistoric feature of the *gēr* in Deuteronomy and DtrH. What is more, he elucidates the fact that *foreign birth* is a feature of the *nŏkrî* in ancient Israel. Yet he indicates that *gēr* and *nŏkrî* delineate different persons. This belief leads him to define the *foreignness* of the *gēr* by domestic criteria: to treat the *gēr* in a local milieu, i.e., in regard to the local village where he/she takes up permanent residence. Bultmann argues that this type of person in Judah did not come from a distant country or region and resettle in the South. In short, he suggests that the *gēr* came from within the borders of Judah. This type of per-

---

35. Bultmann, p. 22.

son immigrated to an area in Judah from a site elsewhere in Judah. What is more, Bultmann maintains that the DC differentiates the *gēr* from the local comrade *('āḥ)*, and that this differentiation supports the idea that the *gēr* is to be understood in relation to the host village that he/she inhabits.[36]

Since Bultmann reasons that *gēr* in Deuteronomy denotes a type of person from a village elsewhere in Judah, he argues that refugees from the North or from elsewhere in Syria-Palestine did not constitute the *gērîm* in the South during the seventh century B.C.E. This claim parts company with de Vaux, Kellermann, and Spina, for these scholars argue that refugees from the North fled to the South after the fall of Samaria. For Bultmann the *gēr* in Deuteronomy and DtrH is from a village in Judah and is of low socioeconomic rank. Regarding this type of person in the South, he states: "The social type of the *gēr* as representative of a lower class in a local environment during the political scene of the Judean monarchy turns out to be a view which is supported by the extant sources. In relation to this area, that is to a single village, the strangeness of the *gēr* is to be understood."[37]

Thus Bultmann proffers that *gērîm* were a distinct element in the social order. This class of people was economically disadvantaged. While he is unclear on the problem that accounts for this circumstance, one cannot but suspect that these persons owned no land, and that landlessness contributed to their dilemma. Bultmann, however, contends that the goal of laws in the DC where the *gēr* appears was to provide opportunity for the acquisition of goods and to integrate this type of person into the local community. Bultmann, accordingly, argues that he/she was a protected citizen in ancient Israelite society.[38]

---

36. *"Ortsgenossen"* is Bultmann's translation of אח, and "local comrade" is my translation of *Ortsgenossen.*

37. Bultmann says: "Einer auf diesen Quellenbestand gestützten Betrachtung erweist sich der soziale Typus des *gēr* als Vertreter einer Unterschicht im lokalen Milieu der Landschaft der judäischen Monarchie. In der Relation zu diesem Raum, und d.h. zu den einzelnen Ortschaften dort, ist die Fremdheit des *gēr* zu bestimmen." See Bultmann, p. 213. 2 Chr 30:25, however, implies that *gērîm* from the North settled in Jerusalem during the time of Hezekiah. This passage raises questions about Bultmann's position on the geographic origins of the *gērîm* in Judah during the seventh century B.C.E.

38. Bultmann, p. 215.

Assessment and Proposal

Robertson-Smith, Pedersen, Weber, de Vaux, Kellermann, Spina, van Houten, and Bultmann show that a long-standing discussion is present among scholars of the HB on the delineation and rights of the *gēr* in the DC. The debate about this type of person has several main points: (a) he/she immigrated from one location and settled in another in the biblical communities; (b) he/she was a member of a different ethnic group; (c) he/she was landless, impoverished, and an unequal member of Israelite society; and (d) he/she, either agreeably or disagreeably, became a protected citizen in the host community.

This study concurs with the aforementioned scholars on the notions that the *gēr* in the DC immigrated into a society from elsewhere, and that he/she had neither kinship ties nor full enfranchisement in the host community. It, however, argues that immigration into Israel from a site elsewhere in Syria-Palestine is a dubious criterion for delineating the *gēr* in the DC. This basis for understanding this term does not consider the response of the immigrant to the cultural phenomena of the dominant group in the community she/he inhabits.

Is it possible that the *gēr* in the DC immigrated into Israelite territories but retained ideas and norms that were distinct from and in competition with these same phenomena in the larger society she/he inhabited? That is to say, did the deprecation of the local customs and cultural norms of the mainstream in the host community, not the geographic origin of this type of person, demarcate the *gēr* from the Israelite in the DC? This study claims that the attitude of the *gēr* toward the culture of the mainstream is the issue that delimited this type of individual in the biblical communities. That is to say, cultural distance, or what G. Simmel describes as "the absence of commonness," should be the distinguishing feature of the *gēr* in the DC.[39] Simmel argues that the *other* in human societies does not seek to assimilate

---

39. Simmel published his study on outsiders in host communities about seventy-five years ago, but its impact reaches into the present. For an English translation of Simmel's work on the outsider in host communities, see Kurt H. Wolff, ed., "The Stranger," in *The Sociology of Georg Simmel*, ed. K. H. Wolff (New York: Free Press, 1964), pp. 402-8. For a review of the literature spawned by the Simmelian concept of the *Other*, see Donald N. Levine, "Simmel at a Distance: On the History and Systematics of the Sociology of the Stranger," in *Strangers in African Societies*, ed. William A. Shack and Elliot P. Skinner (Berkeley: University of California Press, 1979), pp. 21-36.

into the mainstream, and that he/she is likely to meander and not to have a specified or conclusively determined status in the host community. "The stranger is, so to speak, the *potential* wanderer: although he [*sic*] has not moved on, he has not quite overcome the freedom of coming and going. He is fixed within a particular spatial group, or within a group whose boundaries are similar to spatial boundaries. But his position in this group is determined, essentially, by the fact that he has not belonged to it from the beginning, that he imports qualities into it, which do not and cannot stem from the group itself."[40] Simmel proffers that the *outsider* clings to the culture of his ethnic group, but G. Allport suggests that this type of person is indefinable. The ever-changing identity of the in-group is at the heart of this problem. Allport demonstrates that several bases for delineating subgroups are present in human societies.[41] He indicates that sociocultural ties, however, are major criteria for group identification and for demarcating the *Other*. "So far as life's problems have to do with group relations, the answers are likely to be ethnocentric in tone. This is natural enough. Each ethnic group tends to strengthen its inner ties, to keep bright the legend of its own golden age, and to declare (or imply) that other groups are less worthy. Such readymade answers make for self-esteem and for group survival."[42]

Simmel and Allport shape the conceptual framework for identifying the *gēr* in this study; consequently, this project translates *gēr* as "stranger" instead of "immigrant" or "alien," and it argues that this rendition best articulates the sociospatial predicament of the *gēr* in the North or the South prior to the Babylonian captivity. The major point is that he/she shared a proximity with the in-group but maintained cultural distance from this entity. Although the *gēr* in the DC was a member of a host community in a spatial sense, he/she adhered to the culture of his/her ethnic group: he/she had customs, language, religion, and ideas about moral behavior that opposed understandings of these phenomena among the mainstream in the village, city, or tribe in Israel into which he/she immigrated. Immigrating into a village or city in Israel from elsewhere in Syria-Palestine, therefore, was a minor social feature of the *gēr* in the DC; the major issue was that this person was not integrated into the society in a cultural sense.

40. Kurt H. Wolff, p. 402.

41. Gordon W. Allport, *The Nature of Prejudice* (Reading, Mass.: Addison-Wesley, 1954; reprint, 1990).

42. Allport, p. 285.

Deut 14:21a and 23:7 (= Hebr. 23:8b) inform this delineation of the *gēr* in the DC. Deut 14:21a says: "Do not eat anything that died a natural death. You will give it to the *gēr* who is in your gates, and he can eat it; or you can sell it to a *nŏkrî*, for you are a holy people (*'am qādôš*) to Yahweh your God."

Three categories of individuals appear in Deut 14:21a, the *gēr*, *nŏkrî*, and the *'am qādôš*. Two of these groups, namely, the *gēr* and *nŏkrî*, could eat animals that died a natural death; the holy people, however, could not consume these corpses. The rationale is that the former two groups were not members of the holy community. The implication of this issue is noteworthy. What becomes probable is that the *gēr* and *nŏkrî* enjoyed a religiousness and an ethos that differed from the same phenomena in the *'am qādôš* or at least from these features of social life among individuals in the *in-group*. Deut 14:21a therefore lends support to the idea that ethnocentric phenomena differentiated social subgroups in the DC, and that the *gēr* did not assimilate into the mainstream.

Deut 23:7 (= Hebr. 23:8b) states: "Do not hate the Egyptian because you were *gērîm* in his land." This text draws analogies between the dilemma of "Israel" in Egypt and the predicament of the stranger in Israel. While identifying the "Israel" that the Egyptians enslaved is a complex task, it is probable that the Egyptians subjugated a small sociocultural subunit which later escaped and became a constituency of a religio-political entity that appeared in Syria-Palestine at the end of the Late Bronze Age/ beginning of the Iron Age. The account about the escape of this subgroup from the "house of bondage" became one of the many traditions that shaped the identity of the biblical community according to the DC.[43] Working from the assumptions that the nucleus of the biblical community was present in Egypt and that the Egyptians oppressed this social subgroup, it becomes plausible that a sociocultural commonness created a sense of belonging among the enslaved group, and that this point of connection differentiated the enslaved social collectivity from the Egyptians. The idea that a group could not remain distinct from the mainstream if they adopted the worldviews, norms, language, and other cultural phenomena of the dominant group is the basis of this claim, for conforming to the prevailing customs, language, and norms of the dominant group can render one inconspicuous. Deut 23:7 asserts that "Israel" was a *gēr* in

43. Reference to "Israel" as *strangers in Egypt* appears in Deut 10:19 also.

Egypt, and this declaration accordingly leaves open the possibility that a cultural distinction was present between "Israel" and the Egyptians. This passage ideally becomes a basis for arguing that "Israel" was a distinct sociocultural subgroup in Egypt, and that the refusal to assimilate was a major characteristic of the *gēr* in the DC and in the biblical communities before 587 B.C.E.

Summary

Robertson-Smith, Pedersen, Weber, de Vaux, Kellermann, Spina, van Houten, and Bultmann shape the conceptual framework for delineating the *gēr* in the DC. These scholars show that the *gēr* emigrated from a location in Syria-Palestine and lived among a host tribe, village, or city in Israel. Yet this delineation brings into play a constellation of issues. The phenomenon that causes a person to be in juxtaposition with the mainstream in the host community is at the center of this problem.

Simmel, Allport, the scholars mentioned earlier on the *gēr* in the DC, and texts in the DC provide a basis for arguing that he/she immigrated into a host community from elsewhere in Syria-Palestine but did not assimilate into that community. This study therefore proposes that the commitment of this type of person to maintaining his/her ethnic identity was the distinctive feature of the *gēr* in the Deuteronomic Code.

The Orphan in the Deuteronomic Code

History of Scholarship

H. Ringgren and J. Renkema inform contemporary viewpoints on the orphan *(ytwm)* in the HB.[44] Ringgren surveys ancient Egyptian, Mesopotamian, Ugaritic, and Phoenician texts for occurrences of terms that have social and etymological points of contact with the Hebrew term *yātôm*. Furthermore, he states that this term appears forty-two times in the HB. He shows that the usage of this word is widespread in the legal and poetic

---

44. Helmer Ringgren, "יתום," in *TDOT* 6, pp. 477-81; and J. Renkema, "Does Hebrew *YTWM* Really Mean 'Fatherless'?" *VT* 45, no. 1 (1995): 119-22.

texts in the HB, but that its appearance in narrative texts is sparse. Lam 5:3 is the key piece of evidence for understanding Ringgren's idea about the social characteristics of the *yātôm* in ancient Israel: "In Lam 5:3, the people lament: 'We have become orphans, fatherless [*'ēn 'āb*].'"[45] He accordingly argues that *yātôm* means a minor who is fatherless, and that God is his/her protector. Ringgren indicates that two terms for a fatherless child are present in the Egyptian literature — *tfn* and *tfn.t* — and they delineate helpless and impoverished children. He indicates also that *ekûtu* appears in Akkadian texts and means either a homeless or destitute girl.[46] He also points out that *ytwm* is present in the Ugaritic and Phoenician literature. In both instances data are not present on the social characteristics of this individual. Ringgren argues that care for the orphan was the duty of the king in the Egyptian, Mesopotamian, and Ugaritic literature.[47]

Renkema differs with Ringgren. 2 Sam 20:19; Lam 1:1; 5:2-3; and 5:20 shape Renkema's theory on the meaning of this term in the HB. 2 Sam 20:19 says: "I am one of the peaceful and faithful in Israel; you are seeking to destroy a city, a mother in Israel. Why do you swallow up the inheritance of Yahweh?" Renkema uses this passage to argue that cities are considered to be *mothers* in the biblical communities. He points out that Yahweh is considered to be the father of the biblical community. He argues that these beliefs elucidate the meaning of *yātôm* in Lam 5:3, and that this notion is a basis for understanding the meaning of this word in the HB. Lam 5:2-3 implies that the inhabitants of Judah lost their cities, inheritance, and homes, i.e., their mothers, and Lam 5:20 suggests that the people of Judah lost the protection of Yahweh, i.e., their father. Renkema therefore proposes that *yātôm* refers to a child who is bereft of his/her

---

45. See Ringgren, p. 481.

46. It is noteworthy that the *CAD* and the *AHW* introduce competing information on the word for orphan in the Mesopotamian literature also. The *CAD* indicates that only the feminine form of *ekû*, e.g., *ekûtu*, appears in the Mesopotamian literature, and it argues that *ekûtu* denotes a homeless or destitute girl. The *AHW*, however, cites the masculine *ekû/ikû*, and it contends that *ekû/ikû* denotes a fatherless orphan *(vaterlosen Waisen)*. See *CAD*, vol. 4 (Chicago: Oriental Institute, 1958), pp. 72-73; and *AHW*, vol. 1 (1965), pp. 195-96.

47. The Mesopotamian and Egyptian terms for orphan are not cognates of *ytwm*. The fact that words for orphan in the Mesopotamian literature and in biblical Hebrew have different radicals, however, does not exclude the possibility that points of contact were present between the social features of this type of person in Egypt, Mesopotamia, and ancient Israel. In short, context, not derivation, is the major clue on the meaning of these terms. See Barr, p. 107.

mother and father. Thus he translates *yātôm* as "parentless," not as "father-less," because "parentless" considers the plight of children who are bereft of their mothers in ancient Israel.

Ringgren and Renkema isolate the major issue for delineating the *yātôm* in the Deuteronomic Code: Is this type of person a fatherless child or a minor who is bereft of both parents? To reach a plausible belief concerning this issue, this section explores several pieces of information: (a) texts in the ANE where no Semitic cognate for *yātôm* is present but where information is present that might help in delineating this person in the biblical communities; (b) texts in the ANE where Semitic cognates for *yātôm* are present; and (c) texts in the HB where evidence about the family situation of the *yātôm* is present.

Orphans in the Mesopotamian Literature

Concern for orphans is present in the Laws of Ur-Namma (LU) and the Laws of Hammurabi (LH). Information regarding the presence of parents and guidelines for behavior toward the orphan are absent in these texts. A marked interest for the well-being of the orphan, however, appears in the prologues or epilogues of these law collections from Mesopotamia. This phenomenon provides insight into the meaning and dilemma of the orphan in Mesopotamian communities.

The prologue to LU says: "I did not deliver the orphan to the rich. I did not deliver the widow to the mighty. I did not deliver the man with but one shekel to the man with one mina (i.e., 60 shekels). I did not deliver the man with but one sheep to the man with one ox."[48]

The epilogue to LH says: "In order that the mighty not wrong the weak, to provide just ways for the *waif* and the widow, I have inscribed my precious pronouncements upon my stela and set it up before the statue of me, the king of justice, in the city of Babylon, the city which the gods Anu and Enlil have elevated, within the Esagil, the temple whose foundations are fixed as are heaven and earth, in order to render the judgments of the land, to give the verdicts of the land, and to provide just ways for the wronged."[49]

---

48. Roth, p. 16.
49. Roth, pp. 133-34. For an alternative reading of this pericope, see *ANET*, p. 178.

These two texts list the orphan with the widow and the weak person, and thus intimate that the orphan was among the vulnerable in Mesopotamian societies. The LU and LH, however, are silent on the social characteristics of the orphan. These texts, however, link the predicament of the orphan to that of the widow in Mesopotamian societies; thus it is plausible that the *yātôm* was bereft of a male protector.

Orphans in the Ugaritic Literature

The consonantal pattern *ytwm* appears in the Keret legend:

> The lad *Yaṣṣib* departed,
> he entered into (the presence of) his father,
> (and) he lifted up his voice and cried:
> "Hear, I beseech you, o noble Keret, . . .
> While bandits raid you turn (your) back,
> and you entertain feuding rivals.
> You have been brought down by your failing power.
> You do not judge the cause of the widow,
> you do not try the case of the importunate.
> You do not banish the extortioners of the poor,
> you do not feed the orphan *(ytm)* before your face,
> nor the widow behind your back."[50]

In this text *Yaṣṣib* inculpates Keret. It is noticeable that Keret allows the mistreatment of the *ytm*. He deserts the widow and fails to provide sustenance for the *ytm*. Again, this type of person appears with the widow in texts from elsewhere in the ANE. While listing the *ytm* with the widow might be a literary practice that is widespread in the ANE, it is possible also that points of contact are present between the predicaments of these individuals. This might be the reason for the appearance of these individuals together in this text.

The consonantal pattern *ytm* appears in the Aqhat cycle also.

> And behold! on the seventh day,
> thereupon Daniel, man of Rapiu,

---

50. The Keret Legend, tablet 16, col. vi, ll. 39-50. See Gibson, p. 102.

thereat the hero, man of He-of-Harnam,
raised himself up (and) sat at the entrance of the gate,
beneath the trees which were by the threshing-floor;
he judged the cause of the widow,
tried the case of the orphan *(ytm)*.[51]

While Keret abandons the cause of the *ytm*, Daniel adjudicated his/her cause. The Keret and Aqhat legends, then, bolster the claim that a concern for this person was present elsewhere among individuals in Syria-Palestine. While this study infers from the Keret and Aqhat legends that the *ytm* was defenseless, it can only speculate about the identity and socioeconomic dynamics that account for his/her predicament. These legends leave the question on the father of the *ytm* unanswered, for no statement regarding the presence or absence of this person is present in these narratives.

Orphans in the Phoenician Literature

The *ytm* consonantal pattern appears in a Phoenician text about Ešmun'azar, a king of Sidon: "I have been snatched away before my time, the son of a *number* of *restricted* days, an orphan *(ytm)*, the son of a widow. I am lying in this casket and this grave, in a place which I (myself) built."[52] While certainty on the meaning of *ytm* in the Ešmun'azar text is a formidable challenge, the self-description by the Sidonian king suggests that the monarch was bereft of his father, not of his mother. The Ešmun'azar text therefore contains the notion that the *ytm* was fatherless but not parentless. Only one relative appears with the *ytwm* in the Mesopotamian, Ugaritic, and Phoenician literature: the biological mother in a Phoenician text. The Ugaritic evidence groups the *ytwm* with the widow but offers no evidence that suggests that the widow in the text is the mother of the *ytwm* in the text.

---

51. The Aqhat Legend, tablet 17, col. v, ll. 4-8. See Gibson, p. 107.
52. See *ANET*, p. 66, and Ringgren, col. 1077.

Orphans in the Poetic Texts in the HB

The usage of *yātôm* is widespread in the HB.[53] Only Lam 5:3; Job 24:9; 29:12; Pss 68:5 (= Hebr. 68:6); and 109:9, however, contain information about the social features of this person. Consequently, this study turns its attention to these passages.

Lam 5:3 says:

We are orphans *(yĕtômîm)*, fatherless,
Our mothers are truly widows.

As was mentioned above, Lam 5:3 mourns the condition of Jerusalem and Judah, and it suggests that several points of contact were present between the predicament of the *yātôm* and the predicament of the inhabitants of Jerusalem and Judah. This passage says the inhabitants of the South were without a father *('ên 'āb)*. Note that it places this phrase in apposition to *yĕtômîm*. The fact that *'ên 'āb* elucidates *yĕtômîm* suggests that the *yātôm* was not parentless but only without a father. This passage conveys the idea that the *yātôm* has a mother, albeit a widow. Furthermore, it is probable that either many fathers died during the Babylonian onslaught of Jerusalem and Judah or that the Babylonians carried several of them away into Mesopotamia. Lam 5:3 therefore allows this problem to illustrate the condition of Judah. By doing this it supports the conclusions that the father of the *yātôm* is either dead or absent.

Job 24:9 says:

They snatch the *yātôm* from the breast,
They demand collateral from the poor.

Job 24:9 protests the abuse of the vulnerable by calling attention to acts of injustice committed against two defenseless subgroups in the biblical communities. This text asserts that wicked people wrenched the *yātôm* from the breast, and that these sinister individuals demanded collateral from the poor. Information about the social condition of the *yātôm* is present in the

---

53. The highest concentration of texts that treat the *'ănāwîm* is in Deuteronomy. It is possible that this phenomenon signals a growing concern in Deuteronomic literature with the *'ănāwîm* or a numerical increase of this group in the biblical community during the emergence or codification of texts in Deuteronomy that treat this individual.

complaint about inhumanity toward this person in Job 24:9a, where corrupt persons in the biblical communities yank him from the breast. Since this datum does not state who nursed this type of person, it leaves open the probability that the biological mother was alive. What is more, Job 24:9a lends support to the claim that either the *yātôm* was fatherless or the father was incapable of protecting the child.

Job 29:12 says:

> I delivered the afflicted who were crying,
> And the *yātôm* because none helped him.

Job 29:12 associates personal piety with ameliorating the circumstances of the *yātôm*. This text is silent about the issues that caused his defenselessness. The present suspicion is that no adult male was present to champion his cause, and that sparse socioeconomic resources were available to the mother of the *yātôm*. Job 29:12b therefore becomes a basis for arguing that the absence or incapability of the father of the *yātôm* to protect his child contributed to the defenselessness of this type of individual. Thus Job 29:12b indicates that Job performed the duties of a father to this type of person. In doing so this text lends weight to the claim that the father of the *yātôm* is either dead or is incapable of defending and supporting his child.

Ps 68:5 (= Hebr. 68:6) says:

> A father of *yĕtômîm*, and a judge of widows,
> is God in his holy dwelling.

Ps 68:5 (= Hebr. 68:6) praises the deity. In doing this it suggests that the deity protects defenseless elements in the biblical communities. Ps 68:6a contends that the deity is the father of *yĕtômîm*. This notion brings into play two propositions: (1) the biological fathers of these individuals were absent or dead; or (2) they were present but incapable of providing protection for their children. While Ps 68:6a bolsters the position that the *yātôm* was fatherless, it is silent about the status of his mother.

Ps 109:8-9 says:

> Let his days be few,
> and another take his possessions.
> Let his children be *yĕtômîm*,
> and let his wife be a widow.

Ps 109:8-9 requests the death of the false accuser, and that someone else confiscate his possessions. This text argues that the family of the false accuser should suffer for the accuser's injustices. It requests that his children become *yĕtômîm*, and his wife a widow. This piece of evidence, then, supports the notion that the death or absence of the father is the distinctive attribute of the *yātôm*. Thus the earlier mentioned passages suggest that the *yātôm* is without the protection of an adult male.

To summarize, the only relative that appears with orphans in major poetic texts in the HB is the mother (Lam. 5:3; Job 24:9; Ps. 109:8-9).

Summary

The Deuteronomic Code contains the words *'almānâ*, *gēr*, and *yātôm*. These terms appear in English as "widow," "stranger," and "orphan." While these types of persons often appear as a group in this legal corpus, texts where these terms appear are often silent about the circumstance that warrants listing these persons together as a social group. Data in the HB, evidence from elsewhere in the ANE, the secondary literature about the meanings of these terms in the HB, and recent sociological theory informed, not controlled, the delineation of the terms *'almānâ*, *gēr*, and *yātôm* in this study.

The present study proposes: (a) if the *'almānâ* in Deut 12–26 had living adult male relatives, they were either unable or reluctant to provide economic support for her; (b) the *gēr* in Deut 12–26 avoids acculturation into the host community; consequently, this type of person had no adult male protector in the community he/she inhabited; and (c) if the *yātôm* in Deut 12–26 had a living father, he was either powerless or hesitant to protect him.

Thus this study proposes that the absence of an adult male protector is the common social characteristic of the *'almānâ*, *gēr*, and *yātôm* during an epoch in ancient Israelite history. This common thread among these types of individuals provoked the drafters of Deut 14:22-29; 16:9-12, 13-15; 24:17-18, 19-22; and 26:12-15 to list these persons as a social group. Furthermore, the absence of an adult male protector affected the circumstances of these persons, for it guaranteed that they were a category of socially weak, vulnerable individuals in the biblical communities. This absence limited the access of these persons to commodities in the biblical communities, and it undermined their chances for emancipation from debt slavery and for exculpation in litigation. It is plausible that the inaccessibility to commodities affected the socioeconomic ranking of the *'almānâ, gēr,* and *yātôm,* and that this situation cleared the way for the exploitation and oppression of this subgroup by other persons, groups, or institutions in ancient Israelite society.

As was said above, Fensham, von Waldow, Craigie, Mayes, Malchow, Epsztein, and Crüsemann propose that the *'almānâ, gēr,* and *yātôm* constituted a vulnerable, socially weak subgroup. These scholars, however, neither treat the levels of socioeconomic inequality nor discuss the socioeconomic ranking of these types of individuals in the biblical communities. They provide information that aids us in reaching provisional closure about the hierarchical relationship among social subgroups in the biblical communities. These critics convey the idea that ancient Israel was an agrarian community, and that marked social inequality was present in the biblical communities. This research project therefore introduces N. Gottwald, G. Lenski, E. Wolf, and R. Stavenhagen into the discussion.[54] These scholars delineate strata in agrarian societies, and they delineate a framework that aids the present project in determining the socioeconomic ranking of the *'almānâ, gēr,* and *yātôm* in ancient Israel. It is to a discussion about the socioeconomic rank of these types of persons that this study now turns.[55]

Social Subgroupings and the Socioeconomic Ranking of Widows, Strangers, and Orphans in the North during the Ninth Century B.C.E.

Norman K. Gottwald is the pioneering scholar on the study of social stratification in ancient Israel for the present generation. He introduces class as

---

54. Norman K. Gottwald, "A Hypothesis about Social Class in Monarchic Israel in Light of Contemporary Studies of Social Class and Social Stratification," in *The Hebrew Bible in Its Social World and in Ours* (Atlanta: Scholars, 1993), pp. 139-64; Gerhard Lenski, *Power and Privilege: A Theory of Social Stratification* (Chapel Hill: University of North Carolina Press, 1984); Rodolfo Stavenhagen, *Social Classes in Agrarian Societies,* trans. Judy Adler Hellman (Garden City, N.Y.: Anchor Press/Doubleday, 1975); and Eric Wolf, *Peasants* (Englewood Cliffs, N.J.: Prentice-Hall, 1966).

55. Since this study advocates the view that Deut 14:22-29; 16:9-12, 13-15; 24:17-22; and 26:12-15 appeared in the North during the ninth century B.C.E., it explores socioeconomic subgroups and their ordering in the biblical communities after the tenth century B.C.E.

a key analytical concept and interpretive principle for evidence in the HB and for reconstructing society in ancient Israel during the monarchy.[56] Gottwald builds his argument regarding social stratification in the biblical community on the work of A. Mansueto and particularly contends that three major social classes were present in ancient Israel during the monarchy. Regarding strata in the biblical communities, Gottwald writes:

a. ruling class groups: the Israelite royal houses, during the monarchic period, together with priestly sectors, dependent on taxes and corvées from the peasant communities; the metropolitan ruling classes of the various empires which dominated Israel, dependent on tributes levied on the population and collected by the indigenous ruling classes or imperial administrators; and latifundaries, dependent on rents from more or less private estates;

b. middle layers: craftsmen, functionaries, and lower clergy dependent on benefices which do not provide income sufficient to maintain an aristocratic style, and independent craftsmen and merchants;

c. exploited classes: two principal kinds of peasantry:
   * peasants protected by redistributional land tenure and other community guarantees;
   * tenant farmers on the estate of latifundaries; and marginated rural people who have no regular access to the land.[57]

According to Gottwald, three major subgroups were present in ancient Israel: the ruling class groups, intermediate-level groups, and the exploited classes. The monarch, cultic officials in the royal administration, and bureaucratic elites constituted the ruling class subgroup. Craftsmen, disenfranchised cultic officials, and merchants composed the second major socioeconomic subdivision. Farmers who worked the land and who supported privileged social subgroups and other ruling elites constituted the exploited class, the third identifiable substratum in the biblical communities. While Gottwald delineates a framework for identifying and dis-

---

56. See his groundbreaking *The Tribes of Yahweh* (Maryknoll, N.Y.: Orbis, 1979). Gottwald's approach to the HB cleared space for readings of the HB with a special sensitivity to gender, ethnicity, and methods available for studying the HB. For readings that stand in "Gottwaldian tradition," see David Jobling et al., *The Bible and the Politics of Exegesis* (Cleveland: Pilgrim Press, 1991).

57. Gottwald, "A Hypothesis," pp. 159-61.

cussing the hierarchical relationship of subgroups in the biblical communities, his framework neither adverts to widows, strangers, and orphans nor treats the socioeconomic ranking of these individuals. What is more, he pays no particular attention to the ways that socioeconomic inequality arose and persisted in ancient Israel.

Lenski, Wolf, and Stavenhagen show that agrarian societies are economically asymmetric. They link the ranking of socioeconomic subgroups in this type of community to wealth, to income, and to ownership of the means for acquiring commodities. Lenski, however, identifies the hierarchical distinctions among socioeconomic subgroups in agrarian societies. This study builds upon his work, for he provides detailed information for understanding economic subgroups, economic ranking, modes for acquiring commodities, patterns for the distribution of goods, and the treatment of vulnerable underclass subgroups in biblical Israel during the ninth century B.C.E.

Lenski's theory on the social composition of agrarian states is a compromise between the functional and conflict models of social structuring, and it suggests that class differentiation and social ranking are both inevitable and intentional.[58] He therefore shows that prominent discrepancies in levels of existence are present among economic subgroupings in "typical" agrarian societies. "One fact impresses itself on almost any observer of agrarian societies, especially on one who views them in a broadly comparative perspective. This is the fact of *marked social inequality*. Without exception, one finds pronounced differences in power, privilege, and honor associated with mature agrarian economies. These differences surpass those found in even the most stratified horticultural societies of Africa and the New World, and far exceed those in simple horticultural or hunting and gathering societies."[59]

Lenski's model on agrarian societies, as it now stands, indicates that animal-drawn plows, trade, commerce, metallurgy, chariot warfare, urban

58. Lenski examines human societies over time, and he suggests that technological development differentiates one type of society from another. He contends also that four types of societies were present in history: hunting and gathering, horticultural, agrarian, and industrial. The issue that drives Lenski, then, is how to account for the distributive processes in these societies. Thus the controlling question in Lenski's study on distributive processes in human communities is: Who gets what and why?

59. Lenski, pp. 189-210. The parenthetical page references in the following text are to Lenski's *Power and Privilege*.

areas, urban-village cultural dichotomy, monarchy, ruling elites, money as the dominant method for economic exchange, moneylending, guilds, religious pluralism, divisions of labor, and increased structured inequality were socioeconomic and technological features of "typical" agrarian societies. Lenski argues also that several conspicuous social aggregations are present in "typical" agrarian societies: (1) the ruler, (2) a governing class, (3) a retainer class, (4) a commercial class, (5) an artisan class, (6) a priestly class, (7) a peasant class, and (8) a class of expendables (pp. 189-296).

Lenski suggests that the monarch, emperor, or ruler was a distinct class, and that this individual was at the apex of the socioeconomic ranking system in "typical" agrarian societies. Furthermore, he argues that this person enjoyed significant property and business rights in his/her kingdom, and that a plethora of sources contributed to his/her material endowment. "The exercise of proprietary rights, through the collection of taxes, tribute money, rents, and services, undoubtedly provided the chief sources of income for most agrarian rulers. However, these sources were often supplemented by others. First and foremost among these was *booty* obtained through foreign conquest. Not every agrarian ruler has been militaristic, and those who were, were not always successful. However, for those who triumphed in military ventures, the rewards were tremendous" (p. 217). When Lenski's delineation of the monarch in agrarian societies is taken as correct, a conceptual framework is present for contending that the monarch had entitlement to all sources of income in the biblical communities. Consequently, it becomes probable that commodities in biblical Israel, tariffs, and booty taken in war were the main sources for the material endowment and self-aggrandizement of monarchs.

Lenski argues that politico-economic and religious elites constitute the governing class. He argues that most of the ruling class lived in urban areas, and that this economic collectivity made up about 2 percent of the population. Large property owners, monarchs, priests, and other individuals from socioeconomic classes who amassed significant economic resources were among its constituents. Moreover, Lenski implies that politico-economic and religious elites shaped instruments for social control and exercised a decisive influence on the distribution of goods in agrarian societies. What is more, their economic standing positioned them to own efficient tools and weapons and to subsist off rents and taxes collected from the masses. "On the basis of available data, it appears that the governing classes of agrarian societies probably received at least a quarter of the national income of most agrarian states, and that the governing class and ruler together usually received not less than half" (p. 228).

Lenski indicates also that politico-economic elites exploited the masses. This piece of information warrants the claim that they devised stratagems to enable them to control the distribution of *surplus* in agrarian communities. This claim attracts attention, for discussing the control of *surplus* in a subsistence economy brings into play the issue of power.

Lenski argues that the dominating class hired servants, soldiers, and additional persons to protect their interests. Persons in the employ of the governing class constituted the retainer class and made up 5 percent of the population in agrarian societies. Lenski contends that this class was located economically at some point between the ruling class and the peasantry in "typical" agrarian societies. He argues that ranking among individuals in this subgroup by income is a complex task, for an association was present between the wealth of the individual and his/her service to political and economic elites. Thus he argues that service to the politically and economically affluent, not service to the masses or to other elements in the society, was the basis of income for individuals in the retainer class. The intermediary function of the retainer class abetted the accumulation of wealth also. Basic to this claim is that the retainer class collected taxes, distributed prebends, and administered the policies of the ruling class. This function of the retainer class often prevented contact between the political and economic elites and the subordinate socioeconomic elements in "typical" agrarian societies. What is more, this intermediary function broke ground for individuals in the retainer class to create schemes for personal profit, namely, devices for cheating and wresting exorbitant money, goods, and resources from other individuals in agrarian societies (pp. 243-48).

Lenski indicates that a commercial class was present in agrarian societies. Mercantile activity was the focus of this socioeconomic subdivision. Thus knowledge of markets, prices, and systems for the exchange of goods positioned this substratum to accumulate wealth and to be free from the immediate authority of the governing class. Merchants were in a market relationship with and not employees of the governing class, and this circumstance contributed to the relative autonomy of the commercial class in agrarian societies. It therefore comes as no surprise that Lenski argues that merchants competed with the ruling class for commodities in agrarian communities. The present project suggests that merchants were perpetrators of financial crimes in agrarian societies, for special knowledge of weights and measures breaks ground for unrestrained pursuit of wealth, i.e., greed gone amok.

While Lenski indicates that the socioeconomic origins of the commercial class in "typical" agrarian societies are obscure, he leaves open the possibility that individuals in this class emerged from landless men or peasants. Moreover, he argues that merchants were not very active in the political arena, and that some of them were poor. He contends that identifying their socioeconomic location in relationship to other economic substrata in "typical" agrarian societies is a formidable challenge, for the basis of their economic standing proceeded from the exchange of goods, not from land ownership or from their relationship to political and economic elites (pp. 248-56).

Lenski maintains that cultic officials were a prominent class in agrarian societies. He contends that identifying the duties of this stratum is a complex enterprise; consequently, he suggests that their function depended upon the society under examination. He suggests that cultic officials presided at sacrifices and directed rituals, and pronounced blessings and cursings, promulgated doctrine, and provided divine legitimization to the policies of monarchs. While Lenski suggests that their power and privilege is difficult to adjudicate, he argues that several factors positioned this subgroup to procure material resources and to influence their distribution in most agrarian societies. These factors included private knowledge about the deity, special insight into rituals for personal healing, the literary skills to produce sophisticated texts, and the power to inculcate ideas about morality in moral agents. Priests motivated by materialism, greed, and the preservation of power and privilege, therefore, had tools for the creation and promulgation of ideology, and for the validation of values, alternative belief systems, and social conventions that could serve their interests (pp. 256-78).

Lenski indicates that peasant farmers or common people were a major socioeconomic subgroup in "typical" agrarian societies. He points out that 90 percent of the population made up this subgroup, and that a vast economic chasm was present between peasant farmers and the dominant class. He argues that the masses eked out their existence, and that levels of impoverishment were present among this socioeconomic substratum.

Moreover, Lenski argues that the payment of taxes and the performance of duties to ruling elites were major responsibilities of the peasantry in "typical" agrarian societies. He indicates also that this phenomenon often provoked the masses to action, and consequently the peasantry often resisted the established economic order. Lenski therefore states that their contempt for exploitation by ruling elites found expression in diverse disruptive measures. "Usually these struggles were nonviolent in character, at least on the peasant's side. For the most part, their efforts consisted of little more than attempts to evade taxes, rents, labor services, and other obligations, usually by concealment of a portion of the harvest, working slowly and sometimes carelessly as well, and similar devices" (p. 273). While the masses commonly used subterfuge to deal with ruling elites, they used violent uprisings to counter instances of extreme exploitation; when ruling elites extracted exorbitant levies from the common people, the masses abandoned trivial artifice for outright physical conflict with the governing class. Regarding the reactions of the common people to the demands of elites for intolerable taxes and obligations, Lenski declares: "A still more extreme response on the part of peasants was open revolt. Though these are often forgotten or ignored, a careful reading of the history of agrarian societies indicates that they were by no means uncommon" (p. 274). Most people in agrarian societies, therefore, were peasant farmers. These individuals produced food and other items for their personal consumption and for the fulfillment of obligations to ruling elites. What is more, the common people in agrarian communities often used a plethora of devices to show their discontent with intolerable demands placed on their crops, livestock, and services by ruling elites.[60]

Lenski suggests that artisans were a socioeconomic subdivision in "typical" agrarian societies. He argues that points of contact were present between the plight of this socioeconomic substratum and the plight of the peasantry. Furthermore, he implies that artisans were poor, and that camps were present in the artisan subdivision. He indicates that the knowledge of trades or possession of similar skills united individuals into guilds; that many artisans were employees of the merchant class; and that craftsmen provided services for peasants also. It therefore becomes probable that some artificers fared better than others in "typical" agrarian com-

---

60. Lenski argues also that economic stratification was present among the peasantry. The presence of inequality and intraclass difference among the masses, then, leaves open the possibility that the identification of the ruling class only as perpetrators of injustices in agrarian societies may be a misrepresentation of social history in the biblical communities.

munities, for the market in which they participated, and the degree of skill involved in their craft, cleared space for difference in compensation. Moreover, Lenski argues that dispossessed peasants and noninheriting sons provided recruits for the artisan element in agrarian communities, and that apprenticeships controlled the admission into this class. Lenski says also that artisans made up from 5 to 10 percent of the population (pp. 278-80).

Lenski proposes that a class of expendable persons was a feature of agrarian communities. He implies that individuals for whom other members of society had little or no need, or who were unemployable, constituted this stratum. This social subdivision of nonessential persons included petty criminals, beggars, itinerant workers, individuals with physical and mental handicaps, women with children but who were without husbands, and other individuals that political and economic elites forced to lived by charity. What is more, Lenski argues that marginality was characteristic of expendables in an agrarian society. According to Lenski, marginality denotes unemployability: it is the absence of skills or special knowledge regarding a vocation.[61] He suggests that a concentration of expendable individuals was present at urban centers. Moreover, he indicates that this category of persons made up from 5 to 10 percent of the population, and that this group was at the lowest level of the socioeconomic ranking system in the agrarian state (pp. 281-84).

Lenski posits that agrarian societies are collections of diverse and competing economic strata. These subgroups include the ruler, governing class, merchants, artisans, retainers, cultic officials, peasantry, and expendable individuals (p. 260). Lenski groups people by their occupation and relation to economic resources, and he argues that a continuum of power and privilege was present in agrarian societies. Thus he argues against superimposing classes in agrarian societies rigidly on one another. He contends that a rural agriculture-based element, an urban privileged element, and other socioeconomic subdivisions whose bases of social standing and economic affluence were not dependent upon land ownership were part of the social fabric of agrarian societies.

---

61. While this definition of marginality implies that the onus for marginality rested upon the shoulders of the individual who was without employment, this study suggests that marginality in "typical" agrarian communities proceeded from a plethora of factors external to the moral agent who was unemployable. Thus gender, language, religious beliefs, bigotry, and other sociohistorical phenomena broke ground for marginality and for the exclusion of individuals from the labor force in agricultural societies.

Many points of contact are present between the ideas of Gottwald and Lenski about social strata in agrarian societies. What is more, their ideas about the social composition of these types of human communities are consistent with the evidence about the social composition of the North during the Omride administration. This logical connection therefore provides a framework for delineating the social strata in the type of society from which the widow/stranger/orphan regulations in the Deuteronomic Code might have emerged.

Gottwald and Lenski argue that monarchs were a distinct class. These scholars contend that they were at the apex of the socioeconomic ranking system in agrarian societies. 1 Kgs 16:21-34; 18:3, 15-20; and 20:14-15 treat Omri (885-873 B.C.E.) and Ahab (873-851). 2 Kgs 3:4-27 treats Jehoram (849-843). While scant information is present in DtrH about the reign of Omri, the Assyrian data imply that he was a successful ruler, for these data call Israel the land of Omri.[62] Thus evidence in the HB and in the Mesopotamian literature suggests that autocrats were present in the North during the ninth century B.C.E., and that these individuals played a major role in the circumstances in the biblical communities.

Gottwald and Lenski argue that a governing or ruling class was present in agrarian societies. 1 Kgs 20:14-15 implies that royal officials constituted the Omride administration, for it suggests that provincial governors were a subgroup in the Omride administrative apparatus. The relationship of this passage to the reign of Ahab, however, is at the center of debate. J. M. Miller and G. Ahlström propose that 1 Kgs 20:1-34 delineates an Ahab who contrasts with the description of this individual in literature from elsewhere in the ANE, and that 1 Kgs 20:14-15 reflects conditions in Israel that postdate the Omride administration.[63] Miller and Ahlström posit that 1 Kgs 20:1-12 implies that Ahab was subservient to the Syrians; but the Moabite Stone and the inscriptions of Shalmaneser III delineate a fortified and powerful Ahab. The Assyrian evidence states that Ahab contributed two thousand chariots and ten thousand soldiers to the coalition to prevent the Assyrian westward advance at Qarqar in 853 B.C.E. Mesha concedes that Ahab occupied territories in Moab.[64] Miller and Ahlström

---

62. *ANET*, p. 285.

63. J. M. Miller, "The Elisha-Cycle and the Accounts of the Omride Wars," *JBL* 35 (1966): 441-54; and Gösta Ahlström, *The History of Ancient Palestine* (Minneapolis: Fortress, 1993), pp. 575-81.

64. *ANET*, pp. 278-79 and 320.

therefore conclude that 1 Kgs 20:1-12 depicts a powerless Ahab, and that this delineation is inconsistent with the extrabiblical evidence. The historical reliability of 1 Kgs 20:1-12 is suspect.

Furthermore, Miller and Ahlström maintain that 1 Kgs 20:34 incorrectly ascribes the reclamation of Israelite territories from the Syrians to Ahab.[65] Miller brings into play 2 Kgs 10:32-33 and 13:24-25; consequently, he contends that Jehu, not Omri, lost Israelite territory to the Syrians. Thus no Israelite cities were available for Ahab to recover from this group. Miller claims that Jehoahaz defeated the Syrians three times, and that he is the Israelite monarch who reclaimed Israelite territory from the Syrians. According to Miller, the return of Israelite properties to Israel by the Syrians happened after the death of Ahab. Consequently, texts that recount the transfer of Israelite cities from the control of the Syrians to Israel, e.g., 1 Kgs 20:34, postdate Ahab.

It is possible to argue that this passage is a window on the reign of Ahab. On the one hand, this study argues that cycles might have been present in the reign of Ahab, and that 1 Kgs 20:1-34 might deal with a period in the early regime of Ahab. As was said above, Miller and Ahlström introduce the extrabiblical data and allow these texts to inform their notions about the military strength of Ahab. While this study contends that the evidence in the Assyrian annals on soldiers that Ahab contributed to the effort to stymie the Assyrian advance at Qarqar in 853 B.C.E. is questionable, the present project concedes that the report of Shalmaneser III is a window on the Israelite army during the end of the reign of Ahab. 1 Kgs 20:15-21 indicates that Ahab inflicted an uncompromising defeat on the Syrians and on the thirty-two kings that were in a league with the Syrians, and that he confiscated chariots and horses from this campaign. Ahab's victory over the Syrians and other features of his domestic and foreign policy, then, possibly account for the increase in the size of his army. It, then, is possible to argue that 1 Kgs 20:1-12 reflects a period in the reign of Ahab before the increase in the size of his military machine.

On the other hand, 1 Kgs 15:20 indicates that Baasha lost territory to the Syrians. This text states that Ben-Hadad captured Ijon, Dan, Abel Beth Maacah, land near the Sea of Galilee, and the whole territory of Naphtali. 1 Kgs 15:20 provides a basis for arguing that Ben-Hadad I captured cities from Israel. This phenomenon undermines assigning 1 Kgs 20:34 to a pe-

---

65. Miller, pp. 441-54, and Ahlström, p. 575.

riod that postdates Jehu, for 1 Kgs 20:34 indicates that Israel lost territory to the Syrians before the birth of Ahab. Thus the defeat of the Syrians by Ahab positioned him to recover the cities from Syria that Baasha lost to Ben-Hadad I. Two phenomena might account for the return of Israelite cities to Ahab by Ben-Hadad II: (1) it was a response to the political kindness of Ahab, for Ahab spared the life of Ben-Hadad I; (2) it was an endeavor to clear the way for the anti-Assyrian coalition that was to emerge later between Israel and Syria.[66]

This study therefore argues that 1 Kgs 20:1-34 is a window on the administration of Ahab; it consequently extrapolates information about the administrative apparatus of Ahab from this text. As this section mentioned above, 1 Kgs 20:14-15 indicates that provinces and provincial governors were present in the North during the reign of Ahab. Administrative districts and governors, however, were not originally introduced into the North by Ahab, for geographic divisions were in the northern part of the Israelite state during the reign of Solomon.[67] While evidence is not present in the HB and in literature from elsewhere in the ANE on the duties of these officials in the Omride administration, it becomes plausible that a governing class was present in the North during the Omride reign. It is plausible that this component mustered troops for the Israelite army and aided the Omrides in accomplishing their political and economic goals on the local scene.

Gottwald and Lenski argue that royal functionaries were present in a "typical" agrarian society. Without doubt a retainer class was present in the Omride administration. Furthermore, 1 Kgs 18:3 introduces Obadiah and suggests he was the supervisor of the palace. What is more, 1 Kgs 21:1 suggests that a palace for the Omrides was present at Jezreel. It therefore is probable that cooks, bakers, perfume makers, field hands, and other types of domestic servants were present in the Omride administration, and that Obadiah or some other person managed these retainers and superintended the physical upkeep of the royal residences.

66. Moreover, it is possible to argue that 1 Kgs 20:1-12 depicts a diplomatic Ahab, for this text implies that Ahab wanted to bring about a peaceful solution to the crisis with the Syrians.

67. John Bright, "The Organization and Administration of the Israelite Empire," in *Magnalia Dei, the Mighty Acts of God: Essays on the Bible and Archaeology in Memory of G. Ernest Wright,* ed. Frank M. Cross, Werner Lemke, and Patrick D. Miller, Jr. (Garden City, N.Y.: Doubleday, 1976), pp. 193-208.

1 Kgs 20:15 and the report of Shalmaneser III concerning the Battle of Qarqar in 853 B.C.E. state that Ahab mustered seven thousand soldiers for the Israelite conflict with the Syrians. These data suggest that he contributed two thousand chariots and ten thousand soldiers to the Syria-Palestinian effort to stop the Assyrian westward advance at Qarqar.[68] While certainty on the numerical strength of the army and chariots of Ahab is a formidable obstacle, it is probable that Ahab had a sizable army, and that it suppressed potential uprisings and contributed to efficacious rule of the Omride regime.

What is more, DtrH, Palestinian inscriptions, and archaeological finds suggest that a resurgence in state building projects was a feature of the Omride dynasty — the construction of royal residences, housing for the retainers and domestic servants of the Omride administration, the fortification of outlying villages, and the repair of other administrative and defensive structures in the North being paramount among them. It, then, is plausible that artisans and royal functionaries were elements in the socioeconomic fabric of the North during the Omride administration.[69]

Gottwald and Lenski argue that merchants were a major stratum in agrarian societies. Evidence is present for claiming that a mercantile class was present in the North. 1 Kgs 20:31-34 declares that Syrian merchants operated markets in Samaria. Insight into items for sale at these bazaars is absent in 1 Kgs 20:34. This datum suggests that merchants were present in Israel, and that they constituted the mercantile subgroup in the North during the Omride administration.

Gottwald and Lenski affirm that royal priests and prophets constituted a major socioeconomic subdivision in agrarian communities. 1 Kgs 18:15-20 indicates that cultic officials made up the Omride bureaucracy. While this text declares that they promulgated the veneration of Baal, it is silent about which Baal they worshiped. 1 Kgs 18:15-20 links them to the Phoenician princess, Jezebel, and this association clears space for the claim that they promulgated the worship of Melqart of Tyre or Baal Shamem of Sidon.[70] While 1 Kgs 18:15-20 implies that Jezebel was a worshiper of Baal, it is silent on the religiosity of Ahab. DtrH states that

---

68. *ANET*, pp. 278-79.

69. More will be said about the building activities of the Omrides in chapter 5 of this study.

70. Ahlström, pp. 586-88.

Ahab bestowed Yahwistic names on his sons: Ahaziah ("Yahweh seizes"; 1 Kgs 22:51) and Joram/Jehoram ("Yahweh is high"; 2 Kgs 8:16). The names of Ahab's sons imply that he was a member of the Yahweh cult. The fact that cultic functionaries were a prominent feature of the administrative apparatus of Ahab leaves open the possibility that they were a subgroup in the regimes of Omride kings who succeeded Ahab also. 1 Kgs 18:15-20, then, suggests that cultic officials were present in the administrative apparatus of Ahab, and that these individuals constituted an important subgroup in the biblical communities in the North during the ninth century B.C.E.

Gottwald and Lenski propose that the peasantry is a major subgroup in agrarian societies, and both scholars contend that stratification is present among persons in this stratum. A mountain of evidence is present in the HB from which to infer that the peasantry was a major socioeconomic stratum in the North during the Omride administration, and that this collectivity was diverse. Amos illuminates circumstances in Israel during the time of Jeroboam II (786–746/45).[71] Amos 2:6-11; 4:1-3; 5:10-15; and 8:4-8 suggest that socioeconomic asymmetry, rampant injustice, and widespread vulnerability were features of Israel during the eighth century. Amos, however, is silent about the moment at which these phenomena became symptomatic of human communities in the North. It is improbable that many economic circumstances in Israel during the eighth century B.C.E. originated during that century, for 1 Kgs 16:21-34; 18:3, 15-20; and 20:14-15 show that sufficient conditions for eco-

---

71. For the sake of this analysis, "Amos" refers to the literature, not the prophet. Assumptions that guide the present discussion are that multiple editors may be responsible for the arrangement of the prophecies in Amos; this does not mean, however, that the speech units were not spoken by the prophet during the eighth century B.C.E.; moreover, the shift of focus from socioeconomic injustice to cultic hypocrisy does not suggest a different epoch in the ministry of Amos, for it is probable that both layers, that is, pronouncements on exploitation and on cultic misbehavior, were spoken during the reign of Jeroboam II. What is more, since the North is the culprit in speeches in Amos, announcements of deportation and return from exile could have been spoken during the eighth century B.C.E. also; treatment of Amos and the critical discussion on this literature are available in John H. Hayes, *Amos: The Eighth-Century Prophet* (Nashville: Abingdon, 1988); Hans W. Wolff, *Joel and Amos* (Philadelphia: Fortress, 1977); Robert B. Coote, *Amos among the Prophets* (Philadelphia: Fortress, 1981); Shalom Paul, *Amos* (Philadelphia: Fortress, 1991); David N. Freedman, *Amos*, Anchor Bible Commentary Series (Garden City, N.Y.: Doubleday, 1989); and Philip J. King, *Amos, Hosea, Micah: An Archaeological Commentary* (Philadelphia: Fortress, 1988).

nomic antitheses were prominent in the North during the ninth century B.C.E.

Amos 2:6-11; 4:1-3; 5:10-15; and 8:4-8, then, become windows on the peasantry in the North during the ninth century. These texts imply that impoverished and vulnerable persons made up this subgroup, and they use different terms to denote these human beings. On the one hand, the usage of *'ĕbyôn* (needy person) is widespread. In Amos 4:1 and 8:6 this term appears with *dal*. These passages suggest that the *'ĕbyôn* was the victim of crimes in the economic sphere, and that the dignity of this type of person was an object of contempt.

Amos 4:1; 5:11; and 8:6 mention the *dal*. This term has the second-highest frequency among those terms that denote exploited persons in Amos. Amos 5:11 states: you trample the *dal*, and you take portions of grain from him/her. Amos 8:6 implies that this type of person was the target of fraud. Amos 8:4-6 declares:

> Hear this, you who trample the needy and do away with the humbled
>   of the land. You say:
> "When will the New Moon be over
> that we may sell grain,
> and the Sabbath be ended,
> that we may market wheat?"
> reducing the measure,
> and increasing the price,
> and cheating with dishonest scales,
> buying the weak person *(dal)* for silver,
> and the needy for a pair of sandals,
> and selling the refuse of corn.

Thus Amos 5:11 conveys the idea that the *dal* was the target of extortion, and 8:6 indicates that this type of person often sold himself/herself into slavery. Perhaps this circumstance arose as a result of this type of person having to eke out his/her existence on a daily basis with insufficient resources.

The humbled person *('ănāwîm)* appears in Amos, and this term denotes a peasant who experienced some type of injustice in the North. This word appears only twice in Amos; this is striking, for the usage of this term for persons who experienced oppression in ancient Israel is widespread elsewhere in the HB. In 2:7 *'ănāwîm* appears with *dal.* In 8:4 *'ănāwîm* is paired with *'ĕbyôn.* The prophetic corpus and the Psalter frequently pair *'ănāwîm* with *'ĕbyôn.*[72]

The denunciation of exploitation is a feature of speeches in Amos. This document is helpful for identifying elements among the peasantry in the North. Amos contains many terms that symbolized the impoverished masses, and it denounces the injustices that this element suffers. Amos 2:6-11; 4:1-3; 5:10-15; and 8:4-8 convey the idea that the peasantry, a lower socio-economic stratum, was present in the North during the eighth century B.C.E. It is probable that it was present during the ninth century B.C.E. as well, and that several categories of people constituted it.

Lenski suggests that a subgroup of expendable persons was present in "typical" agrarian societies, and that women with children but without husbands and other individuals who had to live by charity made up this collectivity. It is important to add that the Elijah-Elisha narratives declare that widows and orphans were present in the North during the Omride administration. These narratives convey the idea that widows had children and experienced poverty. What is more, they portray Elijah and Elisha as local folk heroes and as friends of widows and orphans. These prophets allegedly suspend or influence the laws of nature in order to benefit this class of socially weak persons (1 Kgs 17:8-24 and 2 Kgs 4:1-7). These texts therefore imply that a subgroup of expendable persons, e.g., widows and orphans, was present in the North during the reign of the Omrides.

Summary

Gottwald and Lenski imply that the access to and command over economic resources are the major criteria for identifying levels of socioeconomic inequality in the biblical communities. Neither Gottwald nor Lenski, however, examines the relationship of gender and age to economic ranking in the biblical communities or in agrarian societies. It, however, is probable that a disproportional number of those on the lower end of the power and privilege continuum in ancient Israel and in typical agrarian societies were females and minor children.

Lenski advocates the position that foreigners were a major element

---

72. See J. David Pleins, "Poor, Poverty," in *ABD,* 5:402-14.

among the peasantry in agrarian societies also. He argues that differences in ways of thinking and speaking, social conventions, and norms separated foreigners from the dominant group in the larger societies they inhabited. The work of Lenski lends support to the idea that the cultural allegiance of foreigners, i.e., the degree to which they assimilated into the larger society, differentiated them from the in-group, and that the nonassimilation of foreigners into the mainstream contributed to their socioeconomic inferiority in agrarian communities. This study adopts Gottwald and Lenski's model of the agrarian society and uses it to identify social subgroups and to discuss socioeconomic ranking in the biblical communities in the North during the ninth century B.C.E.

Working from the assumptions that Lenski's model of the agrarian state and Gottwald's delineation of the social composition of the biblical communities after the formation of the state are clues on social stratification in the North, this study contends that widows, strangers, and orphans were present among groups in the lower economic stratum in ancient Israel. It is noteworthy that Lenski's paradigm for understanding the hierarchically organized levels of socioeconomic inequality in agrarian communities conveys the idea that the social location of the 'almānâ, gēr, and yātôm was beneath the socioeconomic location of the peasantry. Furthermore, it is probable that this social location trapped these persons in a web of injustice and mistreatment, and increased their susceptibility to oppression.

Propounding that Deut 14:22-29; 16:9-12, 13-15; 24:17-18, 19-22; and 26:12-15 contributed to the oppression of widows, strangers, and orphans, a subgroup of vulnerable underclass individuals in ancient Israel, raises questions about the facts of the investigation. Concern with the empirical evidence, therefore, brings into play the literary features of these texts, for these data are the main pieces of information for discussing the effects of these legal injunctions in biblical Israel. Chapter 3 delineates, examines, and provides insight into salient ideas, literary formulas, and pedagogies in the widow, stranger, and orphan laws in Deut 12–26 — phenomena that provide a window on the Deuteronomic response to tithing, cultic pilgrimages, and items left in the fields by reapers.

Chapter 3

TEXTS AND ADJUDICATION

*Examining Innovations in the Widow, Stranger,
and Orphan Laws in the Deuteronomic Code*

Introduction

Critical theory about law contends that legal sanctions advance frequently
the politico-economic interests of social subgroups in human societies.
Since this study uses critical theory to discuss the regulations that deal
with the *'almānâ, gēr,* and *yātôm* in the Deuteronomic Code, it proposes
that these legal injunctions convey biased ideas. Also I contend that the
distinct literary features of these codes disclose these tenets and provide
clues about the identity of the camp that formulated these points of view.
In this chapter I analyze the codes and call attention to the major literary
peculiarities of these regulations. This chapter has three aims: to discuss
tithes, the festival calendar, and gleanings in a manner that provides a
background for understanding the plight of the *'almānâ, gēr,* and *yātôm* in
the Deuteronomic Code; to translate these regulations and treat textual
problems that have relevance for this study; and to delineate the distinctive
formulas, terminology, and pedagogies of these legal sanctions.

Critical Issues for Understanding Laws on Tithes in the DC

One matter that warrants attention regarding the tithing regulations in the
DC is the sociohistoric origins of tithes in ancient Israel. Scant data are
present in the HB on these origins. It is noteworthy that regulations on

73

tithes do not appear in the BC, the oldest body of law in the HB.[1] This absence plus the presence of such in the DC and in Priestly law, bodies of legislation that postdate the BC, imply that tithing was nonextant, voluntary, or not widespread during the formative period in the history of ancient Israel.[2] Thus the BC is inconclusive for discussing the sociohistoric origins of tithing in ancient Israel.

Data elsewhere in the HB, however, suggest that tithing was present in the biblical communities prior to the appearance of the state. Gen 14:18-20 and 28:18-22 imply that tithing was a custom of subgroups that composed the biblical communities. The former passage states that Abram paid tithes to Melchizedek.[3] The latter recounts Jacob's vow at Bethel and shows Jacob setting up a pillar and pouring wine and oil on it. It is important to notice that Jacob proposed to give the deity a tithe of his possessions. Gen 14:18-20 and 28:18-22, however, are silent on how and when Abram and Jacob came into contact with tithing. This silence on the emergence of tithing in these narratives can take the conversation on tithes in different directions. It could mean that the readers, hearers, or codifiers of Gen 14:18-20 and 28:18-22 were either familiar with the sociohistoric origins of tithing and needed no more information, or that they knew nothing about these origins or the factors that accounted for tithing's presence in the Abram-Melchizedek and Jacob stories and did not want to speculate.[4]

1. It is axiomatic in critical scholarship that the BC contains regulations from the tribal period in ancient Israel, and that these regulations were codified during the early Israelite monarchy. The BC therefore proceeds from the early Israelite monarchy; consequently, the present project will use that period as the date of the codification of the BC, and for discussing chronological relationships between regulations in the BC and in the DC. For full discussion on the monarchic date of the Covenant Code, see Rainer Albertz, *A History of Israelite Religion in the Old Testament Period,* trans. John Bowden, vol. 1, OTL (Louisville: Westminster/John Knox, 1992), pp. 60-61.

2. Exod 23:19 treats firstfruits of cattle and agriculture; yet it is unsafe to claim that these regulations cover tithes. The study will return to a discussion of firstfruits in the section below on the feast of weeks in the DC.

3. Treatment of the literary and historical problems of Gen 14 will take us beyond the scope of our discussion. The fact that Abram is described as engaged in a military exploit might be a clue as to who preserved this tradition. For discussion on the historical-critical problems of Gen 14, see Gerhard von Rad, *Genesis,* trans. John H. Marks, OTL (Philadelphia: Westminster, 1972), pp. 174-81.

4. Publications that explore the origins of tithing in biblical Israel are: H. Jagersma, "Tithes in the Old Testament," in *Remembering All the Way,* ed. B. Albrektson (Leiden: E. J. Brill, 1981), pp. 116-28; J. G. McConville, *Law and Theology in Deuteronomy* (Sheffield: JSOT

The custom regarding the payment of tithes was present elsewhere in the ANE, and it is possible that cross-fertilization happened.[5] H. Jagersma discloses that information concerning tithing appears in texts that come from the third dynasty of Ur, and that 90 percent of the relevant information about the payment and collection of tithes in Mesopotamia emerged from the sixth century B.C.E. Jagersma delineates a possibility for the sociohistoric origins of tithing in Mesopotamia by linking the beginnings of this practice to a tax for the support of the state or to an assessment for the material endowment of religious institutions in Mesopotamian societies.[6] Although these texts emerged from the late Babylonian period, it is probable that tithing was much older than the Mesopotamian documents in which the data on it appear. Regarding the custom of tithing elsewhere in the ANE, Crüsemann states: "It is only when we examine what we know about the tithe from other sources that we can begin to understand what happens in these peripheral regulations of deuteronomic law. The tithe existed in a few other contemporary cultures. In those places it was to be paid to the king or to a specific temple."[7] The evidence concerning tithing in Mesopotamian communities, therefore, suggests that this practice was present elsewhere in the ANE. Either tithing was a custom of subgroups in the biblical communities, or subgroups in the biblical communities borrowed the custom from subgroups elsewhere in the ANE. Sociological dynamics that account for the presence of tithing in biblical Israel, however, may be forever lost to scholarship.

While it is plausible that tithing was present in ancient Israelite society, a second issue that warrants discussion is the obligatoriness of this phenomenon. The fact that competing data about the payment of tithes are present in the HB is at the center of this problem. As was said above, no regulations on tithing are present in the BC. This fact could mean that

---

Press, 1984), pp. 68-87; Moshe Weinfeld, "Tithes," in *EncJud* (1971), pp. 1156-62; and Julius Wellhausen, *Prolegomena to the History of Ancient Israel* (Gloucester: Peter Smith, 1983), pp. 152-67.

5. For treatment on tithes in Mesopotamia, see *"ešrû,"* in *CAD*, vol. 4 (Chicago: Oriental Institute, 1958), pp. 369-70; M. A. Dandamayev, "Der Tempelzehnten in Babylon während des 6-4 Jahrhundert," in *Beiträge zur Alten Geschichte und deren Nachleben*, Festschrift für Franz Altheim (Berlin: De Gruyter, 1969), pp. 82-90.

6. Jagersma, pp. 116-17.

7. Frank Crüsemann, *The Torah: Theology and Social History of Old Testament Law*, trans. Allan W. Mahnke (Minneapolis: Fortress, 1996), p. 216.

tithing was present among social actors but was voluntary. Gen 12:4-10; 13:2-7; and 35:1-14 throw light on this issue. These passages are windows on the piety, wealth, and religiousness of key figures in the ancestral period. Gen 12:4-10 and 13:2-7 imply that Abram owned slaves and livestock, and that he had a personal militia and a plethora of money. These texts indicate that he built altars throughout Syria-Palestine. None of these narratives, however, shows that Abram presented tithes of his property to Yahweh. It is noteworthy that Gen 14:18-20 is the only text in the HB that recounts the payment of tithes by Abram.

Moreover, Gen 35:1-14 recounts Jacob's return to Bethel. This text shows that Jacob set up a pillar, and that this stone became a memorial of the theophany to him. It is important to notice that Jacob offered no tithes during this ceremony also. This phenomenon attracts attention, for Gen 30:43 says Jacob owned many cattle and slaves. In short, no evidence in the Pentateuch states that Jacob ever offered tithes. These Abram and Jacob stories suggest that these personalities offered tithes on an infrequent basis; therefore, these passages become bases for arguing that subgroups in the North and South preserved these stories to promulgate the voluntariness of offering tithes. Episodes in the Abram and Jacob cycles associate the giving of part of one's property to the deity with a conscious decision of the ancestors, and this citation supports the position that giving tithes of one's possessions was an old spontaneous action: the offerer did it without coercion.

A third issue that arises is the economic function of tithing in ancient Israel. On the one hand, laws in the Pentateuch suggest that tithes were one element in a comprehensive system for the material endowment of the clergy. Num 18:21-24 suggests that these items belonged to them. Lev 27:30-34 implies that cultic officials subjected grain, fruit, and livestock to tithes, and that these items were for their material endowment.[8] Deut 18:3-5 mili-

---

8. I strongly suspect that Num 18:21-24 and Lev 27:30-34 antedate the razing of the Jerusalem temple. Widespread agreement is present on the presence of a tiered priesthood in the postexilic community, and specificity on this phenomenon is characteristic of texts from the Second Temple period that treat cultic ministrants. Moreover, Solomon's temple became a major center for cultic practice both in the united monarchy and in the Southern Kingdom. Thus the temple in Jerusalem operated for over three hundred years before the Babylonian catastrophe. This would permit cultic officials time to gather, organize, classify, and edit independent traditions in the biblical communities that treat tithes. Thus the absence of the priest/Levite dichotomy that is distinctive of postexilic regulations treating the priesthood,

tates against ambiguity on the remuneration of cultic officials by specifying the material entitlements of the clergy. This regulation states that priests should receive remuneration from the cult. This compensation included parts of animals that were sacrificed to Yahweh, e.g., the shoulder, jaw, and stomach, and the earliest produce gathered from the fields. Deut 18:3-5 does not fix the items to which the clergy has entitlement, and this phenomenon allows the farmer or herder to bring whatever portions from the flock, herd, or fields he thought adequate.

On the other hand, DtrH implies that tithes of property became one element in systems for the material endowment of the Israelite monarchy during the administration of Solomon. A professional army, official priesthood, royal retainers, and a large royal family were not features of the administration of Saul. It therefore is probable that his regime did not call for massive quantities of commodities or a plethora of sources upon which to draw for sustenance. Thus, prior to the tenth century B.C.E., it is improbable that any comprehensive system for the material endowment of the Israelite monarchy was present in the biblical communities. Perhaps booty taken in wars against the Ammonites, Philistines, and other political entities was the main source for the material endowment of Saul and his administration.

The state under David, however, became more complex, and it required more sources for its material endowment than the state under Saul. At the center of this problem was a large administration that included a standing army, a priesthood, and royal retainers. 2 Sam 8:15-18 and 20:23-26 provide insight into this issue, for these passages contain separate lists of top officials in the Davidic state. The former passage states: "David ruled over Israel, and he executed justice and righteousness for all his people. Joab, the son of Zeruiah, supervised the army; Jehoshaphat, the son of Ahilud, was the recorder; Zadok, the son of Ahitub, and Ahimelech, the son of Abiathar, were priests, and Seriah was the scribe. Benaiah, the son of Jehoiada, was over the Kerethites and Pelethites, and David's sons were priests." 2 Sam 20:23-26 says: "Joab was over the army of Israel, and Benaiah, the son of Jehoiada, was over the Kerethites and Pelethites.

and widespread cultic activity associated with the temple prior to 587 B.C.E., are central to the present claim that Lev 27:30-34 and Num 18:21-24 are preexilic. For discussion on the priesthood in the biblical communities, see Joseph Blenkinsopp, *Sage, Priest, Prophet: Religious and Intellectual Leadership in Ancient Israel* (Louisville: Westminster/John Knox, 1995), pp. 66-114.

Adoniram was over the labor battalions; Jehoshaphat, the son of Ahilud, was the record keeper. Sheva was the scribe, and Abiathar was the priest. Ira the Jairite was a priest also." These passages indicate that a standing army, a priesthood, royal retainers, and labor battalions were features of the Davidic administration. It is probable that many of these top officials had large staffs also.[9] The political power of David positioned him to capture chariots and soldiers, to seize gold and bronze, and to force tribute from people he conquered in battle. While DtrH is silent on what David did with these goods, I strongly suspect that he used them to pay his lieutenants, militia, royal retainers, and to support the royal family and harem.[10] Tithes therefore supplemented other sources for the economic support of the Israelite state as it became more bureaucratic.

1 Kgs 4:7–5:8 delineates the sources from which Solomon acquired commodities for the material endowment of his administration. It is noteworthy that Solomon organized the empire into twelve administrative districts, and that each province was responsible for the sustenance of the royal bureaucracy for one month during the year. Moreover, 1 Kgs 10:14-29 implies that international trade and maritime enterprises were features of Solomon's administration, and that income from these endeavors contributed to the support of the monarchy. What is more, Solomon supported international trade, a royal priesthood, a large royal harem, a standing army, extensive building projects, retainers, and a plethora of administrative personnel. It becomes probable that he exacted tithes of produce and meat from the local peasantry, and that these items were an element in the system for the material endowment of his administration.

1 Sam 8:11-21 provides insight into the fiscal affairs of centralized government, and it links the payment of tithes to the support of monarchy in biblical Israel also.[11] This study infers from this text that monarchs took tithes of the flocks and agriculture in the biblical communities. While

---

9. See John Bright, "The Organization and Administration of the Israelite Empire," in *Magnalia Dei, the Mighty Acts of God: Essays on the Bible and Archaeology in Memory of G. Ernest Wright,* ed. Frank M. Cross, Werner Lemke, and Patrick D. Miller, Jr. (Garden City, N.Y.: Doubleday, 1976), pp. 193-208.

10. While income from tolls does not appear in these data, it is probable that it was an additional source of revenue for David. Therefore it is likely that these texts do not delineate each source upon which David drew for the material endowment of his empire.

11. Moreover, we have evidence that tithes of property were a resource for the material endowment of governments elsewhere in the ancient Near East. See *"ešrû,"* in *CAD,* vol. 4.

scholars often link this passage to Solomon, it is unsafe to argue that he is the only one to whom this text can apply, for there were other monarchs who ruled subsequent to Solomon and needed immense resources for their daily operations.[12] Thus it is probable that soldiers, retainers, and members of the royal household received sustenance and an income from the tithes of crops, animals, and orchards in the biblical communities.[13]

Subgroups of law in the Pentateuch and narratives in DtrH, then, suggest that the state and religious camps sought to control and appropriate tithes of produce, cattle, and flocks in ancient Israelite society. Competing ideas about the ownership of these items might be at the center of this issue. For example, Crüsemann advances the theory that the tithes of produce, cattle, and flocks in the biblical communities belonged to the deity and the state. He grounds his claim in the role that Bethel played in the collection of tithes in biblical Israel. "This is, of course, one of the most important state shrines (Am 7:13; 1 Kg 12:26). As elsewhere, the tithe here was a tax connected with the legal claim of the kingdom. It was given to the sacral monarchy, whether it went to the state temple or the sacral state, in each case it belonged to God and the king together."[14]

The decentralization of the cult is a fourth issue that composes the backdrop against which to understand the regulations on tithes in the DC. The fact that there were several sites in ancient Israelite society for the presentation and consumption of offerings and tithes of produce and cattle is basic to this problem. Prior to the Josianic reformation, people in the North and South offered sacrifices, paid vows, and performed rituals at sites throughout the biblical communities. 1 Sam 1:3; 7:16; 1 Kgs 12:25-33; and Amos 4:4 state that Shiloh, Bethel, Gilgal, Mizpah, Ramah, and a location in Dan were major cultic sites in the North; thus people gathered at these shrines in order to celebrate festivals, present sacrifices, and make or fulfill vows. What is more, 1 Kgs 3:4 discloses that cultic sites were widespread in the South, and that social actors offered sacrifices and performed rituals at these shrines. DtrH uses the phrase "high place" to denote these venues.[15]

---

12. Deut 17:14-17 places limits on the financial appetite of the king by stating that he should be pious, not greedy. This text thus implies that the financial appetite of the monarch was at the center of much conflict in the biblical community.

13. I will return to the discussion about the monarch to whom 1 Sam 8:11-21 applies shortly.

14. Crüsemann, p. 217.

15. 1 Kgs 3:1-3; 14:21-24; 22:41-44; 2 Kgs 12:1-3; 14:1-6; 15:1-7.

These texts use this term indiscriminately to denote shrines other than the Jerusalem temple.[16] The belief that several sites were present for the presentation and collection of tithes, then, is consistent with the evidence in DtrH.

Many texts in the HB treat tithes. These data, however, are silent on the sociohistoric origins of this phenomenon in the biblical communities. These data delineate clues about the controversies regarding tithing in ancient Israel. It is probable that these issues were: (1) *the moral question* on tithes, i.e., the obligatoriness of the payment of tithes; (2) sites for the collection of tithes; and (3) the distribution of tithes in the biblical communities, i.e., who had entitlement to tithes. Was it the deity or the monarch? The next section therefore examines Deut 14:22-29 and 26:12-15 against the backdrop of the controversies regarding the collection and distribution of tithes in ancient Israelite society.

Laws on Tithes, and Widows, Strangers, and Orphans in the DC

Deut 14:22-29 says:

> 22You must indeed tithe of all your crops that the field brings forth each year. 23You will eat them in the place that Yahweh will choose, the place where the divine name is present. You will give a tithe of your grain, new wine, fresh oil, and the firstborn of your small and large cattle, so that you will learn to fear Yahweh your God forever. 24If the place is too far away, and you are unable to carry the tithe, 25exchange the tithe for silver; bind it in your hand and go to the place which Yahweh your God will choose. 26You may give the silver for whatever you desire, for large or small cattle, wine, or strong drink; you and your household will eat and rejoice there before Yahweh your God. 27Do not abandon the Levite, since he has neither portion nor inheritance among you. 28At the end of three years, bring all the tithe of your increase and leave it in your gates. 29The Levite, since he has neither portion nor inheritance among you, the stranger, orphan, and widow will come; they will eat and be satisfied, so that Yahweh your God will bless you in everything you do.

Deut 14:22-29 includes five major parts:

16. Albertz, p. 84.

Innovations in Deut 14:22-29 suggest that the drafters of this legal injunction adapted an extant regulation on tithing in the biblical communities. Deut 12:5-7, 17-19 are older regulations about the presentation and consumption of tithes in the biblical communities. Deut 12:6a simply admonishes local peasant farmers and herders to carry all the tithes and offerings to the place that the deity chooses. Deut 12:17-19 pays particular attention to the consumption of the tithes of produce and livestock by plainly directing individuals to eat these items at the official cultic site. Neither the form of Deut 12:5-7 nor the grammatical structure of Deut 12:17-19 implies that the presentation of tithes on an annual basis is an obligation. Mayes and Crüsemann argue that Deut 14:22-29 reflects fresh circumstances in ancient Israelite society.[17] Prominent in this passage is the infinitive absolute/finite verb construction "you will indeed tithe" (ʿaśēr tĕʿaśēr). This literary feature stresses the obligation of tithing. Deut 14:22b

17. A. D. H. Mayes, *Deuteronomy* (Grand Rapids: Eerdmans, [1979] 1991), pp. 244-45; and Crüsemann, p. 218.

introduces the word "year" *(šānâ)*, thereby implying that the local peasant farmer should present the tithes of crops and fruits annually. By emphasizing the idea of tithing yearly, Deut 14:22 states that the presentation of grain, wine, oil is an annual duty. Thus innovations in Deut 14:22 suggest that individuals in the Deuteronomic camp had questions about the payment of tithes: these distinctive form-critical features suggest that the drafters of Deut 14:22-29 sought to inculcate ideas in peasant farmers about the ethical dimensions of tithing. Deut 14:22 therefore proposes that tithing is a yearly obligation for social actors in the biblical communities.

Deut 14:23a suggests that a cultic meal accompanied the presentation of tithes at the official shrine. R. Merendino writes, "An independent literary and tradition-historical command is present in Deut 14:23 that schedules a meal of corn, wine, and olive oil in the presence of Yahweh."[18] Thus the presence of "[and] you will eat" in this verse suggests that the tithes of produce belong to the offerer. This is a major inconsistency, for Priestly law states that the tithes were the property of cultic officials.[19] M. Weinfeld states: "The book of Deuteronomy also contains a less sacral conception of tithes than the other Pentateuchal sources. The tithe, which the Priestly document designates as 'holy to the Lord' (Lev. 27:30-3), and which according to a second tradition accrues to the Levites (Num. 18:21-32), remains by deuteronomic legislation the property of the original owner (14:22-7)."[20] It is improbable that the offerer consumed all the tithes; consequently tithes became a source from which cultic ministrants got commodities for their material support. Deut 14:23a, however, associates tithes with a sacred meal in ancient Israel.

Deut 14:23a states that vegetables, fruits, and livestock were items from which people exacted tithes. Deut 14:23a contains many items that appear

18. "In Deut 14:23aa liegt ein überlieferungsgeschichtlich und literarisch selbständiges Gebot vor, das das Essen von Korn, Most und Öl vor Jahwe vorsieht." See R. P. Merendino, *Das Deuteronomische Gesetz* (Bonn: Peter Hanstein, 1969), p. 97. The present scholar, however, parts company with Merendino and proposes that Deut 14:23a is not "ein überlieferungsgeschichtlich und literarisch selbständiges Gebot," but an original part of the verse.

19. Num 18:21-24 is a regulation on tithes in the biblical communities. Although it says every tithe in ancient Israel was for the material endowment of the Levites, it is ambiguous on items subject to tithes.

20. Moshe Weinfeld, *Deuteronomy and the Deuteronomic School* (Winona Lake, Ind.: Eisenbrauns, 1992), p. 214.

in Deut 12:17a also, for the latter text imposes a levy on grain, new wine, fresh oil, and cattle. Legal injunctions concerning items that were subject to tithes appear elsewhere in the Pentateuch. Lev 27:30-34 imposes an assessment on grain, fruit, and livestock. It therefore becomes plausible that Deut 12:17a informs both lists, and that Deut 14:23 reflects an intermediate stage in the development of laws concerning tithes in the biblical communities.[21]

Deut 14:23a states that only one site was acceptable for the presentation and consumption of tithes, and that the deity chose this venue *(bammāqôm 'ăšer yibḥar lĕšakēn šĕmô)*. This ideology and literary feature is consistent with the centralization formulas in the laws on major cultic festivals that appear elsewhere in the DC.[22]

Regardless of how one interprets the centralization phrase in Deut 14:23a, e.g., exclusively or distributively, the denotation forbids offering and eating tithes at family altars or sanctuaries. While the delineation of official sites for the presentation and consumption of tithes is an insurmountable obstacle, data in DtrH and Amos indicate that Shiloh, Bethel, Gilgal, Mizpah, Ramah, and Dan were major cultic sites in the biblical community for festival gatherings, presentation of sacrifices, making of vows, performance of private rituals, and adjudication of legal issues among sociopolitical subgroups.[23] The centralization formula in Deut 14:23a, therefore, is a counterattack against the presentation and consumption of tithes at local sites, for evidence is present in DtrH that family cults were widespread in the biblical communities. The Elijah-Elisha narratives lend weight to the claim that multiple religious communities were present in the biblical communities after the formation of the state.[24] W. Doorly comments: "In premonarchic Israel there were a variety of forms of Baalism. Later, when Yahweh became a god of Israel, different understand-

---

21. The literary history of Deut 12 is at the center of a long-standing debate among biblical scholars. For a recent treatment on this issue, see Bernard Levinson, *Deuteronomy and the Hermeneutics of Legal Innovation* (New York and Oxford: Oxford University Press, 1997), pp. 23-52.

22. For more treatment on the literary features of the centralization formulas in the DC, see Baruch Halpern, "The Centralization Formula in Deuteronomy," *VT* 36, no. 1 (1981): 20-38.

23. 1 Sam 1:3; 7:16; 1 Kgs 12:25-33; and Amos 4:4.

24. For discussion on the cult and piety in the nuclear family, see Albertz, pp. 23-39, 94-103.

ings of Yahweh produced different forms of Yahwism. There was no central authority for orthodoxy, no committee of priests or theologians to decide which theology was correct and which was heretical. There was no institution of religious education for prophets or religious leaders. Practices varied from location to location. On one level religious practices were determined by family tradition."[25] Doorly clears the way for claiming that the pedagogy concerning an official sanctuary in Deut 14:23a emerged against the backdrop of widespread cultic sites on the local level. Consequently, Deut 14:23a provides insight into the Deuteronomic response to questions about the site for this sacred meal, and it declares that only one site was for the consumption of tithes. It is probable that religiousness was diverse on the local level, and that Yahweh was among objects of veneration by local family cults.

Deut 14:23b states that acquiring *the fear of the deity* will be a consequence of presenting percentages of produce and animals at the official cultic site *(lĕma'an tilmad lĕyir'â 'et yhwh 'ĕlōhêkā)*. This telic clause implies that a relationship is present between partaking in a meal at the official cultic location and gaining an appreciation for Yahweh, but it is silent about the methodology for acquiring such reverence. Two explanations regarding the modus operandi, however, are possible. On the one hand, by the bringing and consuming of tithes at the official cultic site, individuals position themselves and their family to gain theological maturation and insight into the nature of Yahweh. They develop submission and thankfulness to Yahweh and, by allowing such submission and thankfulness to emerge in their personality, acquire reverence for the deity. This method for acquiring fear of the deity provokes introspection and places the onus for learning about the Holy on the moral agent.

On the other hand, it is possible that individuals who taught and promulgated forms of Yahwism were present at the official cultic site. Deut 14:23b, then, suggests that formal instruction in Yahwism accompanied the presentation and consumption of tithes in ancient Israelite society.[26] When they transported and consumed tithes at these venues, the offerers received oral instruction in Yahwism.[27] Thus cultic functionaries were able

25. William Doorly, *The Religion of Israel* (New York: Paulist, 1997), p. 41.

26. I will say more about cultic officials teaching at the official shrine in chapter 5.

27. It is probable that liturgy, exhortation, and moral instruction were methods for pedagogy in the biblical communities. This may account for rituals, legislation, and laws that have an exhortative dimension in the DC.

to communicate catechisms concerning Yahweh and to inculcate ideas about Yahwism in local peasant farmers and herders in the biblical communities.

Deut 14:24 begins the second major section in this law. While this piece of evidence provides insight into phenomena associated with the presentation and consumption of tithes in ancient Israel, it raises questions about two issues. This verse says: "If the place is too far away, and you are unable to carry the tithe." In the first place, "[if] you are unable to carry the tithe" intimates that people transported these commodities to the official cultic site. In other words, Deut 14:24 directs the offerer to bring the tithes of grains, fruits, and animals to the official sanctuary. Information about the method for collecting tithes is not present in Lev 27:30-33 and Num 18:21-24. Perhaps a different strategy for collection accounts for this inconsistency among Deut 14:22-29; Lev 27:30-33; and Num 18:21-24. Laws in P leave open also the possibility that Levites collected these items from individuals in the biblical communities. The method for the collection of tithes is a central point of difference between Deut 14:24; Lev 27:30-33; and Num 18:21-24.

In the second place, Deut 14:24a implies that travel to the site for the presentation and consumption of tithes was a problem. This datum implies that the official cultic site was not in proximity to many local villages or cities, and that this location frequently persuaded people not to make the trek. Deut 14:24a implies also that a distant authority, to whom the people felt no allegiance, sought to regulate the presentation and consumption of tithes. What is more, the presence of ideology that justifies a distant cultic site affirms that a movement to desecrate local altars was present in the biblical communities.

Deut 14:25 considers problems associated with the location and the transportation of tithes to the official sanctuary. If local farmers and herders could not transport these items themselves, they were to convert the tithes into money and travel to the official sanctuary. Deut 14:25 therefore indicates that neither distance nor problems that proceed from the transportation of tithes to a distant location exempted farmers or herders from the obligation to present and consume tithes at the official cultic site.

Deut 14:26 directs local peasant farmers and herders to exchange their commodities for money, and to buy livestock, grains, fruits, and oils at the official cultic site. This verse authorizes the Israelite to buy anything he/she wants and to consume it at the official sanctuary. I concur with J. G.

85

McConville, who argues that this money was not the redemption money that appears in Lev 27:30-33: "While it is to be eaten only at the sanctuary ([Deut] 12:17f), the concession is made (14:24ff) that those who live at some distance may sell their tithe-produce and, at the sanctuary, use the proceeds to repurchase anything they desire to consume. This is evidently not to be understood as 'redemption' (in terms of Lev 27:30ff) since there is no thought of paying over and above the value of the goods."[28]

The idea that the offerer could convert tithes into money, and that local farmers and herders could buy grains, meat, and fruit with money from the converted tithes and consume these items at the official shrine, is absent in Lev 27:30-33 and Num 18:21-24. While Deut 14:26 instructs the offerer to convert the tithes into money, it does not provide insight into the cost of livestock, grains, fruits, intoxicants, and other items the offerer might buy and consume during the sacred meal. What Deut 14:26 does, however, is to effect and legitimize a steady source of income for the cult. Evidence therefore is present that the goal of presenting tithes of produce, cattle, and flocks at the official sanctuary was to create a basis for the material endowment of cultic officials in ancient Israelite society. This piece of information raises questions about the goal of tithes, for Mayes believes the sharing of a meal by persons in a nuclear family was the aim of Deut 14:22-29. "That the money must clearly be reconverted into food and drink indicates that for the deuteronomic legislator the main purpose of the tithe is not the upkeep of the sanctuary. The priest may indeed have a share in the meal (cf. 18:3), but its essential object is that the offerer himself and his household should eat before Yahweh."[29]

Deut 14:27 introduces the third major subdivision in this legal injunction. This section contains one verse, an admonition on behavior toward Levites. In its present form the verse says not to neglect the Levite because he had no inheritance among the people *(kî 'ên lô ḥēleq wĕnaḥălâ 'imāk)*. While it admonishes concern for the Levite, it does not provide guidance on how to care for him. It does state, however, that Levites were poor and without means for sustenance, and the literary context of the verse associates the distribution of grain, fruit, and livestock with charity toward the Levite.

---

28. McConville, p. 69.
29. Mayes, p. 246.

The suggestion in the verse that Levites were poor attracts attention, for the DC indicates that they were neither landless nor poor.

1. Deut 14:24-26 directs individuals to buy sheep, cattle, wine, and intoxicants for consumption at the official cultic site. These instructions bolster the notion that animals and crops were present at the official cultic site. Yet the DC is silent on the sources of these commodities. Deut 14:22-27 is silent on whether the offerer slaughtered all the animals and consumed all the grain and fruit in the meal between himself and his household. This issue leaves open the possibility that some animals remained alive, and that this livestock remained in the custody of cultic officials and became a basis for the sustenance of Levitical families in the biblical communities.

2. The presence of commodities for sale at the central site could mean that Levites farmed, raised cattle, and produced wine and other intoxicants. If so, it is likely they owned land. What is more, Deut 18:6-8 implies that they could sell their possessions. This passage does not identify these items; however, it is possible they included cattle and small pieces of land. In fact, the probability that Levites had an abundance of property might have been the reason they could sell it. Legal injunctions in the DC that indicate that Levites had possessions to sell, then, lend support to the claim that they had assets.

3. The DC shows that offerings made to Yahweh were a major feature of a comprehensive system for the material endowment of Levites in ancient Israelite society. The list of these offerings appears in Deut 18:3-5. These verses imply that the shoulder, jaw, and stomach of animals sacrificed to Yahweh were for the sustenance of the clergy. This regulation also suggests that cultic officials have an entitlement to the earliest gathered produce from the fields. Since it is difficult to enumerate each occasion on which people offered sacrifices, it is possible that this phenomenon was common and frequent in the biblical communities. Deut 18:3-5, then, supports the position that Levites enjoyed a standard of living and material security that insulated them from the economic problems of the peasantry; consequently, the claim that they were poor is suspect.

Deut 14:28 introduces the fourth subdivision in this regulation. This section contains guidelines for the triennial collection and distribution of annual tithes. As was said above, Deut 14:23 shows that the official sanctuary is the site for the presentation and distribution of annual tithes. Deut 14:28b, however, enumerates the local village as the site of the triennial tithes. That is to say, one year out of three the local towns were the location for the presentation and consumption of tithes. In the other two years the official shrine was the location for the collection, distribution, and consumption of tithes of grains, fruit, and livestock in the biblical communities.

Deut 14:29 is the final subdivision in this law. This verse lists the *'almānâ, gēr,* and *yātôm* as a group. It indicates that one year out of three these persons shared in the consumption of the tithe. Thus Deut 14:29a suggests that two years out of three the offerer and cultic officials consumed tithes of grains, fruits, and livestock. This text brings into play the idea of receiving the *blessing of the deity.* This verse, however, does not state the meaning of this phenomenon; thus this study searches elsewhere in Deuteronomy for insight into its meaning. Deut 7:12-16 and 28:1-14 indicate that blessedness is the condition where individuals and communities are free from disease, premature death, barrenness, and defeat in military conquests. Deut 14:29b claims that providing public assistance to the *'almānâ, gēr,* and *yātôm* once every three years effects the blessing of Yahweh; consequently, it advances the typical Deuteronomic ideology that proffering aid to this category of vulnerable persons positions one to be free from circumstances that might undermine the quality of existence.

While Deut 14:22-29 prescribes guidelines for the collection and distribution of the annual tithe, Deut 26:12-15 governs behavior regarding the triennial collection and distribution of the annual tithe exclusively.

Deut 26:12-15 says:

> 12When you finish taking the tenth of all your increase, in the third year, which is the year of the tithe;[30] give the tithes to the Levite, stranger, orphan, and widow, so that they will eat it in your gates and be satisfied. 13Then you will say before Yahweh your God: "I removed the holy thing from the house and gave it to the Levite, stranger, orphan, and widow according to all your commandments. I have neither transgressed nor forgotten your commandments. 14In my affliction, I did not eat from it; when unclean, I did not remove any of it, and I did not give any of it to the dead. I obeyed the voice of Yahweh, my God. I did according to ev-

---

30. "You will give the second tithe" instead of "the year of the tithe" appears in the LXX. The fact that Lev 27:30-34 and Num 18:21-24 are silent on the annual and triennial distribution of tithes to the *'almānâ, gēr,* and *yātôm,* and the fact that these laws state that tithes are for the material endowment of cultic officials, might account for the wording in the LXX and the implication that a second tithing tradition was present in ancient Israel.

erything you commanded me. [15]Look down from the sky, your holy dwelling place, and bless your people Israel and the ground that you gave to us as you swore to our ancestors, a land that flows with milk and honey."

Deut 26:12-15 has two major parts:

I. Guidelines Regarding the Presentation and
   Distribution of the Tithes Triennially   Deut 26:12
   a. The Year for the Sharing of Tithes with Weak
      Social Subgroups in the Biblical Communities   26:12a
   b. The Site for the Consumption of Tithes   26:12b
II. The Ritual That Accompanied the Presentation
    of the Triennial Tithes   Deut 26:13-15
    a. The Recitation   26:13-14
    b. The Prayer   26:15

Deut 26:12a authorizes the biblical community to share the annual tithe with the *'almānâ, gēr, yātôm,* and *lēwî* triennially. This text is clear about this, for it places the year of the tithe *(šĕnat hamma'ăśēr)* in apposition to the third year *(baššānâ haššĕlîšit)*. Thus I contend that one tithing tradition is present in the DC, but that every third year the annual tithe received a special dispensation in the biblical communities. This arrangement, however, does not dispossess the central religious authorities. They simply moved operations to the local villages and collected these commodities there.

Deut 26:12b includes the phrase "so that they will eat [the tithe] in your gates and be satisfied." This datum indicates that the local villages were the venues for the distribution and consumption of the triennial tithes. Two questions immediately arise: By whom, and upon what bases, were the triennial tithes distributed? At the center of this problem is that Deut 26:12b discloses that the *'almānâ, gēr,* and *yātôm* have a right to the tithes stored in the local villages. This verse, however, is silent on the criterion and method for distributing these commodities. This problem warrants attention, for it brings into play concerns about bias and the abuse of power. It is possible that individuals or groups in the biblical communities developed methods to dominate or manipulate the distribution of tithes to Levites and to socially weak, vulnerable individuals in the local villages.

Deut 26:13a introduces the ritual associated with the presentation of the tithes triennially to the 'almānâ, gēr, yātôm, and lēwî. The association of a ritual with the distribution of the triennial tithe is an addition by the drafters of 26:14. No recitation after the deposition of these commodities is present in 14:22-29. Merendino and G. von Rad contend that the formulators of this law incorporated extant confessions that accompanied offerings at local cultic sites with the deposit of tithes in the local villages.[31] It is noticeable that a series of affirmations and a prayer were elements in this liturgy. The offerer professes that he removed the tithes, i.e., the holy thing, from his house and gave them to the 'almānâ, gēr, yātôm, and lēwî. Furthermore, 26:13a states that he should perform the ritual *in the presence of the deity*. The site for the declaration concerning the proper distribution of the annual tithes in the third year is conspicuous. Mayes and von Rad argue that the requirement to perform this ritual in the presence of the deity is evidence that the offerer made this solemn profession at the official sanctuary.[32] These scholars suggest that the venue for the carrying out of the liturgy associated with the distribution of the tithes triennially was the same as the site for the consumption of the annual tithes and for the celebration of the major cultic festivals. Local settlements were sites for the deposit of the tithe triennially, but the official cultic site was the venue for the execution of the ritual that attended depositing the tithe in the local villages.

Deut 26:14 delineates the two additional declarations that were part of the liturgy associated with the distribution of the tithes to the 'almānâ, gēr, yātôm, and lēwî. The offerer — local peasant farmer or herder — affirmed his innocence by stating that he did not eat it while afflicted and unclean, and that he gave no part of the tithes to the dead. He also affirmed his loyalty to Yahweh by distributing his goods to a category of socially weak, vulnerable persons in the local villages.

Deut 26:15 identifies the final element in the recitation of the ritual that accompanied the deposit of tithes in the local villages. This element is a request for divine favor toward the people and regarding the agricultural yields. 26:15b identifies the foundation of this petition by linking this re-

31. For discussion on stages of redaction in Deut 26:12-15, see Merendino, pp. 371-72, and Gerhard von Rad, *Deuteronomy*, trans. Doretha Barton, OTL (Philadelphia: Westminster, 1966), pp. 159-61.

32. See Mayes, p. 336, and von Rad, *Deuteronomy*, p. 160. For additional treatment on "and you will say before Yahweh your God," see Peter C. Craigie, *The Book of Deuteronomy* (Grand Rapids: Eerdmans, 1976), pp. 322-24.

quest for the fecundity of the land, prosperity, health, and the happiness of the people to a promise that Yahweh made to the ancestors of subgroups in ancient Israelite society.

Deut 26:12-15 therefore bolsters the following reconstruction: (a) the offerer bestowed the triennial tithes in the local village(s); (b) an individual or group in the villages might have distributed the triennial tithes to the *'almānâ, gēr, yātôm,* and *lēwî;* and (c) the offerer executed the ritual at the official cultic site after he deposited the triennial tithes in the local villages.

Summary

An infinitive absolute/finite verb construction; the appearance of the *'almānâ, gēr,* and *yātôm* together in a single literary arrangement; the mandatory payment of tithes at an official cultic site; the tenet that the presentation of tithes at an official cultic site was foundational to fecundity, health, and peace; and the command to distribute tithes every three years to these individuals are the distinctive formulas, terminology, and pedagogy in Deut 14:22-29. Specificity about the distribution of the annual tithes of the third year and a ritual commemorating the distribution of these items are characteristic of this law. Deut 26:12-15, then, earmarks two out of seven years for the distribution of commodities to socially weak subgroups in ancient Israelite society, and this law implies that the deity commanded this arrangement.

As was said in Chapter 1, the placement of the *'almānâ, gēr,* and *yātôm* together is a distinguishing feature of Deut 16:9-12 and 13-15. It is to an examination of these laws that this study turns now.

Critical Issues for Understanding Laws on Major Cultic Pilgrimages in the DC

Much data concerning feasts is present elsewhere in the legal corpora in the Pentateuch. These texts are Exod 23:14-17; 34:18-24; Lev 23:4-44; and Num 28:16–29:39. These data designate three major pilgrimages, and they generally use *hag* (sacred pilgrimage) to denote these festivals. Yet discrepancies appear regarding the specifics of these pilgrimages in the biblical communities, such as: (a) the nomenclature for these major cultic festivals; (b) the offerings to be presented at them; (c) the circle of participants at them; (d) the sites for their celebration; and (e) the motivation for observing them.

While information about these major cultic pilgrimages is present in these texts, insight into the social origins and the historical moment these festivals became present in the biblical communities is absent. R. Albertz and H. Preuss suggest that these festivals stem from ancient agrarian festivals in Syria-Palestine.[33] What is more, these scholars state that subgroups in the biblical communities adapted these agricultural rituals to their theological agendas. De Vaux particularly contends that social subgroups in Israel borrowed these festivals from the Canaanites.[34] Albertz and Preuss declare also that the formulators of laws on important cultic pilgrimages in the biblical communities transferred these rituals from the realm of Syrio-Palestinian fertility rituals to the realm of theological commemoration. Albertz writes: "The three festivals were originally agricultural festivals: they were ritual accompaniments to the harvest and served primarily to secure the powers of blessing for the land and to express joy and gratitude for the produce that had grown and had been gathered in. So first of all these festivals had nothing to do with the particular experiences of historical and political liberation which marked out the Yahweh religion."[35]

As was said above, Deut 16:1-17 identifies and provides insight into three major agriculture celebrations in the biblical communities. These pilgrimages were Passover and the feasts of weeks and booths. I will refrain from examining the Passover codes in the DC because the 'almānâ, gēr, and yātôm do not appear in these laws. Thus, in what follows I investigate the feasts of weeks and booths in the DC, for these persons appear together in these regulations.

---

33. Horst D. Preuss, *Old Testament Theology*, trans. Leo G. Perdue, vol. 2, OTL (Louisville: Westminster/John Knox, 1996), pp. 224-35; and Albertz, p. 89. For additional information on cultic pilgrimages in ancient Israel, see Roland de Vaux, *Ancient Israel: Social and Religious Institutions* (New York: McGraw-Hill, 1965), 2:468-74, 484-506; and Mark E. Cohen, *The Cultic Calendars of the Ancient Near East* (Bethesda: University Press of Maryland, 1996).

34. De Vaux, p. 494.

35. Albertz, p. 89.

Laws on Major Cultic Pilgrimages, and Widows, Strangers, and Orphans in the DC

The Feast of Weeks in the DC

Deut 16:9-12 treats the festival of weeks *(ḥag šābuʿôt)*. This was the second major agrarian pilgrimage of the year. Exod 23:16a and 34:22 call it the feast of harvest *(ḥag haqqāṣîr)*, and Num 28:26 refers to it as the day of firstfruits *(bĕyôm habbikûrîm)*. The fact that "harvest festival" appears as the name for this pilgrimage in the BC, the oldest layer of legislation in the HB, lends weight to the claim that this term was the oldest name for this feast. Perhaps the discrepancy in the name proceeds from the possibility that local peasant farmers presented portions of the cereal harvest at this festival.[36]

Deut 16:9-12 declares:

> 9Count to yourself seven weeks from the time you begin to harvest the standing grain. 10Then observe the festival of weeks to Yahweh your God; you will give a freewill offering in proportion to Yahweh your God's blessing to you. 11You, your son, daughter, servant, maidservant, and the Levite who is in your gates, the stranger, orphan, and the widow who are in your midst will rejoice before Yahweh your God, in the place which Yahweh your God causes his name to dwell. 12Do not forget that you became slaves in Egypt; therefore keep and do these statutes.

Deut 16:9-12 contains the following elements:

a.	The Date for the Feast of Weeks	16:9
b.	The Delineation of the Offering at the Feast of Weeks	16:10a
c.	The Criteria for Determining the Offering at the Feast of Weeks	16:10b
d.	The Circle of Participants at the Feast of Weeks	16:11a
e.	The Site for the Celebration of the Feast of Weeks	16:11b
f.	The Motivation for Keeping the Feast of Weeks	16:12

Deut 16:9 provides a benchmark for determining the beginning of the feast of weeks. It directs individuals to count seven weeks from the time

36. Preuss, pp. 229-30, and de Vaux, pp. 493-95.

they begin to harvest their fields. Shifting weather patterns and ecological disasters, namely, locusts, worms, and inadequate rainfall, however, could devastate the crops or even cause crop failure. These calamities would negatively affect the start of grain harvesting. Moreover, an insufficient supply of labor could affect the harvesting of produce; consequently, climatic, pestilent, and sociological problems would affect the time for the celebration of the feast of weeks. Deut 16:9 therefore is a broad guideline for determining the date for this agricultural festival in the biblical communities.

Deut 16:10a demands that local peasant farmers and herders give *a sufficient freewill offering* at the feast. The meaning of this phrase is ambiguous. The fact that *misat* (sufficient) is a hapax legomenon is central to this dilemma.[37] But evidence for adjudicating this phrase is present in Deut 16:10b, which implies that it is relative; that is to say, the blessing of the deity determines what is *sufficient*. Since the context of this verse implies that "as Yahweh has blessed you" refers to the yields of the harvest, it is probable that the types of *misat* are agricultural. While a relationship is present between *misat* and the yields of the grain harvest, two possibilities for interpreting this term are available. On the one hand, it is possible that it refers to the quality of the gift. Following this line of argument introduces the claim that the condition of the gift and the condition of the yields of the harvest should be the same. On the other hand, it is possible that *misat* refers to the quantity of the gift. This word therefore would be a numerical designation. The volume of the harvest would determine what is sufficient.[38]

Deut 16:11a identifies the participants at the feast of weeks. Comparison of Deut 16:11 with Exod 23:17a; 34:23; Num 28:26-31; and Lev 23:15-21 reveals a significant inconsistency. The Deuteronomic law expands the circle of participants to include the *'almānâ, gēr,* and *yātôm.* Only adult males constitute the participants in Exod 23:17a and 34:23. No list of participants appears in Num 28:26-31 or Lev 23:15-21. Craigie accounts for this discrepancy by suggesting that the drafters of the law in Deuteronomy believed that the festival was a time of rejoicing for all members of the biblical com-

---

37. Craigie, p. 245, and Mayes, p. 260.

38. The presence of competing information on items and amounts of gifts to be presented by the donor at the feast of weeks lends weight to the claim that disputation on types, on quantity, and perhaps on the obligatoriness of gifts at this festival was present. It is possible that these issues spawned the drafting of Num 28:26-31 and Lev 23:15-21, for these laws are specific about the gifts that the donor should bring to the festival of weeks.

munity, especially those without regular means of sustenance.[39] Craigie introduces a psychosocial hermeneutic, and he contends that a special interest in the improvement of the predicament of vulnerable social subgroups accounts for the circle of participants in legal injunctions about the festival in the DC. I part company with Craigie and contend that other possibilities may account for including more people in the celebration of the festival of weeks in Deut 16:11a.[40]

Deut 16:12a invokes the memory of the deliverance from Egyptian slavery, and uses this event to delineate the reason for celebrating the festival. It is notable that Exod 23:16-22; 34:22; Lev 23:15-22; and Num 28:26-31 contain no reference to the deliverance from slavery in Egypt. What is more, these texts are silent concerning any historical reason for keeping this agricultural festival. Thus the association of the liberation from slavery in Egypt with the festival of weeks proceeds from the interests of the drafters of the Deuteronomic legislation. Mayes remarks: "The reference to Israel's slavery in Egypt does not appear any earlier than Deuteronomy in connection with the feast of weeks; moreover, it does not even here explain the observance of the festival, but rather why the Levite and the poor should be invited to join in it — in itself a deuteronomic recommendation. So the reference to Egypt in the context of this festival is of deuteronomic origin at the earliest."[41]

Mayes proposes that this reference is a Deuteronomic addition to an extant regulation on the feast of weeks. I agree. I, however, part company with Mayes on the reason for this innovation in this newly crafted regulation. This disagreement rests on two issues: (1) It is possible to interpret the reference to the deliverance from bondage in Egypt as the motivation for celebrating the festival at the official shrine. This addition implies that observing the pilgrimage at this venue is a moral requirement. (2) It is possible to interpret the reference to deliverance as a veiled threat of renewed

---

39. Craigie, p. 245.

40. Deut 16:11a demands celebrating the festival at the official shrine. This idea appears again at the end of Deut 16:11, for Deut 16:11b demands celebration of the feast at the place where the deity establishes the deity's name. The goal of this innovation is to inculcate in individuals a perspective on the proper place to celebrate the festival. For discussion on the central shrine in Deuteronomy, see the section above on Deut 14:23a. I will return to discussion on the rationale for the presence of the widow, stranger, and orphan in Deut 16:11a shortly.

41. Mayes, p. 260.

enslavement. It reminds local peasant farmers and herders that they could always return to servitude.

The Feast of Booths in the DC

Deut 16:13-15 treats the festival of booths *(ḥag hassukōt)*, the third of the major agricultural pilgrimages in ancient Israelite society. Exod 23:16 and 34:22 call this pilgrimage the festival of ingathering *(ḥag hā'āsip)*, and Lev 23:33-36, 39, and Num 29:12-38 call it the festival of Yahweh *(ḥag yhwh)*. The passage in Deuteronomy provides no additional information on why it uses *ḥag hassukōt* to designate this religious gathering. It is probable that this title proceeded from the custom of viticulturists and horticulturists living in temporary huts during the harvesting of their grapes, figs, and olives. D. Hopkins contends that "The harvest and the processing of grapes are concentrated in a short period of time at the end of the summer and do not stretch out like the harvest and processing of grain. Once grapes have matured, there is considerable pressure to gather them before they fall from the vines, become dehydrated, or fall prey to insect or animal pests. Surveillance is vital as the grapes ripen and harvest begins, and the vinegrower or harvesters likely spent the night in the vineyard in specially constructed shelters."[42] Evidence is present elsewhere in the DC that indoctrination occurred at the feast of booths. For instance, Deut 31:9-13 says:

> And Moses wrote this law, and gave it to the priests, the sons of Levi, who carried the ark of the covenant of the Lord, and to all the elders of Israel. And Moses commanded them, "At the end of every seven years, at the set time of the year of release, at the feast of booths, when all Israel comes to appear before the Lord your God at the place which he will choose, you shall read this law before all Israel in their hearing. Assemble the people, men, women, and little ones, and the sojourner within your towns, that they may hear and learn to fear the Lord your God, and be careful to do all the words of this law, and that their children, who have not known it, may hear and learn to fear the Lord your God, as long as you live on the land whither you are going over the Jordan to possess it."

42. David C. Hopkins, *The Highlands of Canaan* (Decatur: Almond Press, 1985), p. 229.

The festival of booths occurred in the autumn, at the end of the agricultural year. It is important to mention that de Vaux and Preuss argue that the Israelites celebrated the Day of Atonement and the New Year's festival during the feast of booths.[43] If a recitation of the "law" occurred at this festival, it is probable that this pilgrimage drew diverse socioeconomic groups together for distinct purposes.

Deut 16:13-15 says:

> 13Once you have gathered the produce from your threshing floor and wine vat, keep the festival of booths for seven days; 14you, your son, daughter, servant, maidservant, the Levite, stranger, orphan, and widow who are in your gates will rejoice with you during this feast. 15Seven days you will keep the festival to Yahweh your God in the place that Yahweh will choose; for Yahweh your God will bless you in all of your harvest and in everything that you do; you will be joyful indeed.

The following elements are present in Deut 16:13-15:

a.	The Command to Observe the Festival of Booths	16:13
b.	The Command to Rejoice at the Festival of Booths	16:14a
c.	The Participants in the Festival of Booths	16:14b
d.	The Duration and Site for the Festival of Booths	16:15a
e.	The Motive for Keeping the Festival of Booths	16:15b

Deut 16:13a directs the biblical community to observe the festival of booths. What is more, it demands that members of ancient Israelite society celebrate this pilgrimage for seven days. Although this verse delimits the celebration of this feast, it is unclear about when this festival happens. While the month and the date for keeping it are absent in the law in Deuteronomy, Lev 23:39-43 states that it began on the fifteenth day of the seventh month of the year. The command to celebrate it for seven days in Deut 16:13a, then, provides a legal basis for keeping donors and celebrants at the sole sanctuary for an extended period.

Deut 16:14a orders jubilation and revelry during the feast. The command to rejoice is absent in Exod 23:16; 34:22; Lev 23:39-43; and Num 29:12-38. The absence of a command to rejoice in the BC shows that the drafters

---

43. De Vaux, pp. 504-10, and Preuss, pp. 230-31. See also Mayes, p. 261.

of Deut 16:14a added this clause to an extant regulation on this pilgrimage. What is more, in Deut 16:14a the command to rejoice implies that the participants in the feast should dance, eat, and consume intoxicants. It therefore is probable that drunkenness was widespread during the celebration of the feast of booths. Regarding the ambience at this pilgrimage, Albertz writes:

> The festal climax of the year was the Feast of Tabernacles at the end of the harvest season, when the work in the winepress and on the threshing floor was complete (Deut. 16.13). Its name derives from the custom of constructing huts at the sanctuary from leaves and palm branches which were decorated with fruits (Lev. 23.40-32 [sic]; Neh. 8.14ff). So this was a regular wine festival, and we have evidence of the relaxation and joy which prevailed during the seven-day period. Thus there was a custom at the autumn festival of Shiloh for the young girls to run out into the vineyards to dance in a ring at the feast of Yahweh; this was regarded as a good opportunity for the young men to get wives (Judg. 21.19ff). So we must imagine that this annual cult was very colourful: the whole population of a village or a region met together to celebrate Yahweh with music, singing, dancing, opulent sacrificial meals and drinking as well (cf. I Sam. 1.14).[44]

Deut 16:14b delineates the circle of participants at the feast. Specifically it includes the 'almānâ, gēr, and yātôm among the celebrators. This literary innovation expands the older regulation on the feast, for Exod 23:16b is silent regarding persons who could attend. For the position of this study on the appearance of these individuals together in this law, please see the section above on Deut 16:11a.

Deut 16:15b links receiving blessings from Yahweh to keeping the festival at the official sanctuary. What is more, the drafters of Deut 16:15b stipulate that the deity commanded the celebration of this pilgrimage at the sole sanctuary. It is important to note that this command is absent in the BC and in the subgroup of laws that treats Yahweh's privilege (Exod 23:16 and 34:22). Thus the idea that the deity commanded individuals to observe the festival at an official cultic site becomes a theological base upon which to build pedagogy concerning proper moral action. This ideology delineates

---

44. Albertz, pp. 90-91. The fact that drunkenness was common at the feast of booths provided opportunity for cultic officials to fleece drunken donors also.

a criterion for identifying obedient and disobedient persons, and it informs a strategy that could influence persons to behave in a manner that was consistent with ideas about proper morality among the drafters of Deut 16:15b. This literary feature of Deut 16:15b, therefore, advocates the typical Deuteronomic view that a relationship is present between obedience and blessings; conversely it lends support to the notion that a relationship is present between catastrophe and disobedience.[45]

Summary

Deut 16:9-12 and 13-15 are guidelines on the festivals of weeks and booths. Important points characterize these laws: (a) the presence of the *'almānâ, gēr,* and *yātôm* among the circle of participants; (b) the admonition to celebrate these pilgrimages at the official cultic sanctuary; (c) the periodic distribution of goods to these persons: one day for allocating commodities to these vulnerable, socially weak individuals during the feast of weeks, and seven days for sharing commodities with them during the festival of booths; and (d) the usage of retribution as motivation for celebrating these feasts.

I now explore a subgroup of miscellaneous laws that purport to govern morality toward the *'almānâ, gēr,* and *yātôm* in ancient Israelite society. These regulations are Deut 24:17-18 and 19-22.

Critical Issues for Understanding Laws against Depriving Widows, Strangers, and Orphans of Legal Protection in the DC

As was said in Chapter 1, Fensham points out that the protection of widows, orphans, and the poor was a common theme in literature throughout the ancient Near East.[46] Deut 24:17-18 reflects this tradition, for it enjoins justice toward the *'almānâ* and *yātôm,* and it includes the *gēr* in this list of vulnerable groups. Proper understanding of this code, however, calls for a working definition of justice; consequently, deducing the meaning of this

---

45. See Deut 14:29b for treatment of this issue, for this study examined the obedience-blessing pedagogy in its discussion on laws in the DC that govern the distribution of the triennial tithe in the biblical communities.

46. F. C. Fensham, "Widow, Orphan, and the Poor in Ancient Near Eastern Legal and Wisdom Literature," *JNES* 21 (April 1962): 129.

term is central to evaluating the relationship of this law to the dilemma of these persons in the biblical communities.

Laws on the Rights of Widows, Strangers, and Orphans in the DC

Deut 24:17-18 says:

> [17]Never deprive the stranger or orphan of justice, and do not take the garment of a widow in a pledge. [18]Remember that you became slaves in Egypt, and that Yahweh your God delivered you from there; therefore I command you do this thing.

This passage has the following structure:

Admonition for Legal Justice	**Deut 24:17-18**
a. The Proper Treatment of the *gēr* and *yātôm*	24:17a
b. The Proper Treatment of the *'almānâ*	24:17b
c. The Motive for Justice toward the *'almānâ*, *gēr*, and *yātôm*	24:18

Deut 24:17a proscribes depriving the *'almānâ, gēr,* and *yātôm* of justice *(mišpāṭ)*. Explication of this term, however, is not present in this code. To find a plausible answer to this issue, this chapter analyzes passages elsewhere in the DC where this word appears in the accusative case.

The wording "never deprive of justice" is present in Deut 16:19a. The structure of Deut 16:19a is characteristic of prohibitions, negative commands, or other texts in biblical Hebrew that express absolute prohibitions, in that the negative particle *lō'* appears with the imperfect and *mišpāṭ* follows in the accusative case. Elsewhere in the passage, legal injunctions against showing favoritism and taking hush money are present. Points of contact are present between the structures of these codes, for *mišpāṭ* appears in the accusative case. The present view, then, is that this term in Deut 16:19a refers to a nonbiased juridical decision wherein a person avoids preferential treatment of a litigant. It is the result of weighing the evidence and reaching an impartial decision about an issue in a legal proceeding. Working from the assumption that the meaning of *mišpāṭ* in Deut 16:18-20 elucidates the meaning of this term in Deut 24:17-18, it becomes plausible that Deut 24:17a refers to reaching nonbiased decisions regarding the 'almānâ, gēr, and yātôm in lawsuits.

On the other hand, it is possible that mišpāṭ carried other shades of meaning in the biblical communities, and that these understandings shape the meaning of this term in Deut 24:17a. Underlying this quagmire is the extensive history of the debate on *justice* among theologians, philosophers, and ethicists in contemporary human societies. In short, these individuals give conflicting answers to this question: What is justice?[47] Therefore, certainty about the nuance of mišpāṭ in this legal injunction is a formidable challenge.

Deut 24:17b places limitations on the items that creditors can use as security for payment of debts from the 'almānâ. This code contains also the permanent prohibition formula, namely, the negative *(lō')* + second-person imperfect + object, without any mention of motivation for banning the use of the garment *(beged)* as security for a loan.[48] Yet this text is silent on the meaning of *beged*. Elsewhere in the HB this term denotes a garment or refers to clothing of any type. BDB indicates that this word refers often to the robes of the high priests and to the dirty and defiled clothing of lepers. What is more, BDB declares that *beged* designates the plain and unpretentious clothing of the poor.[49] It therefore is difficult to determine if this law bans the taking of the loose-fitting outside garments of the 'almānâ only, or if it forbids taking any of her clothing in a pledge for a loan. Without doubt this law condemns creditors who demand that she pawn her clothes. It intimates that she was not to surrender in a pledge for her indebtedness those items that were essential for comfort and for the preservation of dignity.

Deut 24:18 specifies that the deliverance from slavery in Egypt is the correct basis for proper conduct toward the 'almānâ, gēr, and yātôm. This innovation is consistent with warrants for moral action that are present elsewhere in the DC. As mentioned above, the DC uses this tradition to encourage compliance with codes that govern moral action. This feature is unlike H, which uses the self-identification and purity of the deity to justify laws that identify right moral action. Deut 24:18 is proof again that the

---

47. Ronald H. Nash, "The Economics of Justice," in *Economic Justice and the State,* ed. J. Bernbaum (Grand Rapids: Baker, 1986), pp. 9-23.

48. For detailed discussion of the forms of law in the HB, see W. Malcolm Clark, "Law," in *Old Testament Form Criticism,* ed. John Hayes (San Antonio: Trinity University Press, 1974), pp. 99-139.

49. BDB, pp. 93-94.

threat of returning to bondage is a major basis for proper social behavior in the DC.

Critical Issues for Understanding Laws on Gleanings in the DC

Deut 24:19-22 contains three regulations on gleanings. It is noteworthy that laws governing gleanings are absent in the BC, but that a collection of legislation on this subject is present in H. These texts are Lev 19:9-10 and 23:22. Cross-fertilization between the DC and H may account for the presence of injunctions on gleanings of produce in these legal codes also. It may explain their presence in either the DC or H. The absence of such injunctions in the BC, then, raises two important questions: Was gleaning unknown to the codifiers of the BC? And did regulations about gleanings originate with the drafters of the DC or H?

Mayes believes the prohibition on harvesting all the yields of the field proceeds from an ancient custom of leaving behind a portion of crops for deities or for the fertility spirits of the fields.[50] Working from the claim of Mayes, this study contends that customs on gleanings of produce were present in the biblical communities prior to the BC, DC, and H, and that the codifiers of the DC and H incorporated local customs on gleanings of produce into their legal collections.

It is axiomatic among scholars on ancient Israelite society that the harvesting of crops was a permanent feature of the socioeconomic landscape of the biblical communities. Underpinning discussion on gleaning regulations in the DC, then, is conversation on the harvesting of fields, orchards, and vineyards in ancient Israel. Hopkins examines agriculture in ancient Syria-Palestine, and he provides insight into techniques for the harvesting of crops in the biblical communities. He proposes that the gathering of crops in Syria-Palestine involved a series of acts: (a) reaping and picking ripe grains and fruits; (b) collecting the harvested stalks; (c) transporting the harvest to the threshing floor; (d) drying the harvest; (e) threshing to disarticulate the spikelets and remove the hulls; (f) winnowing and sieving to separate the grain from the chaff and to clean the grain; and (g) measuring and storing the grains.

Moreover, Hopkins contends that the staggered sowing of crops and

50. Mayes, pp. 326-27.

the difference in maturation rates for cereals and fruits spread the harvesting of fields out over a long period. Thus horticultural communities in Syria-Palestine might have spent much of the summer harvesting ripening crops. What is more, Hopkins contends that the ingathering of crops was a labor-intensive project: picking crops by hand and the use of two kinds of sickles *(ḥermēš* and *maggāl)* were major methods for the ingathering of crops from the fields, and this contributed to the drudgery of harvesting field crops in the biblical communities. Hopkins indicates also that points of contact were present between methods for the harvesting of orchards and vineyards and the ingathering of crops from the fields. The picking of fruits and grapes was by hand also. The harvesting of olives involved beating the tree branches with sticks and collecting the olives that fell. Thus Hopkins abets understanding methods and issues involved in the harvesting of fields and vineyards in Syria-Palestine. He therefore delineates a sociohistoric context for discussing regulations on gleanings in the DC.[51]

Laws on Gleanings and Widows, Strangers, and Orphans in the DC

Deut 24:19-22 says:

> [19]When you harvest your crops and forget a sheaf, do not go back into the field to get it; it is for the stranger, orphan, and widow, so that Yahweh your God will bless you in every work of your hands. [20]When you harvest your olives, do not go back and get the olives; it is for the stranger, orphan, and widow. [21]When you harvest your grapes, do not return to gather the grapes that you left; it is for the stranger, orphan, and widow. [22]And you shall remember that you were a slave in Egypt; therefore I command you to do this thing.

Deut 24:19-22 includes four major parts:

I. The Regulation on Forgotten Sheaves	Deut 24:19
a. The Protasis	24:19a
b. The Apodosis	24:19a
c. The Motive for Leaving Gleanings for the Widow, Stranger, and Orphan	24:19b

51. Hopkins, pp. 223-35.

Deut 24:19 treats the gleanings of crops in the biblical communities. This law provides insight into the disposition of wheat, barley, grain, and other crops that remained in the fields after harvesting. An important inconsistency is present among laws in the Pentateuch that treat this phenomenon in ancient Israelite society. Deut 24:19a demands that the harvester not return to collect crops that she/he overlooked or forgot and left in the fields. Lev 19:9-10 and 23:22 advance the idea that the reapers leave produce in the fields intentionally. Furthermore, Deut 24:19a shows that the gleanings were part of a social welfare system. The regulation in Deuteronomy parts company with the legal injunctions in Leviticus on the beneficiaries. Deut 24:19a legitimizes an entitlement program, and Lev 19:9-10 and 23:22 indicate that the gēr and poor (ʿānî) have right to the gleanings. The ʾalmānâ and yātôm are absent in Lev 19:9-10, and the ʿānî is absent in Deut 24:19a.

Deut 24:19b delineates the incentive for leaving gleanings in the fields or in the orchards. Consistent with regulations that appear elsewhere in the DC, Deut 24:19b links prosperity to individual moral action also. Thus Deuteronomic phraseology regarding material retribution appears in Deut 24:19b. This motif implies that an association is present between yields of the land and not returning to collect gleanings of the fields, e.g., portions of grain and other staples.[52] This verse ends with a basis for moral action, and this innovation suggests that the drafters of this legal injunction allowed their ideas about proper morality to shape codes on the distribution of gleanings in ancient Israel.

52. For a list of typical Deuteronomic phraseology on retribution and material motivation, see Weinfeld, *Deuteronomy*, pp. 345-50.

Deut 24:20 treats the gleanings of olives. This regulation provides insight into techniques for the removal of these items from the trees. Deut 24:20a contains the wording "when you beat out your olives" *(kî taḥbōṭ zêtĕkā)*. This clause implies that beating branches with sticks or other objects was an efficacious method for severing olives from their branches. Lev 19:9-10 and 23:22 are silent on gleanings of olives; consequently, Deut 24:20 is the sole regulation in the HB that clearly governs the gleaning of olives. What is more, this text admonishes harvesters to go over the olive trees only once *(lō' tĕpā'ēr 'aḥărêkā)*. Thus the reapers would beat the olive trees, and the olives that fell to the ground were the property of the farmers or the owners of the orchards. The olives that remained on the trees after the initial sweep, however, were ineligible for collection by farmers in the biblical communities. They belonged to the *'almānâ, gēr,* and *yātôm.*

Deut 24:21 treats the gleanings of grapes. Since Lev 19:10 also treats this matter, it helps to elucidate the distinctive features of Deut 24:21. Points of contact are present between these two passages on the procedure for distributing the grapes that remained in the vineyards after the initial sweep. Deut 24:21a says: "When you harvest your grapes, do not return to gather the grapes that you left." It is difficult to determine if Deut 24:21a refers to grapes left on the vines or grapes that fell and were overlooked by farmers as they harvested their vineyards. Lev 19:10, though, presents no such ambiguity, for it directs farmers to leave fallen grapes in the vineyards, for this fruit was for the sustenance of the *gēr* and *'ānî.*

Deut 24:22 reiterates the fact that the memory of Israelite enslavement in Egypt should inculcate proper notions about morality in people in ancient Israelite society. The regulations on the gleanings in Leviticus do not introduce a motive for moral action but close with a statement in which the self-identification of the deity is paramount. Deut 24:19-22 parts company with Lev 19:9-10 and 23:22 over the issue that makes an act morally required. Perhaps the presence of competing bases for moral action in these injunctions is a clue as to competing bases for moral action in the biblical communities. As this section has shown, the DC often appeals to the memory of Israelite enslavement in Egypt as the basis for moral decision making. This leads me to conclude that the memory of enslavement in Egypt claimed an authority for moral action that few other phenomena could claim for the drafters of Deut 24:19-22.

Summary

The *'almānâ, gēr,* and *yātôm* appear together, in a single literary formula, in legal injunctions in the Deuteronomic Code. These laws are responses of social subgroups to disputes on the presentation and distribution of tithes of crops, fruits, and cattle; the celebration of cultic pilgrimages; and entitlement to gleanings. In their treatment of tithes, major cultic pilgrimages, and gleanings, these regulations contain distinctive terminology, formulas, and pedagogy. Ideas associated with charity toward this class of people are the conspicuous innovations in these laws. Hence these features invited past research on these texts to claim that the drafters of these regulations had a concern for ameliorating the plight of these vulnerable, socially weak individuals in ancient Israelite society.

At first glance the claim that Deut 14:22-29; 16:9-12, 13-15; 24:17-18, 19-22; and 26:12-15 rectified the plight of the *'almānâ, gēr,* and *yātôm* seems correct. An investigation into the socioeconomic effects of these legal injunctions, however, introduces a new possibility on the reading of these laws. It is now possible to show how these codes exacerbated, not rectified, the plight of these types of persons. In the next chapter I read these legal injunctions with a special sensitivity to the ways in which the innovations in these laws contributed to the circumstances of this category of socially weak persons in ancient Israelite society.

Chapter 4

TEXTS AND INTERPRETATION

Deuteronomy and the Oppression of Widows, Strangers,
and Orphans in the Biblical Communities

On Oppression in the Biblical Communities

As was said in the prolegomenon, critical theory about law proposes that legal injunctions contribute to the oppression of social subgroups in human societies. It avers that this phenomenon is the perennial disadvantaging of a social subgroup. Although widespread agreement is present on the meaning of oppression among scholars who use critical theory about legal injunctions to explore the interplay between codes and society, variance is present among these camps concerning the specific forms that oppression takes. The belief that the identity of oppressed peoples and the circumstances that contribute to the oppression of social subgroups vary from epoch to epoch is at the center of this issue.[1] This project uses critical theorizing about a type of moral injunctions to contend that the regulations in the Deuteronomic Code that prescribe behavior toward the *'almānâ, gēr,* and *yātôm* — a category of vulnerable underclass persons in the biblical communities — contributed to the dilemma of this social subgroup. In this chapter I delineate a framework for identifying the

1. For examples of difference of opinion about the identity of oppressed peoples and about the conditions that account for the oppression of these social subgroups among critical legal theorists, see Cornel West, "Race and Social Theory," in his *Keeping Faith: Race and Philosophy in America* (New York: Routledge, 1994), pp. 251-70; and Angela Y. Davis, "Keynote Address: Third National Conference on Women of Color and the Law," *Stanford Law Review* 43 (July 1991): 1175-81.

forms that oppression might take regarding these persons and for understanding how the regulations could work to the perennial disadvantage of this social subgroup in ancient Israelite society during the ninth century B.C.E.

The concern about oppressed groups and about the forms this phenomenon took regarding socioeconomic social subgroups that composed ancient Israelite society is not novel. For instance, Gottwald and E. Tamez use oppression as a hermeneutical principle for discussing events in the history of ancient Israelite society.[2] Gottwald's most impressive application of this principle appears in his *Tribes* — in his theory about the constituents and socioeconomic issues that led to the fusion of distinct categories of people into a political entity in Syria-Palestine during the Iron Age. He contends that indigenous Canaanite peasants, mercenaries and social misfits (*'apiru*), and recently liberated slaves from Egypt coalesced and formed Israel. While the term "oppression" appears throughout *Tribes*, Gottwald does not delineate the social-scientific framework that governs his understanding of this concept. Yet he uses the term "oppression" when he speaks about the conditions of the slaves who were present in Egypt, native lower-class Canaanites, and the *'apiru* who were present in Syria-Palestine. Gottwald situates his discussion of oppression in an economic context, and he proposes that "oppression" is the exploitation of a subgroup by another, more powerful socioeconomic entity. At the heart of his understanding of oppression is the idea that a dominant socioeconomic group takes advantage of a subordinate social group: the superior camp procures food and other items of material endowment from the labor of a vulnerable, subdominant social category of people in a human society. According to Gottwald, economic arrangements in human societies, then, become structures of oppression.

Tamez explores the notion of oppression in ancient Israel. She contends that degrees of this problem were present in the biblical communities. It comes as no surprise that she shows that several terms for oppression appear in the HB. These words are *dk'* (he crushed), *'nh* (he afflicted), *'šq* (he extorted), *ynh* (he maltreated), *lḥṣ* (he pressed), *ngś* (he exacted), and *rṣṣ* (he mashed). Tamez adverts to the literary contexts of these terms in order to introduce possibilities about the identity of the oppressors and

---

2. Norman K. Gottwald, *The Tribes of Yahweh* (Maryknoll, N.Y.: Orbis, 1979), pp. 210-21; and Elsa Tamez, *Bible of the Oppressed* (Maryknoll, N.Y.: Orbis, 1982), pp. 1-30.

to delineate the methods these individuals use to accomplish their goals. She contends that the HB mentions two levels of oppression: an international level and a local level. On the international level one country exploits another country; on the local level a person or a camp within a society, which holds power, dominates a weaker individual or subgroup of persons within the same society. Moreover, Tamez argues that privileged persons used stealth, force, and influence to increase their wealth, and that avarice was the motivation for oppression. She adds a new approach and a fresh body of scholarship to the debate about oppression in the biblical communities. Tamez identifies the range of terms in biblical Hebrew that denote oppression, and she shows that the oppressed were generally persons of low socioeconomic standing in ancient Israelite society.

Gottwald and Tamez use different methods to examine oppression; their claims about the forms this phenomenon takes, however, are the same. According to these critics, oppression denotes the extraction of goods and services from a vulnerable individual or social subgroup by a more powerful person or politico-economic subgroup in a human society. These scholars advocate the position that oppression finds expression in economic circumstances; therefore, economic subjugation and peonage become the forms that oppression takes.

Gottwald's and Tamez's ideas about oppression and the forms it takes, however, attract attention. These scholars posit that oppression is an economic phenomenon. Arguing that oppression is a purely economic circumstance robs this phenomenon of its distinction. Indebtedness is a fact of life. It is certain also that creditors use a variety of strategies to collect money from delinquent debtors; therefore, the idea that oppression is a circumstance in which a person or social subgroup provides goods and services to elites or creditors involuntarily provides a basis for arguing that everybody with financial obligations is oppressed. Such a definition of oppression conceals the onus for perpetuating this problematic, and it fosters disregard for the circumstances of vulnerable social subgroups in ancient Israelite society.

The definition of oppression and the circumstances of this phenomenon regarding widows, strangers, and orphans in ancient Israel, therefore, are central philosophical questions for this chapter. In this book I advocate a different position about oppression and the forms it took regarding the 'almānâ, gēr, and yātôm in biblical Israel. I. Goldenberg, M. Frye, I. Young, and the lived experience of the writer help to sculpt the understanding of oppression in this study.[3] These different sources of knowledge converge to inform a plausible theory about the meaning of oppression, and to delineate this issue with respect to widows, strangers, and orphans in ancient Israel.

The Theoretical Framework

Goldenberg published his views about oppression the same year that *Tribes* appeared. Goldenberg draws from sociology and psychology, and he introduces a distinct delineation of oppression into the discourse about this issue in human societies. His theory is an interactional analysis in which diverse intellectual and sociohistoric issues intersect and describe oppression in America. "Oppression is, above everything else, a condition of being, a particular stance one is forced to assume with respect to oneself, the world, and the exigencies of change. It is a pattern of hopelessness and helplessness, in which one sees oneself as static, limited, and expendable. People only become oppressed when they have been forced (either subtly or with obvious malice) to finally succumb to the insidious process that continually undermines hope and subverts the hope to 'become.'"[4]

What emerges from a reading of Goldenberg is that oppression is a situation; it is a circumstance in which members of a social subgroup are unable to ameliorate their predicament. This condition confines categories of people to positions of socioeconomic inferiority, and it allows them to be taken advantage of and used for someone else's profit. Oppression therefore impedes one from gaining and maintaining personal dignity.

Goldenberg contends that certain conditions spawn oppression. These circumstances are containment, expendability, and compartmentalization; although ideology is not a circumstance, he includes it among those phenomena that contribute to the oppression of social subgroups. Containment refers to a predicament that increasingly restricts the possibilities that a human being can consider; it effects a situation in which the governed have hardly any options available to them through which they can in any significant manner change their circumstances. Expendability pertains

3. I. Ira Goldenberg, *Oppression and Social Intervention* (Chicago: Nelson-Hall, 1978); Marilyn Frye, *The Politics of Reality: Essays in Feminist Theory* (Trumansburg, N.Y.: Crossing Press, 1983); and Iris M. Young, *Justice and the Politics of Difference* (Princeton: Princeton University Press, 1990).

4. Goldenberg, pp. 2-3.

to a social arrangement that emphasizes the fact that individuals or sub-groups of people can be replaced without any significant injury to the whole. It creates a situation where the dilemma of vulnerable individuals or subgroups becomes unimportant to the oppressors. Compartmentalization refers to isolating aspects of one's existence; it implies that social arrangements often divide a person's life into sections, and that this segmentation undermines any sense of community among moral agents. In short, compartmentalization promotes incongruity between personal and public worlds, i.e., it invites a sharp distinction in the reality/life of a moral agent, by encouraging a marked differentiation between a person's disposition and his/her occupation. An ideology is a system of ideas that bolster and legitimize a particular worldview. It is a set of opinions that can shape value formation and offer guidance on common, everyday socioeconomic issues, and on those situations that occur infrequently. An ideology, therefore, becomes an invaluable means for social control and for legitimizing the interests of ruling elites regarding key socioeconomic issues. An ideology, according to Goldenberg, can inculpate vulnerable oppressed groups by placing the onus for their circumstances on these individuals, and it can exculpate ruling classes by justifying their positions of privilege and domination. Goldenberg therefore implies that ideology is the most effective tool for social control and for oppressing a class of people.

> We come, finally, to what may be the most important of the essential structures through which the oppressive experience is mediated: ideology. Ideology, obviously, is not a "thing." It is neither material nor does it assume any definite or predictable form. It is, nevertheless, a structure, for it serves to shape and control our responses to events which impinge themselves upon our consciousness. Stated differently, without an appropriate ideology to fall back upon and to use as an overarching interpretive schema, such other structures as containment, expendability, and compartmentalization would not suffice to produce the oppressive experience.[5]

While Goldenberg draws from the dilemma of oppressed social sub-groups in general, Frye builds her understanding of oppression upon the plight of lesbians and heterosexual women in America. In the preface to her collection of essays on feminist theory, Frye says she discusses oppres-

---

5. Goldenberg, p. 11.

sion from the perspective of a white, college-educated lesbian female.[6] She therefore introduces critical viewpoints developed in other fields of study in analyzing the relationship between social institutions, gender, and oppression. Frye challenges the belief that oppression includes all human experience of limitation or suffering, despite the cause or consequence. She suggests that in one degree or another, all human beings suffer frustration and restriction and come upon obstacles; consequently, she posits that individuals can be disconsolate without being oppressed.

Frye therefore differentiates oppression from instances of unjust interactions between two human beings. "The experience of oppressed people is that the living of one's life is confined and shaped by forces and barriers which are not accidental or occasional and hence avoidable, but are systematically related to each other in such a way as to catch one between and among them and restrict or penalize motion in any direction. It is the experience of being caged in: all avenues, in every direction, are blocked or booby trapped."[7] Thus Frye avers that oppression is the habitual domination of a social agent over another; it is the systemic relegation of subgroups to positions of socioeconomic inferiority. She describes it as the long-standing condition of subordinate social actors in which a plethora of factors converges and undermines the possibility of categories of people escaping powerlessness in a human society. This feature is distinctive of oppression, for it ensnares groups in perpetual dilemmas from which they cannot escape; oppression is a situation in which options are few and each alternative available imperils the oppressed human being. Oppression, then, is more than mere individual human suffering or deprivation in any form.

Frye stresses that membership in an inferior subgroup marks one for oppression. This idea implies that people suffer because they belong to a social category — oppressed individuals experience a perpetual dilemma because they are part of a common socioeconomic subgroup. For Frye, being female and being lesbian are social categories, and belonging to these conceptual social subdivisions works against women in a male-dominated, heterosexual society. While gender is something over which women have the least control, she contends that it becomes the major issue that shapes their circumstances. Membership in a social category, then, provokes a network of circumstances that relegate individuals to positions of subordination.

6. Frye, pp. vii-x.
7. Frye, p. 4.

Similar to Frye, Young, a feminist political philosopher also, contends that oppression is a structural concept: it is the dehumanization and systemic relegation of human beings to positions of inferiority. She does not ascribe oppression exclusively to malice, despotism, or deliberation; she posits that the objectification of social subgroups proceeds often from the everyday, well-intentioned acts of charitable human beings. In other words, Young implies that oppression is not necessarily the result of conscious and intentional acts of brutality. "In this extended structural sense oppression refers to the vast and deep injustices some groups suffer as a consequence of often unconscious assumptions and reactions of well-meaning people in ordinary interactions, media and cultural stereotypes, and structural features of bureaucratic hierarchies and market mechanisms — in short, the normal process of everyday life."[8]

Thus Young introduces an important idea into the discussion: the long-term disadvantages and injustices that groups suffer stem from the common, but unexamined, practices of well-intentioned individuals. She proposes that the collective consequences of following institutional rules indiscriminately sustain oppression, for abiding by social conventions blindly provokes the unquestioned acceptance of norms, habits, and worldviews. Thus just, law-abiding persons can unknowingly participate in the subjugation of categories of people, for when they act they believe they are simply obeying the law, following procedure, or merely doing what is customary. "The conscious actions of many individuals daily contribute to maintaining and reproducing oppression, but those people are usually simply doing their jobs or living their lives, and do not see themselves as agents of oppression."[9]

Similar to Goldenberg, Young argues that oppression fosters a family of conditions, to wit: exploitation, marginalization, powerlessness, cultural imperialism, and violence. Exploitation refers to the ways that the energy expenditure of one group benefits another subgroup and sustains a relationship of inequality, power, and privilege between these social subgroups. Marginalization denotes unemployability or disutility. This phenomenon refers to the lack of skills or resources needed to contribute positively to the material life of a human community; consequently, it precludes social subgroups from useful participation in social life. By pow-

8. Young, p. 41.
9. Young, pp. 41-42.

erlessness Young means the inability of a category of social actors to effect major changes in their circumstances. Thus a subordinate social subgroup becomes an instrument of another subgroup in which the subordinate's situation is that of being used, controlled, or subjugated by another, more powerful social subgroup. Young uses cultural imperialism to advert to the invisibility of the perspectives of subordinate subgroups. That is, this term refers to the universalization of a dominant group's attitudes, beliefs, habits, and ideas about proper morality and other social phenomena. Cultural imperialism disrespects the vantage of subordinate subgroups by legitimizing the worldviews of the privileged group; consequently, angles of vision that proceed from the historical consciousness of oppressed minorities become suspect and unworthy of serious consideration. Regarding violence, Young argues that individuals in subordinate social subgroups are targets of frequent attacks — acts of aggression and dehumanization that seek to destroy or humiliate them. According to Young, the fact that persons are simply members of a subordinate social category designates them as objects of acts of aggression, and the fact that society often rewards or allows the perpetrators of these offenses to go unpunished implies that these types of unjust moral acts are acceptable. Thus members of subordinate social subgroups exist with the constant threat of experiencing physical, intellectual, and emotional brutality. Young therefore posits that the presence of those five criteria in the conditions of a social subgroup determines if that social subgroup is an oppressed class or community of people in American societies.[10]

The Meaning of Oppression with Respect to Widows, Strangers, and Orphans

I weave my understanding of oppression, its causes, the forms it takes, and the relationship of Deut 14:22-29; 16:9-12, 13-15; 24:17-18, 19-22; and 26:12-15 to the oppression of the 'almānâ, gēr, and yātôm from critical theory about law and the scholars cited in this chapter. Young suggests specifically that oppression is not necessarily the result of the malicious behavior of individuals and is more than isolated or random acts of injustice. Frye avers also that well-intentioned individuals are often the perpetrators of oppres-

10. Young, pp. 48-65.

sion in a human society. To support her position she proposes that human beings often practice poor epistemic agency by failing to identify and evaluate the sources that inform their worldviews and ideas about morality. She accordingly posits that human beings often accept ideas and beliefs uncritically: they frequently adopt attitudes, norms, and customs because of their allegiance to a culture or their membership in a human community. A person therefore might hold a set of beliefs that is inconsistent with observable data, or he/she might embrace notions about morality and social life that work to his/her disadvantage. What is more, Frye implies that human beings accept bases for behavior without examining these guidelines. Consequently, she advocates the viewpoint that neglecting to explore and evaluate the sources of one's beliefs and bases for moral decision making positions an individual to play an unconscious role in the dehumanization of other persons.

Yet Goldenberg, Frye, and Young advocate the position that oppression is an institutional or systemic phenomenon in which the distinct and authoritative social arrangements of a human community sanction beliefs, customs, practices, and policies that dehumanize social subgroups. At the center of this claim is the belief that social institutions can inculcate ideas about proper private morality and citizenship in human beings. Thus Goldenberg, Frye, and Young posit that those institutions with the power and resources to instill morality can become structures of domination, for these social arrangements often bolster systems that enforce perspectives about proper behavior. Although Goldenberg, Frye, and Young argue that distinct social arrangements provoke the oppression of categories of people, they leave questions about the identity of these social institutions unanswered. Thus these scholars clear the way for arguing that religious and educational institutions; patterns of kinship subgroupings; systems for the production, distribution, and consumption of commodities; law; and other common social fixtures of human societies can become structures of domination.

Critical theory about legal injunctions advances the idea that law is an important social institution, and that legal sanctions can inculcate ideas about proper morality in human beings.[11] What is more, Lenski and

---

11. For discussion on the relationship between legal proscriptions and normative behavior, see D. Don Welch, "The Moral Dimension of Law," in *Law and Morality*, ed. Welch (Philadelphia: Fortress, 1987), pp. 1-27.

M. Mann argue that legal injunctions themselves are major mechanisms for social control, and that legal codes can bolster ideas regarding the treatment of social subgroups and legitimize programs that protect the vital interests of camps in agrarian societies.[12] Since I contend that oppression is an institutional phenomenon and that law was a key social institution in biblical Israel, discussing Lenski's and Mann's ideas about the role that law can play in agrarian societies is central to my analysis.

Lenski and Mann presuppose that competing understandings of law are present among individuals in agrarian societies. In other words, these scholars posit that conflicting angles of vision might be present on enforceable regulations that govern behavior in moral communities. Persons or groups, on the one hand, ascertain that law can be a device for personal use. Thus these scholars suggest that law can serve the interests of power elites. Mann says: "The few at the top can keep the masses at the bottom compliant, provided their control is *institutionalized* in the laws and the norms of the social group in which both operate. Institutionalization is necessary to achieve routine collective goals; and thus distributive power, that is, social stratification, also becomes an institutionalized feature of social life."[13] Other people, on the other hand, view legal injunction as a source of protection and retribution. The theory of Lenski and Mann about the interplay between law and society, then, brings into play the possibility that control over the legal institution was at the center of conflict in agrarian societies.[14]

Lenski and Mann argue that legal injunctions might be biased toward ruling elites. I, however, argue that it is difficult to prove bias in every piece of legislation in the HB. For example, it is difficult to argue that sanctions on theft, destruction of property, and murder benefited one socioeconomic aggregation more than another. When this research project speaks about law protecting the interests of camps in ancient Israelite society, it speaks circumspectly — it does not argue that every subgroup of regulations in the HB advanced the interests of a socioeconomic subgroup in the biblical communities.

Mann argues that the function of law contains several points of con-

12. Michael Mann, *The Sources of Social Power* (Cambridge: Cambridge University Press, 1986-1993).

13. Mann, p. 7.

14. What is more, it is possible that intraclass conflict is present among elites regarding the control of legal institutions in human societies.

tact with the function of religion. Similar to religion, law requires allegiance, informs norms, and provides grounding for moral decision making and social interaction. Consequently, he suggests that law is a major mechanism for social control and the formation of social conventions. The role law plays in establishing values, and its association with *justice*, positions it to create regular, widely accepted practices in human communities. Lenski and Mann therefore affirm the point made by Frye that well-intentioned, law-abiding human beings often participate in oppressing vulnerable social subgroups, for just persons can objectify socially weak categories of people simply by obeying the law.

The present writer argues that legal injunctions allowed the oppression of the 'almānâ, gēr, and yātôm in ancient Israelite society. When I speak of the oppression of this social subgroup, I refer to the perennial dehumanization of a category of socially weak human beings. I contend that oppression was not merely a *passing phase* in the historical experience of this social subgroup; it was the continuous denigration of a group of human beings by militating against the chances of vulnerable underclass individuals developing self-respect and becoming self-determining moral subjects in a human society. This understanding of oppression provides a common frame of reference — a working definition for discussing conditions of a category of people — during an epoch in ancient Israelite history.

How did Deut 14:22-29; 16:9-12, 13-15; 24:17-18, 19-22; and 26:12-15 exacerbate the dilemma of the 'almānâ, gēr, and yātôm? What circumstances did these codes effect in the situation of this social subgroup? Participant observation is not an option for the present investigation; consequently, I extrapolate information about these issues from the major literary features of these legal injunctions. In the final section in this chapter I read these codes with a special sensitivity to the ways in which the innovations, i.e., major distinctive literary formulas and pedagogy in these laws, allowed and supported a network of circumstances and concepts that dehumanized this category of people in ancient Israelite society during the ninth century B.C.E.

Deuteronomy and the Oppression of Widows, Strangers, and Orphans

Centralization and the Victimization of Widows, Strangers, and Orphans in the Biblical Communities

Deut 16:11b and 15a state that the location that Yahweh chooses is the site for the distribution of material goods to the *'almānâ*, *gēr*, and *yātôm*. This innovation limits venues for the distribution of commodities to these types of people; thus it becomes probable that the implications of this development greaten the chance that these socially weak persons suffered hardship, mistreatment, and personal injury. The belief that travel was especially dangerous for this social subgroup informs this claim. If the *'almānâ*, *gēr*, and *yātôm* were without the protection of adult males, and if this site were a great distance from the local villages or cities in which these individuals lived, traveling to this venue and returning from this site with grain, wine, and other goods placed these persons at the mercy of murderers, rapists, robbers, kidnappers, and other nefarious individuals. Forcing a group of socially weak and vulnerable persons to appear at the official cultic site in order to collect food and other items ignored a main feature of their social dilemma. Therefore issues associated with making the pilgrimage to the official shrine might have influenced the *'almānâ*, *gēr*, and *yātôm* negatively, in that the fear of becoming the victims of crimes kept these defenseless individuals from making the journey to feed at the public trough. The nonappearance of these persons at the official cultic site during the festivals of weeks and booths militated against the possibility that they received grain, oil, wine, livestock, and other commodities that might have increased their assets and ameliorated their socioeconomic conditions.[15] Deut 16:9-12 and 13-15 therefore decontextualize the *'almānâ*, *gēr*, and *yātôm*. These regulations prescribed a solution that appears to be indifferent to the circumstances of this category of people, and this disregard for the practical, everyday implications of calling for defenseless individuals to travel throughout the biblical communities endangered and broke ground for the dehumanization of this social subgroup in ancient Israelite society.

---

15. The restriction of venues for the distribution of commodities to the *'almānâ*, *gēr*, and *yātôm* leaves open the possibility that if these individuals made trips to these sites, they could have remained there and formed permanent settlements.

Centralization and the Indoctrination of Widows, Strangers, and Orphans in the Biblical Communities

The centralization formula in the Deuteronomic laws that treat the *'almānâ, gēr,* and *yātôm* changes the venue for the celebration of major agrarian rituals in the biblical communities. As was said in Chapter 3, regulations on the celebration of major cultic festivals that are in the BC, the oldest body of law in the HB, are silent about sites for the observance of cultic pilgrimages. It therefore is probable that local family shrines were venues for celebrating these feasts. The centralization policy of the legal injunctions, then, relocated the celebration of cultic pilgrimages from family shrines to a central, authorized shrine.

The usage of theology to justify this change of venue, however, encouraged these socially weak, vulnerable persons to believe that this change was the will of the deity. A rationale of this type invited them to overlook the probability that the choice of the site for observing feasts and for distributing public aid proceeded from a private agendum. It conceals the fact that centralizing the celebration of festivals benefited a camp in the biblical community. It positioned cultic ministrants to advance their religio-politico-economic ideas and to diversify the sources from which they could draw material sustenance. By advocating the position that sites for observing major agrarian pilgrimages and for distributing goods to the *'almānâ, gēr,* and *yātôm* were the choice of the deity, these laws inculcated these persons with an otherwise biased, sectarian viewpoint about these codes: this ideology attempts to hide the interests of a subgroup in the Yahweh-alone cult by stating that these legal injunctions derived from the will of the deity and not from the politico-economic program of officials in this camp.[16]

Periodic Assistance and the Oppression of Widows, Strangers, and Orphans in the Biblical Communities

Regulations in the Deuteronomic Code that prescribe morality toward the *'almānâ, gēr,* and *yātôm* link the distribution of grain, wine, oil, and livestock to these persons to periodic events in the biblical communities. Deut 14:22-29 and 26:12-15 associate the allocation of commodities to these indi-

---

16. I will return to the discussion about the ideological aspect of these laws in Chapter 5.

viduals with the presentation of the tithe of the third year. Deut 16:9-12 connects providing public assistance to this social subgroup with one day during the grain harvest, and Deut 16:13-15 links provision of assistance to them to seven days during the harvest of viniculture. Two major interrelated phenomena, therefore, might proceed from assigning dates and periods for distribution of goods to these human beings, and each phenomenon could contribute to the dehumanization of this vulnerable, socially weak category of persons.

Periodic Assistance and Protracted Indigence among Widows, Strangers, and Orphans in the Biblical Communities

According to Deut 14:22-29 and 26:12-15, the *'almānâ, gēr,* and *yātôm* received tithes of produce, cattle, and sheep every three years. According to Deut 16:9-12, these persons could receive part of the cereal harvest in late spring or early summer. It is possible also that they might have received public support at the vintage harvest in the fall (Deut 16:13-15). The question quite naturally arises: From what sources did these types of persons procure sustenance in the meantime? Where did they obtain food and other provisions between the period for the distribution of the triennial tithes and the celebration of cultic pilgrimages? The infrequent distribution of meat, vegetables, and fruits thus contributed to a critical level of deprivation and hardship for these vulnerable, socially weak individuals and forced them into exploitative relationships.[17] Since these legal injunctions spread out the distribution of commodities to the *'almānâ, gēr,* and *yātôm,* it is possible to argue that these moral injunctions contributed to the plight of these types of persons in the biblical communities.

Periodic Assistance and the Protracted Powerlessness of Widows, Strangers, and Orphans in the Biblical Communities

Deut 14:22-29; 16:9-12, 13-15; and 26:12-15 undermined the possibility of the *'almānâ, gēr,* and *yātôm* becoming self-determining moral agents. These

---

17. Perhaps it was from debt slavery, prostitution, or other exploitative economic arrangements that the *'almānâ, gēr,* and *yātôm* obtained sustenance, for it is probable that social conventions that stemmed from these laws provoked these persons to engage in questionable activities in order to eke out their existence.

regulations did not instruct local farmers and herders to distribute the types of goods that would position these individuals to control their own destinies. These laws demanded neither the distribution of seed, land, domesticated animals, and tools for farming nor the allocation of other items that would position these persons to become self-actualizing. These codes, accordingly, guaranteed that these types of persons would be unable to change their historical predicament. They relegated this vulnerable social subgroup to a position of socioeconomic inferiority, and this continued dependency clearly exacerbated the circumstances of this class of people.

Periodic Assistance and the Bolstering of a False Sense of Hope in Widows, Strangers, and Orphans in the Biblical Communities

Deut 14:22-29; 16:9-12, 13-15; and 26:12-15 suggest that farmers and herders were going to share commodities with the *'almānâ, gēr,* and *yātôm* in ancient Israelite society.[18] It is possible that some concern for these vulnerable individuals was present among farmers and herders. It is improbable that the commitment to providing aid for them was widespread among the masses. Two reasons justify this claim. First, most farmers and herders were poor and barely eked out their own existence. Most were peasants, and it is probable that points of contact were present between their standard of living and the plight of the *'almānâ, gēr,* and *yātôm.* Second, most local farmers and herders supported urban elites, and after the formation of the state, supplied the monarchy with food, supplies, and labor.

In this study I contend that local peasant farmers and herders had small amounts of grain, wine, oil, and livestock.[19] The payment of debts to landlords and to persons elsewhere in the local villages or cities, bartering with

---

18. It is notable that field crops, fruits, items from viniculture, and livestock were subject to tithes in Deut 14:22-29 and 26:12-15, and that events during the agricultural year provided benchmarks for determining the beginning of major cultic pilgrimages in Deut 16:9-12, 13-15. These pieces of evidence invite the present project to claim that persons involved in raising crops and livestock were the probable targets of Deut 14:22-29; 16:9-12, 13-15; and 26:12-15. These passages, therefore, convey the impression that the onus for mitigating the dilemma of *'almānâ, gēr,* and *yātôm* was on individuals involved in animal husbandry and the cultivation of the land in the biblical communities. Consequently, this invites the project to argue that one goal of Deut 14:22-29; 16:9-12, 13-15; and 26:12-15 was to mold current understandings of social responsibility among farmers and herders in ancient Israel.

19. I take up the question about claims to the goods of the local peasantry in Chapter 5.

artisans and merchants, and the reciprocation of acts of charity left local peasant farmers with little or no sustenance. Thus it is probable that only the crops and livestock that were present after bartering and after the payment of debts supported the households of local farmers and herders. The laws in Deut 12–26 that prescribe morality toward the *'almānâ, gēr,* and *yātôm* are romantic legal injunctions: they invite these types of persons to ignore what is probable, namely, the fact that peasant farmers and herders had food only enough to share with their families and with those whose services they needed in order to maintain a basic level of existence. Regulations that suggested that the peasantry were going to share their scant goods with the *'almānâ, gēr,* and *yātôm* provoked these socially disadvantaged persons to exercise their imaginative abilities and to create fiction.

Security for Loans and Discrimination against Widows in the Biblical Communities

Deut 24:17 limits those items that the *'almānâ* could surrender in a pledge for credit and restricts those items that creditors could accept as collateral from this woman. This text implies that creditors could not compensate themselves with her garment in exchange for money or the loss of any item loaned to her. Maybe this article of clothing protected her from heat, wind, and rain, and consequently was exempt from pawn. While this regulation seems to consider the dilemma of this type of woman, it also provides a basis for discriminating against her. Deut 24:17 exposes this type of woman to more, and less favorable, forms of mortgage. It encourages her potential creditors either to withhold money, food, tools, and any other items she might want to borrow or to impose other strategies for the collection of debts from her, e.g., the usage of her children as collateral for loans. The need to protect an economic investment is the basis of this dilemma, for it is plausible that lenders used items of value to influence the repayment of debts. Deut 24:17 therefore increases the possibility that the *'almānâ* was the object of economic discrimination, and that she had to adopt strategies for repaying creditors that other persons in the biblical communities did not use often.

Gleaning Regulations and the Dilemma of Widows, Strangers, and Orphans in the Biblical Communities

Gleaning Regulations and the Stigmatization of Widows, Strangers, and Orphans in the Biblical Communities

Deut 24:19-22 implies that corporate generosity was a source for the material endowment of the 'almānâ, gēr, and yātôm. The opinion that these individuals subsisted through welfare or public assistance, however, could contribute to the patronizing, demeaning, and capricious treatment of them by individuals or subgroups in the biblical communities. Legal injunctions on gleanings in the DC invite people to discredit and use negative terms to describe this subgroup of socially weak individuals. What is more, this legal injunction allows seeing them as nonproducers, for these laws imply that these types of persons were always recipients and consumers. These regulations convey the impression that they benefited from the labor of others but gave nothing back to the community. Deut 24:19-22 offers the idea that reciprocity was not a feature of the relationship between the 'almānâ, gēr, and yātôm and the peasantry in the biblical community; furthermore, this code insinuates that these persons exploited the labor and industry of the masses. This law therefore makes it possible for local peasant farmers and herders to argue that the 'almānâ, gēr, and yātôm were parasites and a scavenger class in ancient Israelite society.

Gleaning Regulations and the Humiliation of Widows, Strangers, and Orphans in the Biblical Communities

Deut 24:19-22 could impair the self-respect of the 'almānâ, gēr, and yātôm in ancient Israelite society. This legal injunction conveys the idea that the crops and fruits that remained in the fields were for the sustenance of these types of persons. In short, these regulations posit that these vulnerable, socially weak individuals were to search the fields for vegetables and fruits that might have been left by the reapers. This circumstance raises a serious question about the quantity of crops left or overlooked in fields or orchards, for it is probable that no produce remained after the harvest. Perhaps cultic officials sensed that local peasant farmers were lying about the yields of their crops; consequently, they developed strategies to influence them to gather everything from their fields; and as a result a law appeared which stated that the crops and fruits that remained in the fields belonged to the *'almānâ, gēr,* and *yātôm.*

The effort of local peasant farmers to misrepresent their crop yields is consistent with the behavior of the masses in typical agrarian societies. Lenski argues that these persons often expressed discontent over being exploited and rebelled often against the ruling elites by being untruthful about the yields of their fields. "Usually these struggles were nonviolent in character, at least on the peasants' side. For the most part, their efforts consisted of little more than attempts to evade taxes, rents, labor services, and other obligations, usually by concealment of a portion of the harvest, working slowly and sometimes carelessly as well, and similar devices."[20] Since peasant farmers eked out their existence, it is plausible that they lied to cultic officials in order to retain possession of their produce. Cultic officials, however, sought to defuse this problematic by proposing that items left in the fields were no longer the property of local farmers but were the property of another social subgroup. Thus it is improbable that these persons left huge amounts of vegetables and fruits in the fields and orchards. Yet Deut 24:19-22 indicates that the *'almānâ, gēr,* and *yātôm* had to comb the fields, orchards, and vineyards for produce that the reapers left either by accident or by design. I maintain that having to scour the fields, orchards, and vineyards for gleanings contributed to piecemeal disintegration in the pride of this vulnerable social subgroup in ancient Israelite society.

Summary

Law shaped social conventions and influenced private morality in ancient Israelite society. Since Deut 14:22-29; 16:9-12, 13-15; 24:17-18, 19-22; and 26:12-15 deal with the *'almānâ, gēr,* and *yātôm,* it is plausible that these codes informed views about public assistance and individual morality toward this social subgroup. What is more, the innovations in these legal injunctions bolstered the improbability of these persons becoming self-determining human beings; consequently, there is solid textual evidence for believing that these regulations contributed to their oppression.

20. Gerhard Lenski, *Power and Privilege: A Theory of Social Stratification* (Chapel Hill: University of North Carolina Press, 1984), p. 273.

Four questions quite naturally arise: Who drafted these legal injunctions? What conditions might account for the drafting of these regulations? How did they benefit their formulators? And why might they purport to provide public assistance to the *'almānâ, gēr,* and *yātôm* in ancient Israel? In the next chapter I offer a response to these questions by reconstructing the circumstances that might have spawned the drafting of these laws.[21]

---

21. "Matrix" (pl. "matrices") refers to aspects of the external environments of text. For additional discussion on "matrix" in examination of biblical texts, see D. Knight, "The Understanding of 'Sitz-im-Leben' in Form Criticism," in SBLSP 1, ed. George MacRae (Cambridge, Mass.: Society of Biblical Literature, 1974), pp. 105-25.

Chapter 5

TEXTS AND CONTEXTS

The Societal Matrices of the Widow, Stranger,
and Orphan Laws in the Deuteronomic Code

Introduction

As was said in the prolegomenon, critical theory about legal injunctions argues that laws often reflect social problems and frequently serve class interests. Since these methodological considerations inform my paradigm for examining the laws in Deuteronomy, I work from the position that these legal injunctions reflect conflicts, circumstances, and personal interests. I therefore argue that cultic officials in the Yahweh-alone movement drafted Deut 14:22-29; 16:9-12, 13-15; 24:17-18, 19-22; and 26:12-15 in order to legitimize a public assistance program that guaranteed their material endowment, positioning these intellectual elites to shape the consciousness of local peasant farmers and herders regarding the distribution of goods and to stave off potential uprisings by these persons in the North during the Omride administration.

Thus I attempt to set these laws into the framework of social history in ancient Israel and to show how they established and legitimized the politico-economic program of cultic officials during that epoch. First, this chapter uses the innovations in these codes to identify the issues that occasioned the formulation of these laws and to discuss the role they played in the program of cultic officials in the Yahweh-alone movement. Undergirding this position is the assumption that the distinctive literary formulas, ideas, and pedagogies in these legal sanctions are clues to the dynamics that provoked their drafting. The innovations also are clues to how these codes might have advanced the program of the Yahweh-alone movement during the Omride administration. Chapter 3 identified these data: (a) the pedagogy that Yahweh is the God of the biblical community; (b) the command to present tithes of crops and animals to Yahweh at sites where the name of Yahweh is present; (c) the requirement to keep major cultic festivals to Yahweh and to observe them at venues where his name is present; (d) the notion that obedience to the commandments of Yahweh undercuts the possibility of returning to enslavement in Egypt; (e) the acquirement of the *fear of Yahweh consciousness* pedagogy; (f) the appearance of the *'almānâ, gēr,* and *yātôm* together in a single literary arrangement in texts that prescribe morality on exchangeable goods in the biblical communities; and (g) the remoteness-of-the-deity ideology that finds expression in name theology and in the notion that heaven is the abode of the deity.

Second, I use narratives in DtrH to help illuminate the legal prescriptions in the Deuteronomic Code that treat the *'almānâ, gēr,* and *yātôm.* Widespread agreement is present among scholars of the HB that points of contact are present between theologies and points of view on morality in the DC and DtrH. What is more, texts in DtrH articulate phenomena in the biblical communities that these laws presuppose. In other words, certain sociohistoric assumptions of these legal injunctions mesh with the sociohistoric indications of narratives in DtrH. This methodological presupposition stems from the belief that a relationship between the DC and DtrH exists.[1]

Third, I use texts from Mesopotamia and data from elsewhere in Syria-Palestine to inform the present reconstruction of the milieus of Deut 14:22-29; 16:9-12, 13-15; 24:17-18, 19-22; and 26:12-15. DtrH itself contains a wealth of information regarding circumstances and epochs in ancient Israel; yet this layer of literature is biased and incomplete. Since DtrH provides only a partial picture of conditions in the biblical communities, extrabiblical data that treat the same epochs in Israelite history can illuminate circumstances in the biblical communities about which data in DtrH are sparse or suspect.

Fourth, I build upon secondary literature on the DC and on the social-scientific study of ancient Israelite society. These sources of information

---

1. See Douglas A. Knight, "Deuteronomy and the Deuteronomists," in *Old Testament Interpretation: Past, Present, and Future,* ed. James L. Mayes et al. (Nashville: Abingdon, 1995), pp. 61-79.

identify benchmarks for suggesting a *terminus a quo* and a *terminus ad quem* for these laws. What is more, scholarly social-scientific publications on the HB offer windows on kinship systems, interest groups, commerce, political destabilization, internal social upheaval, and other antitheses in the biblical communities — issues that occasioned the drafting of these laws.

In the next section I piece together the milieus from which these legal injunctions arose. The goal is to elucidate the political matrix of these laws by proposing a point of view about the geographic origins and the period that provoked the formulation of these legal sanctions.

The Political Milieu

The Northern Provenance

Since the work of de Wette, it has become axiomatic in critical scholarship that the DC received its present form in the South, by the seventh century B.C.E.[2] While this view implies that the incorporation of the *'almānâ, gēr,* and *yātôm* regulations into the DC happened in Jerusalem or elsewhere in Judea, it fails to account for the geographic origins of these laws and other subgroups of regulations that are present in the DC. This book proposes that these legal injunctions originated in Israel, namely, in that socio-political and economic element of the Davidic kingdom that became distinct from Judah in 922 and that the Aramaeans destroyed in 722.[3]

Three reasons justify conjecturing that these legal injunctions originated in the North.

1. Theological notions in these laws link these texts to layers of literature in the HB that originated and circulated in the North. Points of con-

2. Crüsemann contends that the DC is a new legal-historical document, and that it is a replacement for the BC. He argues that the people of the land *('am hā'āreṣ)* codified the DC during the sixth century B.C.E. in Judah. Crüsemann therefore links the present form of the DC to conditions in the biblical communities in the South. See Frank Crüsemann, *The Torah: Theology and Social History of Old Testament Law,* trans. Allan W. Mahnke (Minneapolis: Fortress, 1996), p. 215.

3. This is the definition for "Israel" that informs Chapter 5. For discussion on delineations of "Israel" in scholarly study of the HB, see Philip R. Davies, *In Search of 'Ancient Israel'* (Sheffield: Sheffield Academic Press, 1992), pp. 47-56; and Niels Peter Lemche, *The Israelites in History and in Tradition,* ed. Douglas A. Knight (Louisville: Westminster/John Knox, 1998).

tact are present between ideas about the deity in Deut 14:22-29; 16:9-12, 13-15; and 26:12-15 and notions on the deity and religiousness that appear in the Elohist segment of the Pentateuch (hereafter cited as E), Amos, and Hosea. Deut 14:23a, 24a; 16:11b; and 26:15 imply that the deity is distant from earth. This philosophy finds expression in the name theology in Deut 14:23a, 24a; 16:11b and in the pedagogy that heaven is the abode of the deity in 26:15a. These innovations undermine associating earthly venues with the habitation of Yahweh. Regarding the remoteness-of-the-deity theology that appears in the DC, Nicholson writes:

> It has been rightly pointed out that the notion of the "name" as the form of Yahweh's manifestation is not itself unique in Deuteronomy. Already at an earlier period the Book of the Covenant conceived of Yahweh's sanctuaries as the places where he has caused his name to be recorded (cf. Exod. xx 24). What is new in Deuteronomy, however, is the radical definition of this concept whereby not Yahweh himself but his name is present in the sanctuary. In other words, Deuteronomy is concerned with emphasizing the distance between God and the sanctuary and in so doing is attempting to replace, as von Rad has put it, the old crude idea of Yahweh's presence and dwelling at the shrine by a theologically sublimated idea. Yahweh cannot be contained in a temple-heaven and the highest heaven cannot contain him.[4]

The remoteness of the deity is a distinguishing feature of E. At the center of this claim is that Gen 20:1-18; 22:1-19; Num 12:1-16, and other literary units in the Pentateuch that scholarship accepts as E narratives suggest that the deity is a distant Subject. Moreover, these data imply that he maintains commerce with creation and individuals through dreams, angels, and intermediaries.[5] The belief about the remoteness of Yahweh links Deut 14:22-

---

4. E. W. Nicholson, *Deuteronomy and Tradition* (Philadelphia: Fortress, 1967), pp. 55-56. For additional discussion on the abode of the deity in Deuteronomic literature, see Moshe Weinfeld, *Deuteronomy and the Deuteronomic School* (Winona Lake, Ind.: Eisenbrauns, [1972] 1992), pp. 191-209.

5. For additional discussion on the origin and contents of E, see Douglas A. Knight, "The Pentateuch," in *The Hebrew Bible and Its Modern Interpreters*, ed. D. Knight and Gene Tucker (Philadelphia: Fortress, 1985), pp. 263-96; S. E. McEvenue, "The Elohist at Work," *ZAW* 96 (1984): 315-32; A. W. Jenks, *The Elohist and North Israelite Traditions* (Missoula: Scholars, 1977); Hans W. Wolff, "The Elohistic Fragments in the Pentateuch," in *The Vitality of Old Testament Traditions*, ed. Walter Brueggemann and Hans W. Wolff (Atlanta: John

29; 16:9-12, 13-15; and 26:12-15 to E, and this theological point of contact suggests that the geographic origins of these laws lie in the North.[6]

2. Deut 14:23b links a person acquiring the fear of the deity (*yir'at 'ĕlōhîm*) to his bringing tithes to the official cultic site. Similarly this theological concern, as a basis for moral decision making, is a distinguishing theological feature of E, for Wolff contends that this motif is interwoven thoroughly into narratives in this literary stratum that treat the ancestors and other central figures in the histories of the biblical communities.[7]

For instance, three narratives in Genesis and Exodus provide windows on the *yir'at 'ĕlōhîm* motif in E. Gen 20:1-18 deals with Abraham and Abimelech. Gen 20:11 says Abraham answered, "I said this only because there is no *yirat 'ĕlōhîm* in this place, and I thought that they would kill me because of my wife." This narrative suggests that Abraham has a concern for the fear of the deity and depicts him as fearing that Abimelech is an evil man who lacks this basis for moral decision making. Gen 22:1-19, an E passage, treats the offering of Isaac as a sacrifice to the deity by Abraham. Gen 22:12 says: "Do not stretch forth your hand against the lad; do not do anything to him, for now I know that you *fear God* because you have not kept your only son from me." Third, Exod 18:13-27, an E passage, recounts Jethro's advice to Moses regarding the appointment of judges among the people of Israel. Exod 18:21 delineates the characteristics of these judges and includes *yir'at 'ĕlōhîm* among the virtues they must possess. The sentence units where this phrase is present imply that it is a theological viewpoint that shapes beliefs and values and produces acceptable morality.

Weinfeld offers a view on the group in the biblical communities among whom *yir'at 'ĕlōhîm* pedagogy circulated. He argues that this tenet originated with scribes in the biblical community and, moreover, contends that this pedagogy is a common theme in the Wisdom Literature in the HB.[8] Weinfeld is correct in claiming that this idea is a common theme in

---

Knox, 1982), pp. 67-82; J. F. Craghan, "The Elohist in Recent Literature," *BTB* 7 (1977): 23-35; and Robert B. Coote, *In Defense of Revolution: The Elohist History* (Minneapolis: Fortress, 1991).

6. What is more, Mayes suggests that "name theology" originated in the North and is a response by groups there to the loss of the ark of Yahweh. See A. D. H. Mayes, *Deuteronomy* (Grand Rapids: Eerdmans, [1979] 1991), p. 224.

7. See Wolff, pp. 70-76, and Coote, pp. 4-5.

8. Weinfeld, *Deuteronomy and the Deuteronomic School*, pp. 274-81. For a detailed response to Weinfeld, see C. Brekelmans, "Wisdom Influence in Deuteronomy," in *A Song of*

this layer of literature, yet his claim that its origins lie in sapiential circles invites debate. At the heart of this issue is the possibility that sages, priests, prophets, and other religious functionaries contributed to the intellectual and spiritual life of ancient Israel. It is plausible that a common philosophical tradition about proper morality was present in the biblical communities, and that this shared belief found expression in *yir'at 'ĕlōhîm* pedagogy. Thus the origins of the fear-of-the-deity motif may lie in any of the many levels of religious leadership in ancient Israelite society.[9] This innovation — pedagogy — links Deut 14:22-29 to E, and this connection breaks ground for claiming that the origins of this law lie in the North.

3. Deut 16:12a; 24:18a, and 22a stress the deliverance from enslavement in Egypt. This feature of these legal injunctions links these laws to the book of Amos. For example, Amos 2:9-10 declares:

> Indeed I destroyed the Amorite before them,
> though he was tall as the cedars
> and strong as the oaks.
> I destroyed his fruit above,
> and his roots from below.
> I brought you from the land of Egypt,
> and I led you forty years in the wilderness
> to give you the land of the Amorites.

Amos 3:1-2 states:

> Hear this word that Yahweh spoke concerning you, O children
>   of Israel, concerning each family that I brought up from the
>   land of Egypt:
> I knew you only,
> of all the families of the earth;
> therefore I will punish you,
> because of all your perversions.

Amos 9:7-8 asserts:

Power and the Power of Song: Essays on the Book of Deuteronomy, ed. Duane Christensen (Winona Lake, Ind.: Eisenbrauns, 1993), pp. 123-34.

9. For discussion on religious subgroups in the biblical communities, see Joseph Blenkinsopp, *Sage, Priest, and Prophet: Religious and Intellectual Leadership in Ancient Israel* (Louisville: Westminster/John Knox, 1995).

Are you not like the children of Cush to me,
O children of Israel, says Yahweh?
Did not I bring Israel up from the land of Egypt,
and the Philistines from Caphtor,
and Aram from Qir?
Behold the eyes of Yahweh
are on the sinful kingdom.
And I will destroy it
from the face of the ground.
I will not utterly destroy the house of Jacob, says Yahweh.

Likewise, the deliverance of Israel from enslavement in Egypt is a focus in the book of Hosea. Hosea 11:1 says:

When Israel was a lad, I loved him
and I called my son from Egypt.

Hosea 12:9 (= Hebr. 12:10) declares:

I am Yahweh your God,
I [brought you out] from the land of Egypt.
I will cause you to live in tents again.

Hosea 12:11-13 (= Hebr. 12:12-14) asserts:

Is Gilead wicked? Indeed they are worthless.
They sacrifice bulls in Gilgal.
Their altars also are like piles of stones,
on a plowed field.
Jacob fled to the fields of Aram.
Israel served for a wife,
and he watched for her.
Yahweh brought Israel out of Egypt by a prophet,
and Yahweh watched them through a prophet.

Hosea 13:4-6 states:

I am Yahweh your God,
[the one who brought you] out of the land of Egypt.
Do not acknowledge any God except me,

there is no Savior besides me.
I knew you in the wilderness,
in a land of heat;
they were satisfied, when I was pasturing them,
they were satisfied and they became proud,
therefore they forgot me.

Innovations in the regulations in Deut 12–26 that treat the 'almānâ, gēr, and yātôm link these codes to E, Amos, and Hosea, and to literary strata in the HB that circulated in the North. In the next section I propose an earliest possible date for the formulation of Deut 14:22-29; 16:9-12, 13-15; 24:17-18, 19-22; and 26:12-15. I use the secondary literature on the relationship of the DC to the BC and the historical implications of the innovations in these legal injunctions to proffer a position about the provenance of these codes.

The Chronological Boundaries

Critical scholarship contends that the DC received its present form by the seventh century B.C.E. This point of unification among scholars proposes a *terminus ad quem* for the codification of the DC, and it brings into play a date for understanding the incorporation of disparate subgroups of legal injunctions into this corpus of law. This opinion, however, does not resolve issues regarding a *terminus a quo* for the drafting of the separate regulations constituting the DC.

Commonly held opinions about the formulation of the DC and about its relationship to the BC offer a benchmark for dating the subgroups of regulations in Deut 12–26. Crüsemann, D. Patrick, and Weinfeld note that the BC antedates the DC and that the DC draws extensively from the BC.[10] Crüsemann posits particularly that the DC was a replacement for the BC.

The relationship of deuteronomic law to the older Book of the Covenant, viewed as a whole, compels us to regard the more recent document as a replacement for the older one. The decisive features, which

10. Crüsemann, pp. 201-5; Dale Patrick, *Old Testament Law* (Atlanta: John Knox, 1985), pp. 97-98; and Moshe Weinfeld, *Deuteronomy 1–11*, Anchor Bible Commentary Series (New York and Toronto: Doubleday, 1991), pp. 19-24.

made the Book of the Covenant different from other ancient Near Eastern law codes, were adopted by Deuteronomy and expanded. Thus, the whole appears as the command of Israel's God, even if at the same time it appears through the authority of Moses in a new way, having at its center the first commandment, the exclusive veneration of YHWH. The people being addressed are free, propertied Israelites. Just as in the Book of the Covenant, widely disparate traditions of theology, cult, law and ethos are held together in a single law book.[11]

Working from the assumption that Crüsemann is correct and that the DC is the replacement for the BC, it becomes conceivable that laws on cultic festivals and morality toward the 'almānâ, gēr, and yātôm in the DC are later versions or adaptations of regulations in the BC that treat pilgrimages and morality toward this subgroup of vulnerable underclass individuals in the biblical communities. In addition, Patrick and Crüsemann argue that the BC received its present form by the eleventh century B.C.E.[12] Hence it is plausible that the legal injunctions postdate the eleventh century.

What is more, it is important to note that a nexus is present between the sociohistoric assumptions of the innovations of these laws and politico-economic problems in the North during the ninth century. This link becomes the basis for suggesting that the ninth century was the *terminus a quo* of these codes. Their distinctive literary features suggest that disputes over the distribution of exchangeable goods, irreverence for Yahweh, discontent among local peasant farmers, and decline in the circumstances of the 'almānâ, gēr, and yātôm were features of the milieu that led to their formulation.

1 Kgs 16:21–2 Kgs 10:36 and 1 Sam 8:10-17 bring into play several assumptions regarding social conditions in the North. The texts imply that conflict was present between major subgroups over the allocation of commodities. These data suggest that strict Yahwism was gaining a major following in the biblical community. Also, the pieces of evidence proffer that discontent among the peasantry about their circumstances and deterioration in the circumstances of widows and orphans were features of the North during the ninth century. 1 Kgs 16:21–2 Kgs 10:36 is a window on the Omride administration. Regarding 1 Sam 8:10-17 as a window on social

---

11. Crüsemann, p. 202.
12. Patrick, pp. 97-98, and Crüsemann, p. 111.

history in the North during the Omride dynasty and not as a window on the administration of Solomon exclusively, however, requires justification. This speech is placed on the lips of Samuel, and it discloses beliefs about the state of affairs under a tyrant. 1 Sam 8:10-17 has points of contact with Deut 17:14-20, a text that reflects Northern views about monarchy in ancient Israelite society. Considerable agreement is present among scholars of the HB that Deut 17:14-20 is a Northern text, for critics contend that the view of kingship expressed in this text fits better in the context of the Northern rather than the Southern Kingdom.[13] Deut 17:14-20 is hostile to the self-aggrandizement of monarchs; it condemns the procurement of harems and horses and prohibits the acquisition of a large personal treasury by the king.

1 Sam 8:10-17 also has points of contact with Hos 8:4 and 13:9-14 — texts that reflect Northern views about monarchy in ancient Israelite society also. Each text advances the notion that monarchy in the biblical community was not the wish of Yahweh, but that it proceeded from the wish of subgroups in the biblical community. Common views among 1 Sam 8:10-17 and Northern texts about the state, therefore, link 1 Sam 8:10-17 to Israel.[14]

1 Sam 8:10-17 is part of the antimonarchical narratives in DtrH. D. McCarthy and P. K. McCarter posit that the textual antecedents of the antimonarchical narratives in 1 Samuel circulated among groups in the North before 722.[15] In fact, these scholars aver that these traditions proceeded from a prophetic perspective on kingship, an angle of vision that advocates the position that the authority of the prophet is superior to that of the monarch. What is more, McCarter argues that the belief in the superiority of prophetic authority is a distinctly Northern tenet. He therefore links 1 Sam 8:10-17 to prophetic circles in Samaria. He also contends that this narrative reflects an unpleasant historical experience with kingship in Israel.[16]

13. Mayes, p. 270.

14. 1 Sam 10:17-27 and 12:1-25 provide windows on attitudes toward monarchy in the biblical communities. These passages are critical of monarchy, and this issue suggests that antimonarchical subgroups were present in the biblical communities. 1 Sam 8:10-17 therefore is one of the three narratives in DtrH that came down from the North that are adverse to monarchy in the biblical community.

15. See Dennis J. McCarthy, "The Inauguration of Monarchy in Israel," *Int* 27 (1973): 401-12.

16. See P. Kyle McCarter, Jr., *1 Samuel*, Anchor Bible Commentary Series (Garden City, N.Y.: Doubleday, 1980), p. 161.

I maintain that the policies of Solomon spawned suspicions about monarchy, but that the administration of the Omrides confirmed extant misgivings about monarchy and provoked the codification of existent traditions in the biblical communities that were critical of monarchy. It is probable that the experiences of subgroups in the North with the Omrides led to the codification of 1 Sam 8:10-17.

Summary

In this section I offered a view on the provenance of regulations in Deuteronomy that prescribed morality toward the *'almānâ, gēr,* and *yātôm.* I posited that these legal injunctions arose during the Omride administration. Noteworthy is that a nexus is present between the sociohistoric indications in 1 Sam 8:10-17 and 1 Kgs 16:21–2 Kgs 10:36 and the historical presuppositions of the innovations in Deut 14:22-29; 16:9-12, 13-15; 24:17-18, 19-22; and 26:12-15. This concord suggests that events in Israel during the ninth century led to the formulation of these legal injunctions. Since this book argues that these laws arose in the North during the Omride administration, it now identifies the policies of the Omrides that provoked the innovations in these regulations.

The Economic Milieu of the Omride Administration

The Resurgence in Bureaucracy

Chapter 2 identified officials and levels of administration in the Omride administration. To avoid repetition, this chapter simply states that four major subgroups of officials were present in this administration. 1 Kgs 18:3, 15-20; and 20:14-15 suggest that these subgroups were the supervisors of the palaces, district governors, cultic officials, and the military. Certainty on the socioeconomic relationship and on the intragroup dynamics of these classes is elusive. The fact that the Omrides were at the apex of the socioeconomic ladder in the North, and that the concentration of power in the North was with this group, however, is without dispute.

The Resurgence in State Building Projects

1 Kgs 16:24 indicates that Omri bought a hill and began the construction of Samaria on it. D. N. Pienaar contends that the royal quarters built at Samaria were among the great achievements of the Omride dynasty. "Omri built his royal quarters on the summit of the hill of Shemer. He extended the area by means of a series of terraces and retaining walls. The building complex occupied an area of 145 x 76m and shows clear signs of Phoenician influence. The work was of such excellent standard that nowhere in the Near East had it been equaled until Herod the Great appeared on the scene."[17]

1 Kgs 16:24 does not explicitly state Omri's rationale for relocating the capital from Tirzah to Samaria. Perhaps the cessation of war between Omri and Tibni occasioned this project and a plethora of additional state construction projects in Israel. However, the passage does provide information from which to conjecture about the motivation for building his headquarters on this site. It indicates that Samaria was located on a hill. Y. Aharoni indicates that the site was situated along an important trade route in the hill country of Ephraim. "The most important latitudinal road ascends from the vicinity of Socoh in the Sharon to Samaria and Shechem. From here it joins the longitudinal road and goes north-east as far as Tirzah, whence it descends via the wadi Far'ah to the important fords of the Jordan near the city of Adam. This is the most convenient line by which one may cross the central hill country, and this helps to explain the rise of important cities on the sites of Shechem and Tirzah, and later also Samaria, at major highway junctures."[18]

Archaeological digs indicate that a massive wall encircled the royal quarters at Samaria. This was a defensive measure, for 1 Kgs 15:16-21 indicates that armed hostilities between Israel and Aram were a feature of the international scene in the ANE in the ninth century. Thus the location, architecture, and layout of Samaria positioned Omri and future monarchs of Israel to protect themselves, the royal families, and the inhabitants of villages in the North from the Aramaeans, Assyrians, and other aggressors.

---

17. D. N. Pienaar, "The Role of Fortified Cities in the Northern Kingdom during the Reign of the Omride Dynasty," *JNWSL* 9 (1981): 152.

18. Yohanan Aharoni, *The Land of the Bible*, 2nd ed., trans. A. F. Rainey (Philadelphia: Westminster, 1979), p. 60.

What is more, the location of Samaria positioned Omri to control major routes that permitted the movement and exchange of goods in Syria-Palestine.

These features might account for the relocation of the capital from Tirzah to Samaria. But the internal dynamics of Tirzah might also have contributed to the relocation. On the one hand, it is probable that Tirzah was rife with hostilities toward Omri and his supporters, for it is possible that Omri and his supporters ravaged Tirzah. If this were the case, he could have destroyed its defenses, making it useless to him from a military standpoint. On the other hand, Omri and his camp might have perpetrated atrocities against the supporters of Tibni during the struggle for the politico-economic control of the North. Omri therefore might have murdered many of the supporters of Tibni, and the relatives or friends of those he executed might have harbored animosity toward him and his retainers. Thus the possibility of a coup d'etat or assassination in Tirzah might account for the construction of a new headquarters elsewhere in the North by Omri.

As was said in Chapter 2, 1 Kgs 21:1 indicates that the Omrides built a palace for themselves at Jezreel. Ahlström and Aharoni contend that this palace was the winter residence of the Omrides.[19] A. Mazar indicates that archaeologists unearthed a quarried moat and a few structures made of ashlar masonry at Jezreel. Mazar links these material remains to Ahab, and contends that they are evidence of his large-scale building activities.[20]

1 Kgs 16:34 suggests also that widespread construction activity was part of the state policy of the Omrides. This text indicates that Hiel fortified (bānâ) Jericho; that this building activity happened during the administration of Ahab; and that Abiram, the oldest son of Hiel, died when Hiel laid the foundation of Jericho, and Segub, his youngest son, died when he set up the gates of Jericho. Jericho is just northwest of the Dead Sea, in proximity to Moab, and its geographical location may account for its fortification by Ahab, for rebellion against Israel was common in Moab during the ninth century. Thus the constant insubordination of Moab justified the fortification of Jericho, because this building project

---

19. Gösta Ahlström, *The History of Ancient Palestine* (Minneapolis: Fortress, 1993), p. 584; and Aharoni, *Land of the Bible*, p. 334.

20. Amihai Mazar, *Archaeology of the Land of the Bible, 10,000-586 B.C.E.* (New York: Doubleday, 1990), p. 410.

provided a military compound in the southern part of Israel during the reign of Ahab.[21]

Moreover, 1 Kgs 22:39 implies that Ahab built additional cities in Israel. Scholars include building activities at Hazor and Megiddo among those unspecified building activities.[22] Archaeological digs at Hazor uncovered a citadel, solid wall, elaborate gate, and several small buildings. What is more, Pienaar, Mazar, and Ahlström contend that Ahab fortified Hazor, and that it was the main component of his defense system. Perhaps this fortification was a maneuver to stymie any efforts by the Aramaeans to conquer Israel. Megiddo is a very prominent city in the Jezreel Valley, and it is in proximity to other routes for the movement of goods throughout Syria-Palestine.[23] Regarding the building activities of Ahab, Ahlström contends: "To return to Ahab's buildings and fortifications, some of the buildings and defense systems that have been excavated have been dated to the ninth century BCE at places like Megiddo, Hazor, Shechem, Dan, and Jericho, and construction in other places could have been carried out on Ahab's orders."[24]

The Resurgence in International Trade

The political stability introduced into Israel by Omri provided opportunity for the establishment of trade between Israel and other countries. While DtrH provides meager information about how Omri formed economic leagues with nations elsewhere in Syria-Palestine, it is probable that intermarriage between the Omrides and daughters of monarchs in the ANE brought these commercial arrangements into existence. For example,

21. In the Moabite Stone, Mesha claims that he mounted a successful revolt against Ahab. Aharoni indicates that Mesha gained liberation from Israel by a series of battles that included the capture of several Israelite towns. See *ANET*, p. 320, and Aharoni, *Land of the Bible*, pp. 337-40.

22. Mazar, pp. 409-15; Pienaar, p. 156; Graham I. Davies, *Megiddo* (Grand Rapids: Eerdmans, 1986), pp. 85-106; and Yigael Yadin, *Hazor, with a Chapter on Israelite Megiddo* (London: Oxford University Press, 1972), pp. 147-65.

23. Ahlström, pp. 581-87; Mazar, p. 412; and Pienaar, pp. 156-57.

24. Ahlström, pp. 583-84. For additional information on the building activities of Omri and Ahab, see Yohanan Aharoni, *The Archaeology of the Land of Israel*, trans. A. F. Rainey (Philadelphia: Westminster, 1982), pp. 333-40.

1 Kgs 16:31 indicates that Ahab married Jezebel, the daughter of Ethbaal, the king of Tyre. This datum implies that the Omrides used politico-economic marriages to form alliances and to increase mercantile activity between Israel and other nations in Syria-Palestine.[25]

Because Ahab married Jezebel, it therefore becomes probable that there was an economic alliance between Israel and Tyre during the Omride regime, and that the Omrides imported glass, metalworkings, ivories, ceramics, and toiletries from Phoenicia into Israel. M. Silver indicates that the manufacture and exportation of ivory products was a major market in Phoenicia prior to the eighth century.[26] Furthermore, archaeologists unearthed a small royal acropolis at Samaria that dates from the mid-ninth century. In the acropolis these scholars also discovered a building that contained ivory products, most of which were small and were decorations, which Aharoni links to Phoenicia.[27] Mazar writes: "The Samaria ivories must have been produced during the ninth and eighth centuries B.C.E.; a more exact date cannot be determined, although various suggestions have been made. It is tempting to think that they were brought to Samaria from Phoenicia during the time of Ahab and his wife, the Tyrian princess Jezebel, who introduced Phoenician cult practices to the Israelite capital. If this was the case, most of the ivories should be dated to the first half of the ninth century B.C.E."[28] The presence of Phoenician bazaars and ivories in Israel implies that trade between Phoenicia and Israel during the ninth century was substantial.

Inscriptions from Shalmaneser III suggest that Ahab contributed two thousand chariots and ten thousand soldiers to the Syria-Palestinian effort to stop the Assyrian westward advance at Qarqar in 853.[29] As was mentioned in Chapter 2, certainty on the size of Ahab's army is questionable. It, however, is certain that Ahab had an efficient military machine, and that a well-stocked arsenal was at the heart of the success of his army. It is probable that chariots, swords, shields, spears, and other implements for waging war were in the inventory of the military during the reign of Ahab. Treat-

---

25. For discussion on the marriage between Ahab and Jezebel, see Ahlström, pp. 570-71.

26. See Morris Silver, *Prophets and Markets: The Political Economy of Ancient Israel* (Boston: Kluwer-Nijhoff, 1983), pp. 57-61.

27. Aharoni, *Archaeology*, p. 242.

28. Mazar, p. 505.

29. Mazar, pp. 278-79.

ment on weaponry and chariots in the military machine of Ahab, then, brings into play conversation on the sources of these items.

It is possible that individuals with the skill to manufacture chariots, armor, and weapons were present in the North. This leaves open the possibility that affluent individuals made agreements or entered financial contracts with the monarchy, and that these elites sold weapons, chariots, horses, armor, and soldiers to the royal establishment. What is more, it is probable that Ahab needed immense resources to sustain a sizable military from which he could field thousands of soldiers and chariots. It is conceivable that the material endowment of the military during the reign of Ahab contributed to a resurgence in the buying of or bartering for goods by the state during the Omride administration.

Summary

The political stability introduced by the Omrides reintroduced bureaucracy, major building projects, a sizable military, a resurgence in international trade, and the framework for a mercantile economy. While responsibility for supporting the bureaucracy, military, royal construction projects, and internal and external policies of the Omrides rested upon the shoulders of different socioeconomic subgroupings, it is probable that most of the burden fell upon the shoulders of the peasantry. This situation is consistent with circumstances of the peasantry in agrarian societies elsewhere in human history, for Lenski maintains that rulers and other individuals among the governing class placed economic burdens on local peasant farmers and herders. "Ultimately, the burden of supporting the state and the privileged classes fell on the shoulders of the common people, and especially on the peasant farmers who constituted a substantial majority of the population. Even taxes levied on the more prosperous segments of the population were usually shifted to the peasants and urban artisans by one means or another."[30] Such a problematic, then, makes it plausible that Omri and Ahab placed exorbitant demands on local peasant farmers and herders, and that the state confiscated land and crops from these individuals. Concern about sources for the material endowment of the Omrides,

---

30. Gerhard Lenski, *Power and Privilege: A Theory of Social Stratification* (Chapel Hill: University of North Carolina Press, 1984), pp. 266-67.

then, points me squarely to issues regarding the collection and distribution of grain, wine, oil, and livestock in Israel, for it is certain that the material endowment of the Omrides laid the groundwork for flagitious acts of aggression on the masses.[31]

Social life in the North was not compartmental; consequently, the economic policies of the Omrides effected changes in other aspects of the external environment. It, then, is likely that their economic policies were consequential for the distinct patterns of social organization among the masses. The next section explores effects of the Omride economic policies on the collection of households in Israel. This section has several objectives: (a) it identifies socioeconomic units among the masses; (b) it delineates the major socioeconomic unit among the masses in Israel;[32] (c) it indicates how the political and economic policies of the Omride administration contributed to the weakening of the most consequential type of socioeconomic unit; (d) it discusses how the breakdown in the most consequential type of social subgrouping exacerbated the dilemma of widows, strangers, and orphans; and (e) it shows how the disintegration of the most consequential social subgrouping provided a circumstance that contributed to the drafting of regulations that purported to provide a public relief system for widows, strangers, and orphans.

The Social Milieu

The Identification of Kinship Subgroupings

Num 1:1-52; 26:5-65; 1 Sam 10:17-27; Josh 7:16-19, the book of Ruth, Gottwald, D. Hopkins, N. P. Lemche, and C. J. H. Wright inform the pres-

---

31. The Ahab-Naboth episode in 1 Kgs 21:1-29 provides information on oppressive practices of the monarchy, but it is unclear about the complete holdings of Naboth or his socioeconomic status prior to his encounter with Ahab. It is possible that Naboth was part of the affluent stratum of the biblical community. Yet indignation concerning the wrongful exercise of power by the monarchy may account for the presence of the Ahab-Naboth narrative in DtrH.

32. When I speak of the major, or most consequential, socioeconomic subgrouping, I refer to that collectivity or social unit of organization in the biblical communities with the resources to provide financial aid, mutual support, legal protection, and a plethora of benevolent services to its vulnerable constituents.

ent discussion about the major kinship subgroupings among the masses.[33] Two issues are particularly important for this section in its usage of these data and scholars to identify kinship collectivities among the masses during the Omride dynasty. Scholars posit that these data are present in literary traditions that received their final forms in the North; the book of Ruth received its present form in the South, as did the larger literary collections in which Num 1:1-52; 26:5-65; Josh 7:16-19; and 1 Sam 10:17-27 appear. The Southern provenance of these texts raises questions about using them to identify patterns of social organization in the North. The provenance of P, DtrH, and Ruth, however, is inconclusive for determining the geographic origins of the individual traditions that constitute these strata of literature, for it is possible that the laws and smaller narratives that make up these data circulated in the North.

Gottwald, Lemche, and Wright examine social structure in the biblical communities. Wright, on the one hand, especially allows notions in Gottwald on social structure in the biblical community to shape his investigation into kinship subgroupings in ancient Israelite society. Lemche, on the other hand, criticizes Gottwald heavily and parts company with him on terms for understanding patterns of kinship organization in ancient Israel. Hence the points of difference between Gottwald and Lemche delimit the second problematic involved in discussing family subunits in the biblical communities.

Lemche and Gottwald aid in resolving this dilemma regarding terms for social subgroupings. Both scholars concede that three major kinship subdivisions constituted the biblical communities. For Lemche they are the nuclear and extended family and the large lineage group,[34] for Gottwald the tribe, protective association of families, and household. These scholars agree that *šēbeṭ, maṭê, mišpāḥâ, 'elep,* and *bêt-'āb* denote social subunits in ancient Israelite society, but they part company over the referents of these terms.

This confused condition between Gottwald and Lemche stems partic-

---

33. Norman K. Gottwald, *The Tribes of Yahweh* (Maryknoll, N.Y.: Orbis, 1979), pp. 237-92; David Hopkins, *The Highlands of Canaan* (Decatur: Almond Press, 1985), pp. 265-75; Niels P. Lemche, *Early Israel* (Leiden: E. J. Brill, 1985), pp. 245-72; and Christopher J. H. Wright, *God's People in God's Land* (Grand Rapids: Eerdmans, 1990), pp. 48-70.

34. A lineage group is a collectivity of fifty or more individuals who live together as distinct families. What is more, Lemche leaves open the possibility that matriarchies constituted nuclear families in the biblical communities. See Lemche, *Early Israel*, pp. 248-49.

ularly from difference of opinion regarding the kinship subgrouping that *bêt-'āb* labels in ancient Israelite society. Concerning the definition of this term, Gottwald claims:

> A *bêt-'āv* customarily includes the family head and his wife (or wives), their sons and unmarried daughters, the sons's [*sic*] wives and children, and so on, as far as the biological and affinal links extended generationally. Attrition would occur through deaths, marriages out of the group, and separation of members to start new living groups. Addition would occur through births, marriages into the group, and incorporation of outsiders through adoption or the assimilation of *gērîm*, "resident aliens." Although no biblical figures are given, a thriving *bêt-'āv* might easily comprise from fifty to one hundred persons, depending upon the economic support base and the freedom of the community from external threats.[35]

Gottwald concludes that the *bêt-'āv* lived in a common dwelling, practiced exogamy, and maintained a common economic arrangement; consequently he implies that this term designates the smallest socioeconomic unit in the biblical communities.

Gottwald contends that distinct *battê-'ābôt* (fathers' houses) grouped themselves into larger socioeconomic units for mutual support and protection. He suggests that *mišpāḥâ* (protective association of families) refers to a collection of households. "On the one hand, the *mišpāḥâh* designates an entity larger than the *bêt-'āv;* and where the two appear together in a single context, the *mišpāḥâh* is inclusive of the *bêt-'āv.*" He accordingly maintains that the *mišpāḥâ* was the second major subdivision or layer of socioeconomic organization in ancient Israel.[36]

Lemche, however, declares that terminological ambiguity is conspicuous in Gottwald's position on social subdivisions in the biblical communities. The fact that Gottwald uses *bêt-'āb* to refer to households, extended families, and lineage groups and allows *mišpāḥâ* to denote extended families and lineage groups is at the center of this problem. Lemche cites Gen 18:19 and 24:38, 40 to support his critiques of Gottwald regarding the referent of the *bêt-'āb* in the HB. On the one hand, Gen 18:19 implies that *bêt-'āb* refers to a lineage group. On the other hand, Gen 24:38, 40 suggest that

---

35. Gottwald, p. 285.
36. Gottwald, p. 257.

this term denotes an extended family. "Thus בת־אב [*bêt-'āb*] may be used of both lineages and extended families, even though in sociological terms these are two distinct levels in societal structure. The extended family is a residential group, while the other, the lineage, is a descent group which is composed of a number of residential groups."[37] Regarding Gottwald's appropriation of terms in the HB for social subgroupings in Israel, Lemche states:

> Thus in my opinion Gottwald's analysis shows that ancient Israel possessed both nuclear families, extended families, and lineages, and that all three were referred to by the same term, בת־אב. Nevertheless, there is no reason to assume that in every case we shall be in position to determine which of these phenomena we are dealing with, which naturally limits the analytical value of this insight. The subsequent sections of Gottwald's treatment of Israelite social organization emphasize that בת־אב is also used of the lineage, since, as he notes, the term בת־אב sometimes figures metaphorically instead of משפחה [*mišpāḥâ*], and, in a few cases, it even substitutes for שבט [*šēbeṭ*], "tribe." The reason why this is possible is not that בת־אב is a metaphor for משפחה, but that the two concepts overlap because they are both used of the same structural level in Israelite society.[38]

Thus terminological inexactness for kinship subgroupings is at the heart of Lemche's criticism of Gottwald. This censure raises questions about the meaning of relationship terminology in Num 1:1-52; 26:5-65; Josh 7:16-19; 1 Sam 10:17-27, and the book of Ruth. It is probable that the definition of family differed among individuals, and that this variance found expression in competing terms for kinship subgroupings in ancient Israelite society. Consequently, it is no surprise that competing terms for kinship groupings are present in the HB.

Kinship terminology in Num 1:1-52; 26:5-65; Josh 7:16-19; 1 Sam 10:17-27, and Ruth thus suggests that three major kinship groupings were present in the biblical communities. Gottwald and Lemche also propose three major kinship subgroupings: the *šēbeṭ*, *mišpāḥâ*, and *bêt-'āb*. I therefore contend that the *mišpāḥâ* was the major kinship subgrouping in Israel during the ninth century B.C.E. The next section, then, articulates an un-

37. Lemche, *Early Israel*, p. 252.
38. Lemche, *Early Israel*, p. 249.

derstanding of this social subunit and advances a theory on why it was the most relevant kinship pattern in Israel during the Omride administration.

The Significance of Blood Relations among the Collection of Households

This section uses the term "collection of households" to indicate the level of kinship between the household and the large-scale lineage group in biblical Israel. Blood relations and relatives through marriage composed this kinship subgrouping,[39] and this book contends that consanguinity was the main structuring or binding factor among the collection of households.[40] This thesis modifies Gottwald, for he contends that shared interests fused disparate families into the collection of household units in the biblical communities.[41]

The present study argues that compact sociospatiality was a feature of collections of households in the North. That is to say, the constituent nuclear families of local collections of households lived in proximity to each other. This argument is based on the terrain of the Ephraimite territory. The features of the central hill country of Syria-Palestine partitioned the land into sections, and these natural longitudinal fissures in the Ephraim territory subdivided the land into four regions. What is more, many cleav-

---

39. While Num 1 and 26 treat the selection of men for military service in the biblical communities and enumerate the process and criterion for membership in the army, these texts contain direct evidence on the major structuring factor in the collection of households. They indicate that nuclear families/households constituted the association of households. Moreover, they suggest that kinship, not shared interests, was the cohesion among disparate households in the association of households. The fact that the heads of each socioeconomic element in associations of households were biological descendants of the individual from whom the collection of households obtains its name is basic to this claim. While the collection of households was a subgrouping of smaller autonomous socioeconomic units, certainty on the size of the subsidiary units in the collection of households in the biblical communities is a formidable challenge. Thus Num 1 and 26 provide scaffolding upon which the present project bases its claim that common biological descent is the main factor between individual families in the collection of households in the biblical communities.

40. For discussion on kinship terminology in anthropological research, see Robert Parkin, *Kinship: An Introduction to the Basic Concepts* (Malden, Mass.: Blackwell, 1997), pp. 1-35.

41. Gottwald, p. 257.

ages cut latitudinally across Syria-Palestine.[42] Thus features of the terrain, namely, the mountains, rivers, forests, valleys, and other features of the landscape, formed natural boundaries and subdivided the central hill country of Syria-Palestine. It, however, is probable that some sections of land in the central hills were fertile and inhabitable and others were infertile and uninhabitable. The Ephraimite territory contained many small inhabitable districts, and this phenomenon invites the present project to argue that subsidiary socioeconomic units in associations of families cohabited fertile plots and lived within proximity of one another.

The Socioeconomic Functions of the Collection of Households

The present project argues that the socioeconomic potential of the association of households was superior to that of the household/nuclear family, and that the collection of households performed a variety of services that nuclear families/households could not perform. It is probable that a quantitative difference was present between the labor, land, and political influence of the association of households and these same assets among nuclear families in ancient Israelite society. It becomes probable that the association of households controlled more commodities and could alter critical situations that affected the welfare of individuals in the biblical communities.

The socioeconomic and political potential of the collection of families positioned this social subgrouping to provide assistance to its marginal constituents and to respond to circumstances with which they struggled. The Ruth story, for instance, is a window on the socioeconomic functions of the association of households. This saga suggests that the collection of nuclear families served as a social welfare institution, by showing that vulnerable individuals in this social subgrouping appealed to the collection of households for help in crises. The Ruth story implies that the association of nuclear families regularly ameliorated the predicaments of its constituents. This narrative implies that the collection of households: (a) rescued its vulnerable constituents from slavery or servitude; (b) provided males for the carrying out of the levirate institution; and (c) provided food,

42. For discussion on the geography of the central hill country of Syria-Palestine, see Aharoni, *Land of the Bible*, pp. 21-42; and Israel Finkelstein, *The Archaeology of the Israelite Settlement*, trans. D. Saltz (Jerusalem: Israel Exploration Society, 1988), pp. 121-204.

physical protection, and additional socioeconomic services that abetted the humanization of its constituents.

What is more, the Ruth legend refers to Boaz, a kinsperson of Elimelech, Ruth's father-in-law, and indicates that Boaz was wealthy (*'îš gibôr ḥayil*). Ruth 2 identifies the bases of Boaz's affluence, namely, the possession of fields, servants, slave girls, and a personal aide. Ruth 2, then, raises questions about the normativeness of egalitarianism in the association of households. Ruth 2 says clearly that Boaz was a man of considerable means. Working from the assumption that Boaz's nuclear family was a subset of the collection of households of which Elimelech was a member, this could mean that Boaz's nuclear family was one of the more affluent families in the association of households of which Elimelech was a constituent. The socioeconomic status of Boaz suggests that either economic disproportion among individuals or inequality between nuclear families in a collection of households was present in the biblical communities.

Thus the historicalness of the collection of nuclear families provides bases for arguing that it was the most relevant kinship subgrouping among the masses in the biblical communities. Regarding the collection of families, Gottwald writes:

> With all that said, it is clear that the *mišpāḥâ* was nonetheless a social entity of major importance. We have already delineated its salient functions, namely, to protect the socioeconomic integrity of *bēth-'āvôth* threatened with diminution or extinction and to organize troops for the tribal levy. It was organized, not as a cross-cutting sodality, but as an aggregated cluster of *bēth-'āvôth*, all of whose members had mutual obligations to extend the assistance of their own *bēth-'āvôth* to any needy *bêt-'āv* within the *mišpāḥâ*, and to arrange among themselves how they would muster and field a quota of fighting men as required for the tribal and national levy.[43]

It is to an examination of the effect of the Omride regime on the collection of households in Israel that I now turn. At the center of this concern is that treatment on this issue positions me to elucidate the phenomenon that provides a backdrop against which to discuss the drafting of regulations that purport to provide a public relief system for the *'almānâ*, *gēr*, and *yātôm*.

43. Gottwald, pp. 315-16.

The Effects of the Omride Administration on the Collection of Households

The restoration of political stability by the Omrides affected the collection of households in the North in three principal ways.

1. The policies of the Omrides siphoned off manpower in the collection of households/nuclear families. 1 Kgs 16:24 and 22:39 indicate that Omri built Samaria and that Ahab fortified several unnamed cities. As was stated earlier in this chapter, state construction projects were commonplace during the reigns of Omri and Ahab. The building activities of the Omrides raise serious questions regarding the source of labor for these projects. This book suggests that males from the association of households/nuclear families provided this labor. While 1 Kgs 5:13 (= Hebr. 5:27) suggests that the labor gang *(mas)* provided services during the administration of Solomon, DtrH does not use this term in reference to manpower for the state building projects of the Omrides. Yet 1 Sam 8:16 implies that males from the collections of households carried out the policies of the king, for this text states that the monarch would conscript the best young men from the biblical communities into his service. Working from the assumption that this text reflects an attenuated, painful experience with monarchy in the North, this book suggests that the peasantry in the North provided the labor for the building projects of the Omrides. If the association of nuclear families in the North was a major source of this labor, it becomes probable that the supply of manpower in this socioeconomic subgrouping in Israel was depleted.

Reports in DtrH regarding the wars between Ahab and Aram (1 Kgs 20:15-22), the subjugation of Moab by Omri (2 Kgs 3:4), and inscriptions from Shalmaneser III about the contribution of Ahab to the coalition of nations that fought the Assyrians at Qarqar imply that a formidable army was a feature of the Omride administration.[44] DtrH provides insight into the origins of these soldiers, for 1 Kgs 20:15-22 implies that the masses in Israel constituted the Israelite army. Furthermore, 1 Sam 8:10-21 indicates that males from the peasantry served as infantry and cavalry in the military machine of

---

44. 2 Kgs 3:4 indicates that Mesha paid one hundred thousand lambs and a sizable amount of wool to Ahab, and it is probable that a formidable Israelite military machine motivated Mesha to comply with the economic demands of Omri and Ahab. For extrabiblical evidence on the oppression of Moab by Omri, see *ANET,* p. 320.

the monarch. These data warrant claiming that the peasantry was conscripted into the military during the Omride administration. While it is difficult to ascertain the number of men in the North who became a part of the Omride military machine, it is probable that this number was substantial.

While conscription might have been a tactic of the Omrides, it is possible also that men from the association of nuclear families in the North enlisted in the army. The lure of sustenance might have encouraged people to believe that service in the military would improve their material well-being. Enlistment in the Omride military, then, meant that food, land, clothes, and additional commodities were now available to these men. Whether through conscription or enlistment, the staffing of the Omride military machine reduced the supply of men in the association of nuclear families in the North.

2. The funding of state building projects and the remuneration of individuals in the Omride administration placed exorbitant economic burdens on the peasantry. This phenomenon might account for the claim in 1 Sam 8:10-17 that the Israelite monarch would confiscate the choicest vineyards and fertile fields in the North. On the assumption that the origins of this text lie in the North, 1 Sam 8:10-17 supports the claim that the Omrides took a tenth of the crops and viniculture and gave it to their princes or head administrators. While these payments might have been for services rendered, this study opines that they might have been incentives for service and rewards for loyalty to the Omrides. The redistribution of wealth by the Omrides placed fields, vineyards, and orchards in constant danger of confiscation. Viewed from this perspective, 1 Sam 8:10-17 implies that landholdings among the masses in Israel were in decline. The frequent loss of land and crop yields by collections of households weakened the economic power of these kinship subgroupings in Israel.

3. The resurgence in the market economy bolstered an extant system for the acquisition of goods and services in the North. This development effected circumstances which made it unnecessary for persons to align themselves with other individuals in associations of households, for people could bargain with merchants and economic elites for clothes, food, and other commodities. Individuals with technical knowledge could contract their services to the state, merchants, or other skilled workers, and these persons could receive grain, land, and remuneration for their labor. During dearths, skilled laborers could become dependent on their employers. Economic diversification and the burgeoning market economy

under the Omrides opened other avenues for acquiring mutual aid. Thus the market economy encouraged persons in the biblical communities to abandon the tillage of land, and it undermined aligning oneself in kinship systems for mutual aid.

Summary

The ascendancy of the Omrides introduced political stability into a community that was ravaged by civil war. This internal stability effected a governmental organization, military machine, and state building projects. What is more, the Omride administration contributed to a resurgence in commerce and trade. This restoration of a central authority and vibrant mercantile economy might account for the description of Israel as the land of Omri in the Assyrian annals. It becomes probable that the economic recovery and political stability on the local scene had diverse effects on the major kinship subgrouping in the North. I suspect that the economic policies of the Omrides induced a piecemeal disintegration in the collections of households, and that this breakdown in the major kinship subgrouping devastated any extant social welfare systems for the relief of widows, strangers, and orphans. It is interesting to note that H. Schulte draws upon DtrH, and that he proposes that major kinship subgroupings were unable to cope during the Omride administration.

> The story of the woman who was supposed to hand over her two sons to a creditor indicates that old tribal ties offered no more protection (2 Kgs 4:1-7). Otherwise she would have been able to turn to her or her husband's kinship group, rather than to the man of God. Without a doubt clans were being broken up into smaller units at that time, into family units with their own land and homes. Even so, relatives would have helped those in distress, had poverty not assumed the upper hand in the agriculture realm, overtaxing the clan's ability to redeem debts.[45]

This book agrees with Schulte and proposes that the economic policies of the Omride administration depleted the association of nuclear fam-

---

45. Hannelis Schulte, "The End of the Omride Dynasty: Social-Ethical Observations on the Subject of Power and Violence," in *Ethics and Politics in the Hebrew Bible*, trans. Carl Ehrlich, Semeia 66 (Atlanta: Scholars, 1994), p. 140.

ilies in Israel of labor, land, wine, oil, livestock, and leadership. Since social life in the biblical communities was not compartmental, it is probable that these economic policies effected circumstances and affected camps elsewhere in the North. The next section, therefore, examines the interplay between the state cult and religious life in Israel. In short, it offers these claims about the religious dimension of social life in the North: (1) the Yahweh-alone group was a distinct politico-economic subgroup in the North; (2) the Yahweh-alone group opposed aspects of the politico-economic program of the Omride administration; and (3) the Yahweh-alone group drafted Deut 14:22-29; 16:9-12, 13-15; 24:17-18, 19-22; and 26:12-15 in order to establish and legitimize their politico-economic program in Israel during the ninth century B.C.E.

The Religious Milieu

The Yahweh-Alone Cult

The Elijah and Jehu stories (1 Kgs 17–19; 2 Kgs 1–8:15; and 10) suggest that an absolutist religious camp was present in the North during the Omride administration. While these texts divulge no information about either the origins of this camp or its sociopolitical structure, evidence is present about its beliefs and constituency. These data posit that the Yahweh-alone camp was present in the North during the Omride administration.

1 Kgs 18:16-18 says: "Obadiah reported to Ahab, and Ahab went to meet Elijah. When Ahab saw Elijah he said to him: Is it you, the one who is troubling Israel? Elijah said to him: I am not troubling Israel, but you and your household by forsaking the commandments of Yahweh and worshiping the Baalim." 1 Kgs 18:20-21 says: "Ahab summoned the Israelites and gathered the prophets on Mount Carmel. Elijah approached the people and said: How long will you go on undecided about who is God? If Yahweh is God, serve Yahweh. If Baal is God, serve Baal. The people did not answer Elijah."

These texts recount an incident between Ahab, Obadiah, the official cult, and Elijah. They identify the tenet that is at the heart of this intolerant religious consciousness in the North. In 1 Kgs 18:16-18 Elijah inculpates Ahab and his household by accusing them of making a personal commitment to the Baal cult, and of contributing to the paying of homage to the Baalim throughout the North. Josephus thinks Jezebel spawned this situation.

> [Ahab] also took to wife the daughter of Ethbaal, king of the Tyrians and Sidonians, whose name was Jezebel, of whom he learnt to worship her own gods. This woman was active and bold, and fell into so great a degree of impurity and wickedness, that she built a temple to the god of the Tyrians, which she called Belus, and planted a grove of all sorts of trees; she also appointed priests and false prophets to this god. The king also himself had many such about him; and so exceeded in madness and wickedness all [the kings] that went before him.[46]

1 Kgs 18:20-21 implies that separate views on religiousness were present between Elijah and the common people. While this passage implies that Elijah contended for the complete dedication to Yahweh, it suggests that the masses had no urgency about the exclusive worship of this deity. This text, then, proposes that a monotheistic religious element was present in the North, and that this religious subgroup argued for the exclusive worship of Yahweh in Israel during the reign of Ahab.

2 Kgs 1:2-18 recounts an encounter between Elijah and Ahaziah. Ahaziah, the successor of Ahab, falls from his window and injures himself. 2 Kgs 1:2 says Ahaziah sent messengers to inquire of Baal-zebub, the god of Ekron, about his recovery from this accident. 2 Kings 1:3 indicates that Elijah met these messengers while on their way to inquire of Baal-zebub in Ekron. Elijah then contends that the appeal of Ahaziah to Baal-zebub showed disloyalty to Yahweh. The encounter between Elijah and Ahaziah suggests that the Yahweh-alone group was a distinct religious cult in Israel after the death of Ahab. This episode implies also that complete faithfulness to Yahweh was an important aspect of the worldview of this religious subgroup.

2 Kgs 10:18-29 recounts events in Israel during the reign of Jehoram,

---

46. Flavius Josephus, *Antiquities of the Jews,* trans. William Whiston (Grand Rapids: Kregel Publications, 1985), VIII, §13; pp. 189-90. I contend that Ahab was familiar with the Baal cult and that he had henotheistic or polytheistic inclinations anterior to his marriage to Jezebel. Essential to this claim is that religious syncretism was a feature of the biblical communities prior to the ninth century B.C.E. The fact that Ahab bestowed Yahwistic names on his sons, however, is not solid proof that Ahab was a monotheist, namely, a Yahwist. In short, Ahab could have been henotheistic. Thus this section disagrees with Josephus, and contends that Jezebel merely expressed Ahab's own tacit theology.

the successor of Ahaziah. This text indicates that Jehu used deceit to advance his quest for the throne. Jehu insinuates that he is a worshiper of Baal, and that he is hosting a major celebration for this deity. He assembles priests, prophets, and laity of the Baal cult and also clothes them in distinctive attire. These garments distinguish them from the Rechabites and from Jehu's henchmen. The latter then murder the members of the Baal cult and destroy images and places in the North associated with the worship of Baal. It is probable that the presence and growing influence of the Yahweh-alone cult in the North are the backdrop against which to understand this atrocity. The Elijah cycles and the Jehu narrative, therefore, suggest that the Yahweh-alone group was a prominent religious subgroup in the North during the ninth century.[47]

As was said above, DtrH suggests that the Yahweh-alone group was a rising camp in Israel during the ninth century, but this stratum of literature provides sparse evidence on its sociological beginnings. Thus DtrH leaves the question unanswered whether this movement began as a cult headed by a charismatic leader and developed into the established religious movement. DtrH, however, provides insight into its constituents and designates prominent leaders of this movement. 1 Kgs 17:1 introduces Elijah, but it offers meager biographical information about him. It states that he was from a group of sojourners who inhabited Gilead. What is more, DtrH suggests that he was a rainmaker (1 Kgs 17:1 and 18:41-46) and contends that he was a friend of widows and fatherless children (1 Kgs 17:8-24). Most importantly, it indicates that he was a spokesperson for Yahweh (1 Kgs 21:17-28 and 2 Kgs 1:2-18). It is probable that Elijah was a folk hero among subgroups in the North. These data depict Elijah as a prophet and as an advocate for the exclusive worship of Yahweh. These pieces of information bring into play the possibility that cultic functionaries were a conspicuous subgroup in the Yahweh-alone movement in the North during the ninth century.

---

47. For detailed discussion on the Yahweh-alone subgroup, see Morton Smith, *Palestinian Parties and Politics That Shaped the Old Testament* (London: SCM Press, 1987), pp. 21-22; Bernhard Lang, *Monotheism and the Prophetic Minority* (Sheffield: Almond Press, 1983); Mark S. Smith, *The Early History of God: Yahweh and the Other Deities in Ancient Israel* (San Francisco: Harper and Row, 1990); and Rainer Albertz, *A History of Israelite Religion in the Old Testament Period*, trans. John Bowden, 2 vols., OTL (Louisville: Westminster/John Knox, 1994), p. 153. Furthermore, Schulte argues that the appearance of the Yahweh-alone camp in the North was a response to the policies of the Omride dynasty. See Schulte, p. 139.

It is probable that country priests were among those cultic officials who composed the Yahweh-alone cult. The secondary literature on persons responsible for the preservation and codification of the DC informs this claim. G. von Rad, for instance, proposed that the origins of many cultic regulations in the DC lie in the North. What is more, he contends that at the fall of Samaria, country priests fled to the South and brought subgroups of legal sanctions with them. Consequently, rural cultic officials were responsible for the preservation of many regulations in the DC. Von Rad says:

> At any rate, the authors of Deuteronomy are to be sought amongst those Levites. But this means that we have also found a tenable explanation of Deuteronomy's Janus-like character, its combination of what is priestly and cultic with a national and martial spirit. Such tolerably clear indications as we have of the provenance of Deuteronomy narrow the circle of possible "authors" as follows: first, they must have been men invested with full priestly powers who had access to a copious sacral literature, and who also possessed this disparate material in a form in which it was powerfully impregnated with, and integrated by means of, a theology.[48]

Von Rad provides a basis for arguing that Levites in Israel were an element in the Yahweh-alone cult also, for it is probable that this group was familiar with the fund of traditions concerning rituals and ceremonies at cultic sites that venerated Yahweh throughout the North. I therefore argue that priests and prophets were important subgroups in the Yahweh-alone cult, and that a rigid distinction between the duties of these types of persons is unwarranted.[49]

48. Gerhard von Rad, *Studies in Deuteronomy*, trans. D. Stalker (London: SCM Press, 1953), pp. 66-67.

49. The present project uses the term "cultic officials" to denote functionaries in the Yahweh-alone movement. The usage of this term stems from the overlap between the roles of priest and prophet in the cult in ancient Israel. For a discussion on the relationship between these types of persons, see Sigmund Mowinckel, "Cult and Prophecy," in *Prophecy in Israel*, ed. David L. Petersen (Philadelphia: Fortress, 1987), pp. 74-98.

The Yahweh-Alone Cult and the State Cult

The Yahweh-alone sect in the North advocated strict dedication to Yahweh. Without doubt, religious beliefs often inform moral agents about what actions are desirable and what actions are abhorrent. When intolerance is a major religious tenet, it is possible that an entire range of norms that justify this belief appears in human beings. It therefore is no surprise that the Yahweh-alone subgroup existed at various levels of friction with the religious subgroups that promoted henotheistic Yahwism and the worship of the Baalim in the North during the ninth century.

The Yahweh-alone cult, consequently, opposed the state cult, for the Omrides advocated the position that religious syncretism was acceptable in the North. As this section said above, the formation of political and economic alliances with nations elsewhere in Syria-Palestine was a policy of the Omrides. These coalitions found expression in political marriages and in the religious policy of the Omrides. Ahab, the son of Omri, married Jezebel. Athaliah, the granddaughter of Omri, married Jehoram the king of Judah.[50] What is of interest to this section is that Jezebel was the daughter of an Astarte priest.[51] It then is conceivable that she was a patron of Astarte, the consort of Baal, and that she was familiar with rituals in the Baal cult. I suspect that Jezebel practiced the worship of Baal in Israel, for 1 Kgs 16:31b-32 states that Ahab built a temple to Baal in Samaria. Furthermore, 1 Kgs 18:19 alleges that Jezebel supported 850 cultic officials: 450 prophets of Baal and 400 prophets of Asherah. The temple Ahab built in Samaria for Baal provided sacred space for his wife and these prophets to worship Asherah and the Baalim.[52] Put another way, diplomatic syncretism and practical wisdom informed the state cult in Israel during the reign of Ahab. Regarding the diplomatic syncretism of the Omrides,

---

50. 2 Kgs 8:25-26.

51. Flavius Josephus, *Against Apion*, trans. William Whiston (Grand Rapids: Kregel Publications, 1985), I, §18; pp. 612-13.

52. The Omrides formed political and economic alliances with Phoenicia. For discussion on the deity in the Phoenician Baal cult and on the worship of Baal in the North during the ninth century, see F. C. Fensham, "A Few Observations on the Polarisation between Yahweh and Baal in I Kings 17–19," *ZAW* 92 (1980): 227-36; Yehezkel Kaufmann, *The Religion of Israel from Its Beginnings to the Babylonian Exile*, trans. Moshe Greenberg (New York: Schocken Books, 1972), pp. 273-75; and J. Maxwell Miller and John H. Hayes, *A History of Ancient Israel and Judah* (Philadelphia: Westminster, 1986), pp. 250-302.

Albertz writes: "The religious policy of the Omrides also belonged within the framework of their new foreign policy; it, too, was meant to lead to an agreement with Israel's northern neighbours and to consolidate political relationships. Ahab had a temple to Baal built in his capital Samaria (I Kings 16.32; cf. II Kings 10.8ff.), which was probably dedicated to the Baal of Sidon, and it was intended to make it possible above all for his wife Jezebel and her Phoenician entourage to practise their home cult."[53]

Thus the politico-economic alliances of the Omrides paved the way for a state cult that recognized a plethora of deities. During the reign of Ahab, the state cult supported the Baal cult. It legitimized the worship of Asherah, the consort of Baal. It, however, is important to mention that diplomatic syncretism in biblical Israel did not appear first with the Omrides. It was a policy also of David and Solomon. 2 Sam 3:3 implies that David married Maacah, the daughter of the king of Geshur. 1 Kgs 3:1 states that Solomon married a daughter of the pharaohs. The LXX preserves a tradition that suggests that Solomon married Naanan, the granddaughter of the king of Ammon.[54] What is more, 1 Kgs 11:1-10 leaves open the possibility that Solomon entered many diplomatic marriages, and that he demarcated sacred space in Jerusalem for his foreign wives to practice their native religions. At the center of this claim is that 1 Kgs 11:1-10 declares that Solomon built sites for the cult of Chemosh and Molech. Thus the marriages of David and Solomon to princesses from kingdoms elsewhere in Syria-Palestine linked them to royal families elsewhere in the ancient Near East and set a precedent for the diplomatic marriages and syncretism of the Omrides.

The Elisha stories are windows on the religious milieu in the North during the Omride administration also. While the Elijah and Jehu stories suggest that the Yahweh-alone cult was in conflict with competing cults in the biblical communities,[55] the Elisha stories reflect a different religious milieu. The Elisha traditions neither mention the religious policy of the

---

53. Albertz, p. 143.

54. 1 Kgs 12:24a (= Hebr. 14:21). While the LXX indicates that Solomon married the granddaughter of the king of Ammon, it also introduces competing biographical information on Rehoboam. The LXX reports that Rehoboam was sixteen years old when he became the king in Jerusalem and reigned twelve years in Jerusalem. This is in contrast to the biographical data concerning Rehoboam in the MT, for the MT says Rehoboam was forty-one years old when he became the king and reigned seventeen years in Jerusalem.

55. I will say more about Jehu shortly.

Omrides nor contend that people in the North should worship Yahweh exclusively. Moreover, a collection of miracle stories is a feature of the Elisha narrative. This literary stratum includes reports about the purification of poisoned water and food (2 Kgs 2:19-22 and 4:38-41), the feeding of a group of prophets with twenty loaves of bread (4:42-44), the provision of the source of income for an indigent widow (4:1-7), the resuscitation of a widow's son (4:8-37), the healing of Naaman (5:1-19), and the recovery of a lost ax head (6:1-6). As this section showed above, concern for the exclusive worship of Yahweh shaped the religious milieu that provoked the codification of the Elijah and Jehu traditions. This discrepancy between the Elijah and Jehu stories and the Elisha traditions implies that cycles were present in the clash between the henotheistic state cult and the monotheistic Yahweh-alone group in the North during the Omride regime. A mountain of evidence is present in DtrH which bolsters the present claim that the Yahweh-alone cult existed at various levels of tension with religious subgroups in its surroundings, i.e., the state cult and henotheistic or family cults that did not worship Yahweh.[56]

1 Kgs 18:4 therefore states that war was present between the Yahweh-alone movement and the state, for this passage mentions that Jezebel massacred members of the Yahweh cult. It says: when Jezebel was killing the prophets of Yahweh, Obadiah hid one hundred prophets, fifty to a cave, and provided them with bread and water. The Elijah cycle does not point out the date, site, or motivation for this massacre. The narrative presupposes that the reader is familiar with this conflict. Furthermore, 1 Kgs 18:4 does not state if those prophets of Yahweh that Jezebel murdered were religious zealots and advocated the exclusive worship of Yahweh. This, however, appears to be the case, for the notion that Jezebel would murder individuals in the Yahweh cult who were either polytheistic or henotheistic and encouraged both the worship of Baal and Yahweh is suspect. 1 Kgs 18:4 implies that a conflict between the worship of Baal and Asherah and the Yahweh cult lies behind the episode between Jezebel and the Yahweh-alone cult, and that Jezebel used the power of the state to neutralize or annihilate this religious subgroup.

---

56. For more information about the backdrop against which to interpret the Elisha-Elijah stories, see Miller and Hayes, pp. 250-302; Kaufmann, pp. 273-75; and J. Alberto Soggin, *An Introduction to the History of Israel and Judah*, trans. John Bowden (Valley Forge, Pa.: Trinity Press International, 1993), pp. 212-24.

While 1 Kgs 18:4 points out that the Omrides attacked the Yahweh-alone subgroup, 1 Kgs 18:40 records that members of this cult launched offensives against the state during the reign of Ahab. 1 Kgs 18:40 reports the massacre of the prophets of Baal by Elijah: "Elijah said to them, seize the prophets of Baal and let none of them escape; they seized them and Elijah took them down to the wadi Kishon and slaughtered them there." This text is a window on the morality of Elijah and the Yahweh-alone group, for it elucidates their behavior toward members in the Baal cult. It shows that Elijah and a group of his supporters murdered members of the Baal cult, and implies that their motivation was to extirpate that cult. While this might have been their motivation, it is possible that this bloodshed was in retaliation for the murder of prophets in the Yahweh-alone movement by Jezebel.

In addition, 1 Kgs 18:21 (= Hebr. 18:20) suggests that the Yahweh-alone camp was in combat with family cults over the exclusive worship of Yahweh in Israel during the Omride administration. It says: "Elijah approached the people and said: How long will you go on undecided about who is God? If Yahweh is God, serve Yahweh. If Baal is God, serve Baal. The people did not answer Elijah." The claim that the ardent supporters of Yahwism clashed with family cults among the masses in the North proceeds from the probability that competing religious communities were widespread among kinship subgroupings in Israel. Gen 31:22-35, an E passage, shows that Laban accused Jacob of stealing his household idols (těrāpîm). While this text delineates an episode in the Jacob story, it also probably reflects the religious milieu of the North during the eighth century B.C.E. Thus it is possible that local family cults were present in the North before the eighth century. Judg 17:5 reports that Micah, an Ephraimite, had a private shrine, for the text indicates that he forged těrāpîm, made an ephod, and hired a personal cultic functionary. 1 Sam 19:11-14 reports David's escape from Saul. The text shows that Michal used the household idol to deceive the messengers of Saul. She placed hair on the idol, laid it in the bed, and placed a cover over it, then told Saul's messengers that David was sick and in bed. Saul's lieutenants discovered that the household idol, not David, was in bed.[57] These texts provide a basis for arguing that family cults were common in the North, and that representations of deities were present among these religious communities. What is more, necromancy, divination, soothsaying, and child sacrifice might have been common phe-

---

57. Maybe David was small in stature or Michal's household idol was rather large.

nomena in family cults in the North.[58] If these cults worshiped deities other than Yahweh, it is plausible that they became targets of the Yahweh-alone subgroup.

While 1 Kgs 18:4, 21, and 40 imply that clashes between the Yahweh-alone cult, the state cult, and popular religion were aspects of the religious milieu during the reign of Ahab, evidence elsewhere in DtrH suggests that combat between the Yahweh-alone group and the state cult was present during the reign of Jehoram.

For example, 2 Kgs 10:25-28 says: "When Jehu finished presenting the burnt offering, he said to the guards and officers, 'Go in and strike them down; let no man get away!' The guards and the officers struck them down with the sword and threw out the dead bodies; they proceeded to the interior of the temple of Baal. They brought out the pillars of the temple of Baal and burned them. They destroyed the pillars and the temple of Baal and turned the temple of Baal into a latrine. Thus, Jehu eradicated Baal from Israel."

2 Kgs 10:25-28 reports that Jehu and his supporters butchered members of the Baal cult. What is more, 2 Kgs 10:25b implies that the supporters of Jehu were unconcerned about disposing the corpses, for it says they simply threw the dead bodies out of the temple. No condemnation of this atrocity is present in DtrH, and the absence of censure of Jehu and his lieutenants for this horrifying act implies that an element in the biblical community approved of these murders. DtrH is silent on the identity of the individuals or camps that backed Jehu. It, however, is probable that members in the Yahweh-alone subgroup supported Jehu, for this faction hated persons who worshiped the Baalim and Asherah. Thus this faction might have backed Jehu because of their politico-economic interests. Regarding the role that Elijah, Elisha, and the Yahweh-alone group played in the violent overthrow of the Omrides, J. A. Soggin states: "The dynasty of Omri was overthrown by a coup d'état arranged by a certain Jehu, commander of the northern army, who then ascended the throne. There is an interesting note that the disorders arose out of the prophetic groups with Elijah and Elisha at their head (I Kings 19.15-18; II Kings 9.1-10), and were connected with similar movements in Damascus, where a certain Hazael ascended the throne in place of king Ben/Bar Hadad (III?, c. 845?-843?)."[59]

---

58. Practices among family cults in the biblical communities might have provoked the formulation of Deut 18:10-11.

59. Soggin, p. 222.

The larger narrative that contains the Jehu story denounces the Omrides. It also attacks the official cult and defends the exclusive worship of Yahweh. It is probable that the Jehu traditions preserve only the information that the religious absolutists wanted to hand down. Although the bias in these texts for the worship of Yahweh and against the worship of Baal is an obstacle to delineating the interaction between the loyal Yahwists and the ardent supporters of Baal, it is probable that the conflict between these two groups during the ninth century is the backdrop against which to interpret the slaughter of members of the Baal cult by Jehu and his lieutenants.

DtrH implies that ardent supporters of Yahweh and Baal were present in Israel during the Omride administration. Moreover, the Elijah cycle and the Jehu story imply that the Yahweh-alone group and worshipers of the Baalim fought each other. The hostilities between these camps illustrate the belief that the quest to advance one's religious program invites brutality, bigotry, and the systematic destruction of human beings: all in the name of piety. Regarding the relationship of religiousness to dehumanization, Allport writes: "The role of religion is paradoxical. It makes prejudice, and it unmakes prejudice. While the creeds of the great religions are universalistic, all stressing brotherhood, the practice of these creeds is frequently divisive and brutal. The sublimity of religious ideals is offset by the horrors of persecution in the name of these same ideals."[60]

The Yahweh-Alone Cult and the Drafting of the Widow, Stranger, and Orphan Laws

The governmental policies of the Omrides endangered the material endowment of officials in the Yahweh-alone subgroup. The diplomatic syncretism of the Omrides, on the one hand, undermined the exclusive worship of Yahweh in the North. It is probable that the support of polytheism, Baalism, or henotheistic Yahwism by the Omrides cleared space for local peasant farmers to present and consume their offerings, and to celebrate the fecundity of the land, at sites in the biblical communities where the worship of deities other than Yahweh was common. The material en-

60. Gordon W. Allport, *The Nature of Prejudice* (Reading, Mass.: Addison-Wesley, 1990), p. 444.

dowment of the Omrides, on the other hand, reintroduced the struggle for control of the exchangeable goods in the biblical communities, for the payment of bureaucrats and the funding of state building projects dictated that the Omrides control sources from which they could extract the necessities of life. What is more, the Omrides had to extract goods from the masses in order to support functionaries in the state cult. The politico-economic policies of the Omrides, then, overburdened the local peasantry, and this phenomenon jeopardized the sustenance of cultic functionaries in the Yahweh-alone movement.

These cultic functionaries responded to the politico-economic crisis in the North by creating a program that protected their material interests. And the reworking of extant laws on the presentation and consumption of tithes of crops and produce and on the celebration of major pilgrimages in the biblical communities was at the center of this program. As stated at the beginning of this chapter, critical theorizing about law advocates the position that elitist social subgroups can draft legal sanctions that will serve their interests. Lenski also advocates that subgroups in agrarian societies can draft legal injunctions that will advance their programs. "To begin with, by virtue of its coercive power, a new elite is in a good position to rewrite the law of the land as it sees fit. This affords them a unique opportunity, since by its very nature law is identified with justice and the rule of right. Since legal statutes are stated in general and impersonal terms, they appear to support abstract principles of justice rather than the special interests of particular men or classes of men."[61]

Moreover, Lenski and Mann declare that law can bolster an ideology, and that this phenomenon is an important instrument for maintaining social control and for influencing the distribution of commodities in human societies.[62] Lenski submits that ideology is a system of ideas that underpins action, and that it legitimizes the superiority of one group and the subordination of another group.[63] He argues that sustained domination requires ideological justification, for the acquisition of goods through coercion is costly, and it undermines the bestowal of honor upon those who rule by intimidation and physical violence. Consequently, Lenski indicates

61. Lenski, *Power and Privilege*, p. 54.

62. Lenski; and Michael Mann, *The Sources of Social Power* (Cambridge: Cambridge University Press, 1986). For additional discussion on ideology, see Raymond Geuss, *The Idea of a Critical Theory* (Cambridge: Cambridge University Press, 1981).

63. Lenski, p. 54.

that the governing class or those seeking to remain in power and control the distribution of goods in a community must gain the loyalty of the masses, and that these subgroups must adopt refined and complex means for justifying and protecting their interests. This is the nature and function of ideology, for ideology can institutionalize the futility of political uprisings and other forms of social protest. Thus Lenski suggests that ideology is extremely destructive, and that it greatly affects social history in agrarian societies.[64]

Mann argues that ideology elucidates reality and introduces guidelines for social interaction. This rationale identifies an ultimate, final, ahistorical basis of authority, and it creates a sense of common purpose regarding a subgrouping in an agrarian society. What is more, Mann states that ideology is plausible, and that it advances the interests of a group. Mann therefore argues that neither the misrepresentation of reality nor the concern with socioeconomic advantage is the main characteristic of an ideology, although an ideology may serve the interests of individuals in human societies.[65] "Knowledge purveyed by an ideological power movement necessarily 'surpasses experience' (as Parsons put it). It cannot be totally tested by experience, and therein lies its distinctive power to persuade and dominate. But it need not be false; if it is, it is less likely to spread."[66]

Mann implies that characteristics of human beings position them to accept ideology. He suggests that human beings are social creatures and enter relationships with other individuals to accomplish personal goals and fulfill private desires.

> Let us consider some of their needs again. As they desire sexual fulfillment, they seek sexual relations, usually with only a few members of the opposite sex; as they desire to reproduce themselves, these sexual relations usually combine with relations between adults and children. For these (and other purposes) a family emerges, enjoying patterned interaction with other family units from which sexual partners might be found. As humans need material subsistence they develop economic relationships, cooperating in production and exchange with others.[67]

64. Lenski, pp. 50-56.
65. Mann, pp. 22-24 and 519-20.
66. Mann, p. 23.
67. Mann, p. 14.

Mann's theory about human beings, then, leads him to argue that people require bases for moral decision making; consequently, he implies that the human psyche is fertile ground for the implantation of ideology, for ideology can inform value formation and offer guidance on common, everyday moral issues and on those moral situations that occur infrequently. An ideology, therefore, can provide reasons for moral judgment and directives for moral action.[68]

Second, Mann asserts that ideology offers possibilities on meaning in life. At the center of this feature of ideology are answers to questions about the human dilemma, i.e., distress, strife, suffering, alienation, and other issues that are characteristic of the human condition. Because moral agents inquire into issues in life for which there are no easy solutions, the human psyche again becomes fertile ground for the implantation of ideology. According to Mann, theological belief systems, then, are major purveyors of ideology, for religion contains a transcendental element, that is, a link between a "sacred" phenomenon and "ideas about reality."

Cultic functionaries in the Yahweh-alone group drafted Deut 14:22-29; 16:9-12, 13-15; 24:17-18, 19-22; and 26:12-15, positioning themselves to protect their interests; consequently, these laws propagated a network of ideas that could work to the advantage of this subgroup in the North. Since the distinct literary features of these codes are windows on the program of functionaries in the Yahweh-alone cult, the next section shows how these innovations could serve the interests of this subgroup in the biblical communities.

The Widow, Stranger, and Orphans Laws and Their Role in the Program of the Yahweh-Alone Cult

Innovations in Deut 14:22-29; 16:9-12, 13-15; 24:17-18, 19-22; and 26:12-15 suggest that these codes served the interests of cultic functionaries in ancient Israelite society. First, these codes established an annual system that added to the material endowment of the officials in the Yahweh-alone cult. Deut 14:22-29; 16:9-12, and 13-15 treat the yearly presentation and consumption of oil, wine, livestock, and the celebration of cultic pilgrimages, and, as Chapter 3 showed, these legal sanctions contain a centralization

---

68. Mann, pp. 22-23.

formula (Deut 14:23a, 24a; 16:11b, and 15a).[69] This innovation suggests that the annual presentation and consumption of tithes and the yearly celebration of major cultic festivals, which included the exchange of goods, should occur at a site where the name of Yahweh was present. It is improbable that the offerers and their households consumed all the produce and livestock brought to these sites during these cultic celebrations. This claim grounds itself in Mayes's theory about the annual tithe in the DC, for he suggests that if "tithe" in Deut 14:22-29 means "tenth," it is unlikely that the local peasant farmer and his household consumed the entire tithe of grain, oil, wine, and meat at the cultic site.[70] By centralizing the consumption of the annual tithes and the celebration of cultic pilgrimages to a Yahwist sanctuary, officials in the Yahweh-alone movement established a system that could create an influx of grain, oil, wine, meat, and other commodities. The drafters of Deut 14:22-29, therefore, included annual tithes of produce and meat and goods from cultic festivals in an extant system for the material endowment of officials in the Yahweh-alone movement.

Second, the centralization formula in Deut 14:23a and 24a transformed the site for the presentation and consumption of annual tithes into a marketplace; it therefore becomes plausible that this phenomenon contributed to the material endowment of functionaries in the Yahweh-alone movement also. Deut 14:24-26 is at the center of this claim, for these verses indicate that refusing to present tithes of grain, wine, oil, and livestock at the central Yahweh sanctuary yearly is inexcusable. It is noteworthy that Deut 14:24-26 presupposes that people lived in different places throughout the biblical communities, and that many of them lived great distances from the official shrine. It is plausible that there would be many for whom obedience to the command to present annual tithes at the Yahwist sanctuary would be very difficult, for obedience would mean driving cattle and small animals, and transporting grain, oil, wine, and other goods, great distances. Thus Deut 14:24-26 commands these people to sell their tithes at home, proceed to the central cultic site, and purchase items for the sacred meal at the designated cultic location. This innovation, i.e., the command

69. Deut 12 contains two regulations about the presentation and consumption of tithes that antedate Deut 14:22-29 and 26:12-15. These texts are Deut 12:5-7 and 17-19. These legal sanctions, however, contain the centralization ideology. Thus the centralization formula is an innovation in all Deuteronomic regulations that govern tithing in the biblical communities.

70. Mayes, p. 245.

to buy goods for the cultic meal at the Yahweh shrine, implies that a thriving economy might have been present at this site. Centralizing the presentation and consumption of tithes of produce and livestock and the celebration of major pilgrimages to the central Yahwist shrine served the interests of officials in the Yahweh-alone cult, for it positioned them to determine the exchange value of goods and to pursue personal profit.

Third, Deut 14:23b connects acquiring the fear of the deity with the presentation of tithes at the central sanctuary. According to Mayes, this phrase suggests that a reading of the law took place during the presentation of tithes in the biblical communities.[71] Although Mayes never explains what he means by "law," he argues that a link was present between instruction in Yahwism and acquiring the fear of Yahweh, and that schooling in Yahwism was a concomitant of presenting tithes at the central shrine. This book agrees with Mayes on this issue, for Deuteronomy suggests that teaching was the prerogative of cultic officials in the Yahweh-alone movement. For example, Deut 33:8-11 states:

> And of Levi he said,
> "Give to Levi the Thummim,
> and thy Urim to thy godly one,
> whom thou didst test at Massah,
> with whom thou didst strive at the waters of Meribah;
> who said of his father and mother,
> 'I regard them not';
> he disowned his brothers,
> and ignored his children.
> For they observed thy word,
> and kept thy covenant.
> They shall teach Jacob thy ordinances,
> and Israel thy law;
> they shall put incense before thee,
> and whole burnt offerings upon thy altar.
> Bless, O Lord, his substance,
> and accept the work of his hands;
> crush the loins of his adversaries,
> of those that hate him, that they rise not again."

71. Mayes, p. 245.

It therefore becomes plausible that officials in the Yahweh-alone move-ment proclaimed Yahwist propaganda throughout the biblical communi-ties. Also, I suspect that they promulgated this ideology at major festivals and other cultic celebrations when large groups of people were present. Communicating catechisms concerning a brand of religiousness, then, gave officials in the Yahweh-alone cult a mechanism to prohibit religious practices that were inconsistent with the prominent tenets of absolute Yah-wism. What is more, teaching the masses about true piety could serve the interests of officials in the Yahweh-alone cult, for it positioned them to change the consciences of local peasant farmers and herders. Through pedagogy they could convince local farmers to adapt to exploitation and to disregard phenomena that were separating their grain, wine, oil, and live-stock from them. Teaching local peasant farmers to fear Yahweh, then, po-sitioned the Yahweh-alone cult to spread ideas that protected their polit-ico-economic program regarding the distribution of goods in the biblical communities.

Fourth, Deut 24:19-22 commands that local peasant farmers, not offi-cials in the Yahweh-alone cult, care for the 'almānâ, gēr, and yātôm. This attracts attention. Deuteronomy implies that cultic functionaries in the Yahweh-alone movement had a plethora of sources from which to procure items for the support of these vulnerable, socially weak individuals. Deut 18:3-5 says: "And this shall be the priests' due from the people, from those offering a sacrifice, whether it be ox or sheep: they shall give to the priest the shoulder and the two cheeks and the stomach. The firstfruits of your grain, of your wine and of your oil, and the first of the fleece of your sheep, you shall give him. For Yahweh your God has chosen him out of all your tribes, to stand and minister in the name of Yahweh, him and his sons for-ever." This legal injunction implies that the choice parts of animals sacri-ficed to Yahweh belonged to functionaries in the Yahweh-alone movement. Besides which, these officials had a claim to the produce in the biblical communities. Deut 14:24-26 implies that animals, grain, wine, oil, and other commodities were present at cultic sites in the biblical communities, for the DC commands people to buy items for sacred meals at these loca-tions. It is noteworthy that neither Deut 18:3-5 nor Deut 14:24-26 com-mands cultic functionaries to share their grain, wine, oil, and livestock with widows, strangers, and orphans. In fact, Deut 14:24-26 implies that cultic officials should sell these items to local peasant farmers and herders. Deut 24:19-22, however, demands that local peasant farmers share their crops and fruits with widows, strangers, and orphans. This innovation in the DC, therefore, serves the interests of cultic officials in the Yahweh-alone movement by placing the onus for caring for widows, strangers, and orphans on local peasant farmers in ancient Israelite society.

Without doubt the peasantry carried the onus for supporting the Omride administration. What is more, Deut 14:22-29; 16:9-12, 13-15; and 26:12-15 indicate that this social subgroup supported the officials in the Yahweh-alone cult. Furthermore, Deut 24:19-22 implies that peasant farmers carried the onus for providing public relief for widows, strangers, and orphans. It therefore is likely that local farmers and herders suffered considerable deprivation, and that they became outraged about the siphoning off of their grain, oil, wine, and livestock by the Yahweh-alone cult and the monarchy. It therefore becomes plausible that it did not take much to incite an uprising among the masses in ancient Israel. While narratives that recount uprisings by local peasant farmers and herders in ancient Israelite society are absent in DtrH, it is unsafe to assume that revolts did not occur. Knight warns:

> We can hardly speak of a political right of dissent or of civil disobedience under the monarchy. The better question is whether or not the people ever engaged in such protest and, if so, on what grounds and with what effect? Unfortunately our literary sources pose special limitations on our ability to answer this question, for the Hebrew Bible records essentially the viewpoints that were in some way favorable, or at least tolerable, to the power groups who preserved and canonized the literary heritage. There were plausibly any number of individual or group acts of dissent that are lost to history.[72]

It therefore is not beyond reason to assume that the masses became subversive and expressed discontent about carrying the onus for the support of other social subgroups in the biblical communities.

Officials in the Yahweh-alone cult, accordingly, placed ideas in the widow, stranger, and orphan regulations in the Deuteronomic Code. It is likely that these innovations molded the conscience about the presentation of the annual tithes of produce and livestock and about the celebration of cultic festivals at a central Yahweh sanctuary in the biblical communities,

---

72. Douglas A. Knight, "Political Rights and Powers in Monarchic Israel," in *Ethics and Politics in the Hebrew Bible*, p. 104.

positioning these officials to stave off a potential revolt by the peasantry in ancient Israelite society. The next section shows how these codes could influence local peasant farmers and herders to acquiesce to the program of the Yahweh-alone cult in the North during the ninth century B.C.E.

The Widow, Stranger, and Orphan Laws and the Co-opting of Peasant Farmers

Three features of these laws could influence the masses to accept the program of the Yahweh-alone cult uncritically. First, the language of divine obligation is widespread in these legal injunctions. Deut 14:22-29 and 26:12-15 propagate the idea that the annual presentation and consumption of tithes of grain, oil, wine, and livestock at the official site are moral requirements that originated with the deity. Deut 16:9-12, 13-15 suggest that the decree to celebrate major cultic pilgrimages annually at the central site derives from the will of Yahweh. Deut 24:19-22 posits that local peasant farmers should share gleanings with widows, strangers, and orphans because of the action of the deity in their history. Thus these laws imply that local peasant farmers, i.e., individuals in the biblical communities who eked out their existence, should ignore destitution and other features of their circumstances and comply with a set of legal prescriptions that separated grain, wine, oil, livestock, and other goods from them. Grounding these laws in the will of Yahweh, however, suggests that these regulations derived from the deity. This strategy positioned cultic officials to parade their ideas as the will of Yahweh, and using theological language to cloak a private agenda could contribute to the undiscriminating acceptance of a collection of a group of otherwise biased regulations.

Second, Deut 14:24b, 29b; 16:15b; 24:19b; and 26:15 promote the idea that a direct relationship is present between obedience to these legal injunctions and receiving the blessing of Yahweh. These innovations promulgate the belief that if the local peasantry presented and consumed tithes of produce and livestock and celebrated cultic festivals at a central Yahwist cultic site, they could procure the favor of the deity. They also suggest that if the local peasantry shared gleanings with widows, strangers, and orphans, they would be blessed by Yahweh. A cause-effect relationship is implicit in this form of consciousness. Conversely, privation, barrenness, death, and destruction are the results of disobedience to the legislation of the Yahweh-alone cult, for insubordination to these codes implies that local peasant farmers and herders were in defiance of the commandments of Yahweh.

Finally, Deut 14:22-29; 16:9-15; 24:19-22; and 26:12-15 list the *'almānâ*, *gēr*, and *yātôm* as a group. What is more, these laws purport to provide public assistance to these types of persons. This innovation suggests that ameliorating the plight of widows, strangers, and orphans was a significant concern of these laws. These laws could influence local peasant farmers to bring exchangeable goods to a central distribution site. I, however, suspect that ministrants in the Yahweh-alone subgroup wanted to establish and legitimize a set of conventions that bolstered their own material endowment. By centralizing the appropriation of these items, they positioned themselves to oversee the allocation of commodities and to guarantee an influx of grain, wine, and meat into their personal coffers, while using charity toward a category of socially weak, vulnerable persons as a pretext.

The innovations in the widow, stranger, and orphan regulations in Deut 12–26 imply that the self-interest of priests and prophets shaped these laws. Without doubt the command to bring exchangeable goods to a central cultic site and consume them there gave cultic functionaries access to the money, crops, flocks, and herds in the biblical communities. In a word, the mandates to bring wheat, barley, sheep, cows, and wine to, and celebrate the fecundity of the land at, an officially sanctioned cultic site provided a continual supply from which officials in the Yahweh-alone subgroup could draw sustenance.

Summary

The Omrides and the Yahweh-alone cult placed economic burdens on the peasantry, and it is probable that this circumstance exacerbated the situation of local farmers and herders in the North. The monarchy, on the one hand, employed soldiers and owned chariots, and it could use physical coercion to extract goods from the peasantry. Cultic ministrants, on the other hand, could shape the consciences of local peasant farmers and herders, and this advantage positioned them to develop ideologies that could serve their interests.

I have argued that cultic officials in the Yahweh-alone movement drafted a set of legal injunctions that aided them in the establishment and legitimization of a public relief program that guaranteed their material endowment and positioned them to undermine notions about rebellion among local peasant farmers and herders in the North during the ninth century B.C.E. To support my position I brought into play the innovations in the widow, stranger, and orphan regulations in Deut 12–26 — these data lend support to the claims that programs to institutionalize the frequent presentation and consumption of tithes at an official shrine, to indoctrinate individuals with the views of the Yahweh cult, and to provide for the material endowment of the cult were aims of these legal injunctions. These attributes of these laws are compelling evidence against Weinfeld, who claims: "Indeed the very purpose of the book of Deuteronomy, as has been correctly observed, was to curtail and circumscribe the cultus and not to extend or enhance it."[73]

Chapter 6 summarizes my argument. It enunciates the significance of allowing critical theory about law to shape a paradigm for discussing the sociohistoric origins of legal injunctions in the HB and their effects in the biblical communities.

---

73. Weinfeld, *Deuteronomy and the Deuteronomic School,* p. 190.

Chapter 6

CONCLUSION

The present book derived from a concern with the social-scientific study of law in the DC. It explored the relationship of Deut 14:22-29; 16:9-12, 13-15; 24:17-18, 19-22; and 26:12-15 to the conditions of the *'almānâ, gēr,* and *yātôm* during an epoch in ancient Israelite history. I argued that these laws were part of a larger politico-economic program that established and legitimized sources for the material endowment and sustenance of cultic functionaries in the Yahweh-alone sect, a major camp in Israel during the ninth century B.C.E. Consequently, the present analysis arrived at this conclusion: the laws represented in the text used a category of socially weak but politically useful persons as pawns in a scheme to siphon off percentages of produce and livestock from overburdened peasant farmers and herders in the biblical communities during the Omride administration.

Contending that the aforementioned Deuteronomic texts were part of a program of cultic officials in the North during the Omride era proceeded from looking differently at the innovations in these texts and the secondary literature about them. Several important insights, therefore, emerged from this study: (1) since the DC reworks many regulations in the BC and is a replacement for the BC, it is plausible that the tenth century B.C.E. is the *terminus a quo* for these legal injunctions; (2) the widespread acceptance of a seventh century B.C.E. dating for the DC provides a seventh-century *terminus ad quem* for these laws; (3) the literary and theological points of contact among these regulations, E, and Hosea link these regulations to the North; (4) the sociohistorical presuppositions of these codes imply that conflict over the presentation and distribution of goods, proper religiosity, and the plight of widows, strangers, and orphans were features of the milieu from which these laws emerged; and (5) 1 Sam 8:10-21, the Elijah-Elisha narratives, and the Jehu story imply that a burgeoning central administration, breakdown in the socioeconomic support system for widows and orphans, and hostility between the Yahweh-alone subgroup and the Baal cult were important dynamics in the biblical communities during the Omride dynasty.

A legal framework that drew from critical theory gave this project a fresh lens through which to view Deut 14:22-29; 16:9-12, 13-15; 24:17-18, 19-22; and 26:12-15, for questions about the role that law played in creating and maintaining socioeconomic inequality and dehumanization are absent from conventional scholarship but are basic to conceptual frameworks for exploring legal sanctions that stem from critical theory. Critical theorizing about legal injunctions rejects the idea that law and legal sanctions are value-free and above political, economic, and social interests. It therefore declares that they often reflect the politico-economic interests of the persons or subgroups responsible for their formulation. The usage of critical theory about law positioned this research project to view these types of moral injunctions from an angle of vision that is sympathetic and analogous to points of view among needy and vulnerable groups in ancient Israelite society. Moreover, the usage of critical theory for discussing the sociohistoric origins and effects of regulations in Deut 12–26 that prescribe morality toward the 'almānâ, gēr, and yātôm represents a decisive break with conventional scholarship on law and morality in ancient Israel, for to my present knowledge, publications that elucidate these regulations work from a methodological position that does not explore the relationship between politico-economic interests and the formulation of law in ancient Israel. No scholar on law in the HB of whom I am aware has raised questions about these legal injunctions with a special sensitivity to the ways they worked to support and maintain the dehumanization of widows, strangers, and orphans in the biblical communities.

An interpretive framework shaped by critical theory is only one conceptual paradigm available for studying the social origins and effects of these laws in the biblical communities. No single angle of vision on law in human societies can answer every question about the historical origins and interplay between legal sanctions and social subgroups in ancient Israelite society. Scholars, however, can broaden their understandings of legal injunctions in the HB by using critical theory about law to inform conceptual paradigms for discussing legal sanctions in ancient Israelite society, for critical theory about law examines regulations with a concern for the realities of social life in communities that are ethnically heterogeneous and economically and politically asymmetric.

Exploring Deut 14:22-29; 16:9-12, 13-15; 24:17-18, 19-22; and 26:12-15 from a vantage shaped by critical theory about legal injunctions, however, offers insights that can be helpful to individuals with an interest in social history in ancient Israel. This perspective brings questions regarding classism, power, and socioeconomic inequality to the forefront of the debate on the role that law played in human communities where competing socioeconomic interests were present: issues that would not otherwise be at the center of conventional discussions about the social origins and effects of law in the biblical communities.

Ancient Israel was a human community, and the fact that a relationship is often present between law and socioeconomic interests justifies using critical theorizing about legal injunctions to discuss subgroups of law in the HB. Note that the idea that ruling and intellectual elites drafted laws to advantage themselves was present in the biblical communities, for Isaiah of Jerusalem states that certain elite groups created and invoked rules to protect their social and economic agendas. Isa 10:1-4 says:

> Shame on you who make unjust laws,
> and write mischievous decrees,
> to deprive the needy of justice,
> and to rob the oppressed of their rights;
> they turn widows into plunder,
> and they make orphans their prey.
> What will you do in the day of visitation,
> when devastation comes from afar?
> To whom will you run for help,
> and where will you leave your wealth?
> You will crouch among the prisoners,
> and will fall among the slain.
> In all of this his anger will not turn,
> and his hand remains stretched out.

The present writer believes scholars must articulate, and become critical of, their models for studying law in the HB. This approach positions them to pay serious attention to the role law played in producing and sustaining domination, dehumanization, and subordination in ancient Israel, for it is plausible that laws like the ones represented in Deut 14:22-29; 16:9-12, 13-15; 24:17-18, 19-22; and 26:12-15 provoked the aforementioned speech by Isaiah of Jerusalem.

BIBLIOGRAPHY

Abba, Raymond. "Priests and Levites in Deuteronomy." *VT* 27, no. 3 (1977): 257-67.

Ackroyd, Peter R. *Exile and Restoration.* Philadelphia: Westminster, 1968.

Aharoni, Yohanan. *The Archaeology of the Land of Israel.* 2nd ed. Translated by A. F. Rainey. Philadelphia: Westminster, 1979.

————. *The Land of the Bible.* Translated by A. F. Rainey. Philadelphia: Westminster, 1982.

Ahlström, Gösta W. *Royal Administration and National Religion in Ancient Palestine.* Leiden: E. J. Brill, 1982.

————. *Who Were the Israelites?* Winona Lake, Ind.: Eisenbrauns, 1986.

————. *The History of Ancient Palestine.* Minneapolis: Fortress, 1993.

Aichele, George, et al. *The Postmodern Bible.* New Haven: Yale University Press, 1995.

Albertz, Rainer. *A History of Israelite Religion in the Old Testament Period.* Translated by John Bowden. 2 vols. OTL. Louisville: Westminster/John Knox, 1994.

————. "Wer waren die Deuteronomisten? Das historische Rätsel einer literarischen Hypothese." *EvT* 4 (1997): 319-38.

Allport, Gordon W. *The Nature of Prejudice.* Reading, Mass.: Addison-Wesley, 1990.

Alt, Albrecht. *Kleine Schriften zur Geschichte des Volkes Israel.* Vol. 2. Munich: C. H. Beck, 1953.

————. "The Monarchy in the Kingdoms of Israel and Judah." In his *Essays on Old Testament History and Religion,* translated by R. A. Wilson, pp. 311-35. Garden City, N.Y.: Doubleday, 1967.

————. "The Origins of Israelite Law." In his *Essays on Old Testament History and*

Religion, translated by R. A. Wilson, pp. 101-71. Garden City, N.Y.: Doubleday, 1967.

Altman, Andrew. *Critical Legal Studies: A Liberal Critique.* Princeton: Princeton University Press, 1990.

―――. *Arguing about Law: An Introduction to Legal Philosophy.* Belmont, Calif.: International Thomson Publishing Co., 1996.

Andersen, F. I. "The Socio-Juridical Background of the Naboth Incident." *JBL* 85 (1966): 46-57.

Andreasen, N. E. A. "The Role of the Queen Mother in Israelite Society." *CBQ* 45 (1983): 179-94.

Aptheker, Herbert. *American Negro Slave Revolts.* New York: International Publishers, 1987.

Arato, Andrew, and Eike Gebhardt, eds. *The Frankfurt School Reader.* New York: Continuum, 1997.

Aristotle. *Nicomachean Ethics.* Translated by Terence Irwin. Indianapolis: Hackett, 1985.

Arthur, John, and William H. Shaw. *Justice and Economic Distribution.* Englewood Cliffs, N.J.: Prentice-Hall, 1978.

Asante, Molefi K. *The Afrocentric Idea.* Philadelphia: Temple University Press, 1987.

―――. *Afrocentricity.* Trenton, N.J.: Africa World Press, 1996.

Baab, O. J. "Fatherless." In *IDB,* 2:245-46. Nashville: Abingdon, 1962.

Bankowski, Zenon, and Geoff Mungham. *Images of Law.* Boston: Routledge and Kegan Paul, 1976.

Barker, Ernest. *Social Contract.* Oxford: Oxford University Press, 1949.

Barr, James. *The Semantics of Biblical Language.* London: SCM Press, 1983.

Barton, John. "Understanding O.T. Ethics." *JSOT* 9 (1978): 44-64.

―――. "Approaches to Ethics in the Old Testament." In *Beginning Old Testament Study,* edited by J. Rogerson, pp. 113-30. Philadelphia: Westminster, 1982.

―――. *Ethics and the Old Testament.* Harrisburg, Pa.: Trinity Press International, 1998.

Begg, Christopher. "The Significance of the *Numeruswechsel* in Deuteronomy: The Pre-history of the Question." *ETL* 55 (1979): 116-24.

―――. "1994: A Significant Anniversary in the History of Deuteronomy Research." In *Studies in Deuteronomy,* edited by F. García Martínez et al., pp. 1-11. Leiden: E. J. Brill, 1994.

Beirne, Piers. "Marxism and the Sociology of Law: Theory or Praxis?" In *The Sociology of Law: A Conflict Perspective,* edited by Charles Reasons and Robert M. Rich, pp. 471-75. Toronto: Buttersworth and Co., 1978.

Bell, Derrick A. *Race, Racism, and American Law.* New York: Little, Brown, 1980.

―――. *And We Are Not Saved.* New York: Basic Books, 1987.

————. "Racial Realism." In *Critical Race Theory,* edited by Kimberlé Crenshaw et al., pp. 302-12. New York: New Press, 1995.

Belliotti, Raymond. *Justifying Law.* Philadelphia: Temple University Press, 1992.

Ben-Barak, Z. "Status and Right of the *Gĕbîrâ.*" *JBL* 110 (1991): 23-34.

Bender, Leslie, and Daan Braveman, eds. *Power, Privilege, and Law.* Saint Paul: West Publishing Co., 1995.

Bennett, Lerone. *Before the "Mayflower": A History of Black America.* Chicago: Johnson Publishing Co., 1987.

Bennett, Robert A. *God's Work of Liberation.* Wilton, Conn.: Morehouse-Barlow, 1976.

————. "Black Experience and the Bible." In *African American Religious Studies,* edited by Gayraud Wilmore, pp. 129-39. Durham, N.C.: Duke University Press, 1989.

Berger, Peter L., and Thomas Luckmann. *The Social Construction of Reality.* New York: Doubleday, 1966.

Berman, Harold J. *The Interaction of Law and Religion.* Nashville: Abingdon, 1974.

————. "Law and Religion in the Development of a World Order." *Sociological Analysis: A Journal in the Sociology of Religion* 52 (spring 1991): 27-36.

Berry, Mary Frances. *Black Resistance–White Law: A History of Constitutional Racism in America.* New York: Viking Penguin Press, 1995.

Berryman, Philip. *Liberation Theology.* New York: Pantheon Books, 1987.

Birch, Bruce C. *Let Justice Roll Down: The Old Testament, Ethics, and Christian Life.* Louisville: Westminster/John Knox, 1991.

Black, Donald. *The Behavior of Law.* New York: Academic Press, 1976.

Bleiberg, E. "Historical Texts as Political Propaganda during the New Kingdom." *Bulletin of the Egyptological Seminar* 7 (1985-86): 5-13.

Blenkinsopp, Joseph. *Sage, Priest, Prophet: Religious and Intellectual Leadership in Ancient Israel.* Louisville: Westminster/John Knox, 1995.

Bloch, Marc. *Feudal Society: Social Classes and Political Organization.* Translated by L. A. Manyon. Chicago: University of Chicago Press, 1964.

Boecker, Hans J. *Klagelieder.* Zürich: Theologischer Verlag, 1985.

Boff, Leonardo, and Clodovis Boff. *Introducing Liberation Theology.* Maryknoll, N.Y.: Orbis, 1989.

Borowski, Oded. *Agriculture in Iron Age Israel.* Winona Lake, Ind.: Eisenbrauns, 1987.

Bottomore, Tom, ed. *Interpretations of Marx.* New York: Basil Blackwell, 1988.

Boxill, Bernard. *Blacks and Social Justice.* Totowa, N.J.: Rowman and Allanheld, 1984.

Boyd, Neil. *The Social Dimensions of Law.* Scarborough, Ont.: Prentice-Hall Canada, 1986.

Boyle, James, ed. *Critical Legal Studies.* Aldershot, England: Dartmouth Publishing Co., 1992.

Braulik, Georg. "Zur Abfolge der Gesetze in Deuteronomium 16:18–21:23: Weitere Beobachtungen." *Bib* 69, no. 1 (1988): 63-92.

————. *The Theology of Deuteronomy.* Translated by U. Lindbald. North Richland Hills, Tex.: BIBAL Press, 1994.

Brekelmans, C., and J. Lust, eds. *Pentateuchal and Deuteronomic Studies.* Leuven: Leuven University Press, 1990.

Brett, Mark. *Biblical Criticism in Crisis? The Impact of the Canonical Approach on Old Testament Studies.* Cambridge: Cambridge University Press, 1991.

Brettler, M. Z. "The Book of Judges: Literature as Politics." *JBL* 108 (1989): 395-418.

————. "Biblical Literature as Politics: The Case of Samuel." In *Religion and Politics in the Ancient Near East,* edited by Adele Berlin, pp. 71-92. Bethesda: University Press of Maryland, 1996.

Bright, John. "The Organization and Administration of the Israelite Empire." In *Magnalia Dei, the Mighty Acts of God: Essays on the Bible and Archaeology in Memory of G. Ernest Wright,* edited by Frank M. Cross, Werner Lemke, and Patrick D. Miller, Jr., pp. 193-208. Garden City, N.Y.: Doubleday, 1976.

————. *A History of Israel.* Philadelphia: Westminster, 1981.

Brown, Francis, et al. *The Brown-Driver-Briggs Hebrew and English Lexicon.* Peabody, Mass.: Hendrickson, [1906] 1996.

Brueggemann, Walter, and Hans W. Wolff, eds. *The Vitality of Old Testament Traditions.* Atlanta: John Knox, 1982.

Buccellati, G. *Cities and Nations of Ancient Syria.* Studi Semitici 26. Rome: University of Rome, 1967.

Bultmann, Christoph. *Der Fremde im Antiken Juda.* Göttingen: Vandenhoeck & Ruprecht, 1992.

Burcholy, Todd G. "Biblical Laws and the Economic Growth of Ancient Israel." *Journal of Law and Religion* 6, no. 2 (1988): 389-427.

Burns, Haywood. "Black People and the Tyranny of American Law." In *The Sociology of Law: A Conflict Perspective,* edited by Charles Reasons and Robert M. Rich, pp. 353-66. Toronto: Buttersworth and Co., 1978.

Campbell, Edward F. "Archaeological Reflections on Amos' Targets." In *Scripture and Other Artifacts: Essays on the Bible and Archaeology in Honor of Philip J. King,* edited by Michael Coogan et al., pp. 32-52. Louisville: Westminster/John Knox, 1993.

Carmichael, Calum M. "Deuteronomic Laws, Wisdom, and Historical Traditions." *JSS* 12 (1967): 198-206.

————. *The Laws of Deuteronomy.* Ithaca, N.Y.: Cornell University Press, 1974.

————. "'Treading' in the Book of Ruth." *VT* 92 (1980): 248-66.

———. "The Law of the Forgotten Sheaf." In SBLSP 20, edited by Kent H. Richards, pp. 35-37. Chico, Calif.: Scholars, 1981.

———. "Uncovering a Major Source of Mosaic Law: The Evidence of Deuteronomy 21:15–22:5." *JBL* 101 (1982): 505-20.

———. *Law and Narrative in the Bible: The Evidence of the Deuteronomic Laws and the Decalogue.* Ithaca, N.Y.: Cornell University Press, 1985.

Carter, C., and C. L. Meyers, eds. *Community, Identity, and Ideology: Social Science Approaches to the Hebrew Bible.* Winona Lake, Ind.: Eisenbrauns, 1996.

Cartledge, Tony W. *Vows in the Hebrew Bible and in the Ancient Near East.* JSOTSup 147. Sheffield: Sheffield Academic Press, 1992.

Chalcraft, David J. *Social Scientific Old Testament Criticism.* Sheffield: Sheffield Academic Press, 1997.

Chambliss, William, and Robert Seidman. *Law, Order, and Power.* Reading, Mass.: Addison-Wesley, 1982.

Chaney, Marvin L. "Ancient Palestinian Peasant Movements." In *Palestine in Transition: The Emergence of Ancient Israel,* edited by David N. Freedman, pp. 39-90. Sheffield: Sheffield Academic Press, 1983.

———. "Systemic Study of the Israelite Monarchy." In *Social Scientific Criticism of the Hebrew Bible and Its Social World: The Israelite Monarchy,* edited by Norman Gottwald, pp. 53-76. Semeia 37. Decatur: Scholars, 1986.

———. "Bitter Bounty: The Dynamics of Political Economy Critiqued by the Eighth-Century Prophets." In *Reformed Faith and Economics,* edited by Robert L. Stivers, pp. 15-30. Lanham, Md.: University Press of America, 1989.

———. "Debt Easement in Israelite History and Tradition." In *The Bible and the Politics of Exegesis,* edited by D. Jobling et al., pp. 127-39. Cleveland: Pilgrim Press, 1991.

Chang, Robert. "Toward an Asian American Legal Scholarship: Critical Race Theory, Post-structuralism, and Narrative Space." *California Law Review* 81, no. 5 (October 1993): 1241-1323.

Cholewinski, Alfred S. I. *Heiligkeitsgesetz und Deuteronomium: Einevergleichende Studie.* AnBib 66. Rome: Biblical Institute, 1976.

Christensen, Duane, ed. *A Song of Power and the Power of Song: Essays on the Book of Deuteronomy.* Winona Lake, Ind.: Eisenbrauns, 1993.

Clark, W. Malcolm. "Law." In *Old Testament Form Criticism,* edited by John H. Hayes, pp. 99-139. San Antonio: Trinity University Press, 1974.

Clements, R. E. "The Deuteronomistic Interpretation of the Founding of the Monarchy in 1 Sam VIII." *VT* 24 (1974): 398-410.

———. *Deuteronomy.* Sheffield: Sheffield Academic Press, 1989.

———, ed. *The World of Ancient Israel: Sociological, Anthropological, and Political Approaches.* Cambridge: Cambridge University Press, 1991.

Cohen, Mark E. *The Cultic Calendars of the Ancient Near East.* Bethesda: University Press of Maryland, 1996.

Cone, James. *A Black Theology of Liberation.* Philadelphia: J. B. Lippincott Co., 1970. Reprint, Maryknoll, N.Y.: Orbis, 1986.

Cook, Anthony. "Beyond Critical Legal Studies: The Reconstructive Theology of Dr. Martin Luther King, Jr." In *Critical Race Theory,* edited by Kimberlé Crenshaw et al., pp. 85-102. New York: New Press, 1995.

Coote, R. *Amos among the Prophets.* Philadelphia: Fortress, 1981.

——. *Early Israel: A New Horizon.* Minneapolis: Fortress, 1990.

——. *In Defense of Revolution: The Elohist History.* Minneapolis: Fortress, 1991.

——, ed. *Elijah and Elisha in Socioliterary Perspective.* Decatur: Scholars, 1992.

Coote, Robert B., and Mary P. Coote. *Power, Politics, and the Making of the Bible: An Introduction.* Minneapolis: Fortress, 1990.

Coote, Robert B., and David Robert Ord. *The Bible's First History.* Philadelphia: Fortress, 1989.

Coote, Robert B., and Keith W. Whitelam. "The Emergence of Israel: Social Transformation and State Formation following the Decline in Late Bronze Age Trade." In *Social Scientific Criticism of the Hebrew Bible and Its Social World: The Israelite Monarchy,* edited by Norman Gottwald, pp. 107-47. Semeia 37. Decatur: Scholars, 1986.

——. *The Emergence of Early Israel in Historical Perspective.* Sheffield: Almond Press, 1989.

Craghan, J. F. "The Elohist in Recent Literature." *BTB* 7 (1977): 23-35.

Craigie, Peter C. *The Book of Deuteronomy.* Grand Rapids: Eerdmans, 1976.

——. *The Problem of War in the Old Testament.* Grand Rapids: Eerdmans, 1978.

Crenshaw, James, ed. *Studies in Ancient Israelite Wisdom.* New York: Ktav, 1976.

——. "Education in Ancient Israel." *JBL* 104, no. 4 (1985): 601-15.

Cross, Frank M. *Canaanite Myth and Hebrew Epic.* Cambridge: Harvard University Press, 1973.

Crüsemann, Frank. *The Torah: Theology and Social History of Old Testament Law.* Translated by Allan W. Mahnke. Minneapolis: Fortress, 1996.

Dalton, G. "Peasantries in Anthropology and History." *CA* 13 (1972): 385-415.

Dalton, Harlon. "The Clouded Prism: Minority Critique of the Critical Legal Studies Movement." In *Critical Race Theory,* edited by Kimberlé Crenshaw et al., pp. 80-84. New York: New Press, 1995.

Dandamayev, M. A. "Der Tempelzehnte in Babylon während des 6.-4. Jahrhundert." In *Beiträge zur Alten Geschichte und deren Nachleben,* pp. 82-90. Festschrift für Franz Altheim. Berlin: De Gruyter, 1969.

——. "State Gods and Private Religion in the Near East in the First Millennium B.C.E." In *Religion and Politics in the Ancient Near East,* edited by Adele Berlin, pp. 35-45. Bethesda: University Press of Maryland, 1996.

Davies, Graham I. *Megiddo*. Grand Rapids: Eerdmans, 1986.

Davies, Philip R. *In Search of 'Ancient Israel.'* Sheffield: Sheffield Academic Press, 1992.

Davis, Abraham L., and Barbara Luck Graham. *The Supreme Court, Race, and Civil Rights*. Thousand Oaks, Calif.: Sage Publications, 1995.

Davis, Angela Y. "Keynote Address: Third National Conference on Women of Color and the Law." *Stanford Law Review* 43 (July 1991): 1175-81.

Davis, Nanette, ed. *Prostitution: An International Handbook on Trends, Problems, and Policies*. Westport, Conn.: Greenwood Press, 1993.

Deakin, Nicholas. *The Politics of Welfare*. New York: Harvester Wheatsheaf, 1994.

Delgado, Richard, ed. *Critical Race Theory: The Cutting Edge*. Philadelphia: Temple University Press, 1995.

De Ste. Croix, G. E. M. "Karl Marx and the History of Classical Antiquity." *Arethusa* 8 (1975): 7-41.

Dever, William. "The Contribution of Archaeology to the Study of Canaanite and Early Israelite Religion." In *Ancient Israelite Religion*, edited by Patrick D. Miller, Paul Hanson, and S. Dean McBride, pp. 209-47. Philadelphia: Fortress, 1987.

Diamond, Stanley. "The Rule of Law versus the Order of Custom." In *The Sociology of Law: A Conflict Perspective*, edited by Charles Reasons and Robert M. Rich, pp. 239-62. Toronto: Butterworth and Co., 1978.

Doorly, William J. *Obsession with Justice: The Story of the Deuteronomists*. New York: Paulist, 1994.

―――. *The Religion of Israel*. New York: Paulist, 1997.

Dorsey, D. *The Roads and Highways of Ancient Israel*. Baltimore: Johns Hopkins University Press, 1991.

Driver, G. R., and John Miles. *The Babylonian Laws*. Oxford: Clarendon, 1952.

Driver, S. R. *Deuteronomy*. ICC. Edinburgh: T. & T. Clark, 1978.

Duke, Rodney. "The Portion of the Levite: Another Reading of Deuteronomy 18:6-8." *JBL* 106 (1987): 193-201.

Dutcher-Walls, Patricia. "The Social Location of the Deuteronomist: A Sociological Study of Factional Politics in Late Pre-exilic Judah." *JSOT* 52 (1991): 77-94.

Eagleton, Terry. *Ideology*. London: Verso, 1996.

Eissfeldt, Otto. *The Old Testament: An Introduction*. Translated by Peter R. Ackroyd. New York, San Francisco, and London: Harper and Row, 1965.

Elliot-Binns, L. E. "Some Problems of the Holiness Code." *ZAW* 67 (1955): 26-40.

Ellis, Marc H., and Otto Maduro. *The Future of Liberation Theology*. Maryknoll, N.Y.: Orbis, 1989.

Emmerson, G. I. "Women in Ancient Israel." In *The World of Ancient Israel: Sociological, Anthropological, and Political Approaches*, edited by R. E. Clements, pp. 371-94. Cambridge: Cambridge University Press, 1989.

Epsztein, Léon. *Social Justice in the Ancient Near East and the People of the Bible.* Translated by John Bowden. London: SCM Press, 1986.

Falconer, Alan. "Dehumanization." In *The Westminster Dictionary of Christian Ethics,* edited by James F. Childress and John Macquarrie, p. 149. Philadelphia: Westminster, 1986.

————. "Humanitarianism." In *The Westminster Dictionary of Christian Ethics,* edited by James F. Childress and John Macquarrie, p. 283. Philadelphia: Westminster, 1986.

Feeley, Malcolm M. "The Concept of Laws in Social Science: A Critique and Notes on an Expanded View." In *The Sociology of Law: A Conflict Perspective,* edited by Charles Reasons and Robert M. Rich, pp. 13-38. Toronto: Buttersworth and Co., 1978.

Felder, Cain H., ed. *Stony the Road We Trod: African American Biblical Interpretation.* Minneapolis: Fortress, 1991.

Fensham, F. C. "Widow, Orphan, and the Poor in Ancient Near Eastern Legal and Wisdom Literature." *JNES* 21 (April 1962): 129-39.

————. "A Few Observations on the Polarisation between Yahweh and Baal in I Kings 17–29." *ZAW* 92 (1980): 227-36.

Finkelstein, Israel. *The Archaeology of the Israelite Settlement.* Translated by D. Saltz. Jerusalem: Israel Exploration Society, 1988.

————. "The Emergence of the Monarchy in Israel: The Environmental and Socio-Economic Aspects." *JSOT* 44 (June 1989): 43-74.

Fishbane, Michael. *Biblical Interpretation in Ancient Israel.* Oxford: Clarendon, 1985.

Fitzpatrick, Peter, ed. *Nationalism, Racism, and the Rule of Law.* Brookfield, Vt.: Darmouth Publishing Co., 1995.

Flanagan, James W. "New Constructs in Social World Studies." In *The Bible and the Politics of Exegesis,* edited by David Jobling et al., pp. 209-23. Cleveland: Pilgrim Press, 1991.

Foucault, Michel. *Power/Knowledge.* New York: Pantheon Books, 1980.

Frankfort, Henri. *Kingship and the Gods: A Study of Ancient Near Eastern Religion as the Integration of Society and Nature.* Chicago: University of Chicago Press, 1948.

Franklin, John Hope. *Race and History.* Baton Rouge: Louisiana State University Press, 1989.

Frazier, Thomas R. *Afro-American History.* Chicago: Dorsey Press, 1988.

Freedman, David N. *Amos.* Anchor Bible Commentary Series. Garden City, N.Y.: Doubleday, 1989.

Freire, Paulo. *Pedagogy of the Oppressed: Twentieth Anniversary Edition.* New York: Continuum, 1993.

Frick, Frank S. *The City in Ancient Israel.* Missoula: Scholars, 1977.

————. *The Formation of the State in Ancient Israel.* Decatur: Almond Press, 1985.

————. "Social Science Methods and Theories of Significance for the Study of the Israelite Monarchy." In *Social Scientific Criticism of the Hebrew Bible and Its Social World: The Israelite Monarchy*, edited by Norman Gottwald, pp. 9-52. Semeia 37. Decatur: Scholars, 1986.

————. "Widows in the Hebrew Bible: A Transactional Approach." In *A Feminist Companion to Exodus to Deuteronomy*, edited by Athalya Brenner, pp. 139-51. Sheffield: Sheffield Academic Press, 1994.

Frick, Frank S., and Norman Gottwald. "The Social World of Ancient Israel." In *The Bible and Liberation*, edited by Norman Gottwald, pp. 149-65. Maryknoll, N.Y.: Orbis, 1989.

Frohock, Fred. *Normative Political Theory.* Englewood Cliffs, N.J.: Prentice-Hall, 1974.

Frug, Mary Joe. *Postmodern Legal Feminism.* New York: Routledge, 1992.

Frye, Marilyn. *The Politics of Reality: Essays in Feminist Theory.* Trumansburg, N.Y.: Crossing Press, 1983.

Frymer-Kensky, Tikva. "Law and Philosophy: The Case of Sex in the Bible." In *Thinking Biblical Law*, edited by Dale Patrick, pp. 89-102. Semeia 45. Atlanta: Scholars, 1989.

Gaffney, Edward M. "Of Covenants Ancient and the New: The Influence of Secular Law on Biblical Religion." *Journal of Law and Religion* 2, no. 1 (1984): 117-44.

Garbini, Giovanni. *History and Ideology in Ancient Israel.* New York: Crossroad, 1988.

Garrett, William R. "Religion, Law, and the Human Condition." *Sociological Analysis: A Journal in the Sociology of Religion* 47 (March 1987): 1-34.

Gelb, Ignace, et al. *The Assyrian Dictionary of the Oriental Institute of the University of Chicago.* Chicago: Oriental Institute, 1958.

Gemser, B. "The Importance of the Motive Clause in Old Testament Law." *VTSup* 1 (1953): 50-66.

Gerbrandt, G. E. *Kingship according to the Deuteronomistic History.* Atlanta: Scholars Press, 1980.

Gerstenberger, Erhard. "Covenant and Commandment." *JBL* 84 (1965): 38-51.

Geuss, Raymond. *The Idea of a Critical Theory.* Cambridge: Cambridge University Press, 1981.

Gibson, J. C. L. *Canaanite Myths and Legends.* Edinburgh: T. & T. Clark, 1977.

Gieselmann, B. "Die Sogenannte Josianische Reform in der Gegenwärtigen Forschung." *ZAW* 106, no. 2 (1994): 223-42.

Gilbert, M., et al. *Morale et Ancien Testament.* Louvain: Centre Cerfaux-Lefort, 1976.

Glanzman, George. "The Origin and Date of the Book of Ruth." *CBQ* 21 (1959): 201-7.

Glendon, Mary Ann, et al. *Comparative Legal Traditions*. Saint Paul: West Publishing Co., 1982.

Gnuse, Robert. "Jubilee Legislation in Leviticus: Israel's Vision of Social Reform." *BTB* 15 (April 1985): 43-48.

Goldenberg, I. Ira. *Oppression and Social Intervention*. Chicago: Nelson-Hall, 1978.

Goldstein, Bernard R., and Alan Cooper. "The Festivals of Israel and Judah and the Literary History of the Pentateuch." *JAOS* 110 (1990): 19-31.

Gooding, D. W. "Ahab according to the Septuagint." *ZAW* 76 (1964): 269-79.

Gotanda, Neil. "A Critique of 'Our Constitution Is Color Blind.'" In *Critical Race Theory*, edited by Kimberlé Crenshaw et al., pp. 257-75. New York: New Press, 1995.

Gottlieb, Roger S., ed. *Key Concepts in Critical Theory*. Atlantic Highlands, N.J.: Humanities Press International, 1997.

Gottwald, Norman K. "Domain Assumptions and Societal Models in the Study of Pre-monarchic Israel." *VTSup* (1974): 89-100.

———. *The Tribes of Yahweh*. Maryknoll, N.Y.: Orbis, 1979.

———. "The Participation of Free Agrarians in the Introduction of Monarchy to Ancient Israel." In *Social Scientific Criticism of the Hebrew Bible and Its Social World: The Israelite Monarchy*, edited by Norman Gottwald, pp. 77-106. Semeia 37. Decatur: Scholars, 1986.

———. "Sociological Method in the Study of Ancient Israel." In *The Bible and Liberation*, edited by Norman Gottwald, pp. 26-37. Maryknoll, N.Y.: Orbis, 1989.

———. "A Hypothesis about Social Class in Monarchic Israel in Light of Contemporary Studies of Social Class and Social Stratification." In *The Hebrew Bible in Its Social World and in Ours*, pp. 139-64. Atlanta: Scholars, 1993.

———. "Social Class as an Analytic and Hermeneutical Category in Biblical Studies." *JBL* 112, no. 1 (spring 1993): 3-22.

Graham, Carol. *Safety Nets, Politics, and the Poor*. Washington: Brookings Instituion, 1994.

Gutiérrez, Gustavo. *A Theology of Liberation: Fifteenth Anniversary Edition*. Translated by Caridad Inda and John Eagleson. Maryknoll, N.Y.: Orbis, 1973. Reprint, Maryknoll, N.Y.: Orbis, 1988.

Haas, Peter J. *A History of the Mishnaic Law of Agriculture*. Chico, Calif.: Scholars, 1980.

———. "'Die He Shall Surely Die': The Structure of Homicide in Biblical Law." In *Thinking Biblical Law*, edited by Dale Patrick, pp. 67-87. Semeia 45. Atlanta: Scholars, 1989.

Hahn, Herbert H. *Old Testament in Modern Research*. Philadelphia: Muhlenberg, 1954.

Hallo, William W., and William K. Simpson. *The Ancient Near East: A History.* San Diego and New York: HBJ Publishers, 1971.

Halpern, Baruch. "The Centralization Formula in Deuteronomy." *VT* 36, no. 1 (1981): 20-38.

————. *The Emergence of Israel in Canaan.* Chico, Calif.: Scholars, 1983.

Hals, Ronald M. "Is There a Genre of Preached Law?" In SBLSP 1, edited by George MacRae, pp. 1-12. Cambridge, Mass.: Society of Biblical Literature, 1973.

Hamilton, Jeffries M. *Social Justice and Deuteronomy.* SBLDS 136. Atlanta: Scholars, 1992.

Handy, Lowell. "The Role of Huldah in Josiah's Cult Reform." *ZAW* 106, no. 1 (1994): 40-53.

Harding, Vincent. *There Is a River: The Black Struggle for Freedom in America.* New York: Vintage Books, 1983.

Harrelson, Walter. "Blessings and Curses." In *IDB,* 1:446-48. Nashville: Abingdon, 1962.

Harris, Angela P. "Forward: The Jurisprudence of Reconstruction. Symposium: Critical Race Theory." *California Law Review* 82, no. 4 (July 1994): 741-85.

————. "Race and Essentialism in Feminist Legal Theory." In *Critical Race Theory: The Cutting Edge,* edited by Richard Delgado, pp. 253-66. Philadelphia: Temple University Press, 1995.

Hauer, Chris, Jr. "The Economics of National Security in Solomonic Israel." *JSOT* 18 (1980): 63-73.

Havice, Harriet. "The Concern for the Widow and the Fatherless in the Ancient Near East." Ph.D. diss., Yale University, 1979.

Hayes, John H. *Amos: The Eighth-Century Prophet.* Nashville: Abingdon, 1988.

Hayes, John H., and Paul K. Hooker. *A New Chronology for the Kings of Israel and Judah.* Atlanta: John Knox, 1988.

Hayes, John H., and J. Kuan. "The Final Years of Samaria (730-720 BC)." *Bib* 72, no. 2 (1991): 153-81.

Hayes, John H., and J. Maxwell Miller. *Israelite and Judaean History.* London: SCM Press, 1990.

Hayman, Robert. "The Color of Tradition: Critical Race Theory and Postmodern Constitutional Traditionalism." *Harvard Civil Rights–Civil Liberties Law Review* 30, no. 1 (winter 1995): 57-108.

Herion, G. "The Impact of Modern and Social Science Assumptions on the Reconstruction of Israelite History." *JSOT* 34 (1986): 3-33.

Herrmann, Siegfried. *A History of Israel in Old Testament Times.* Philadelphia: Fortress, 1973.

————. "King David's State." In *The Shelter of Elyon: Essays on Ancient Palestinian Life and Literature,* edited by Boyd Barrick and John Spencer, pp. 261-75. JSOTSup 31. Sheffield: JSOT Press, 1984.

Hiebert, Paula S. "'Whence Shall Help Come to Me?' The Biblical Widow." In *Gender and Difference in Ancient Israel,* edited by Peggy L. Day, pp. 125-41. Minneapolis: Fortress, 1989.

Hiskes, Richard. *Community without Coercion.* Newark: University of Delaware Press, 1982.

Hobson, Deborah, and Baruch Halpern. *Law and Ideology in Monarchic Israel.* Sheffield: JSOT Press, 1991.

Hoffner, Harry A. "אלמנה." *TDOT* 1:287-91. Grand Rapids: Wm. B. Eerdmans, 1977.

hooks, bell. *Feminist Theory: From Margin to Center.* Boston: South End Press, 1984.

Hopkins, David C. "The Dynamics of Agriculture in Monarchic Israel." In SBLSP 22, edited by Kent H. Richards, pp. 177-202. Chico, Calif.: Scholars, 1983.

———. *The Highlands of Canaan.* Decatur: Almond Press, 1985.

Hoppe, Leslie J. "The Meaning of Deuteronomy." *BTB* 10 (July 1980): 111-17.

———. "Elders and Deuteronomy: A Proposal." *Eglise et Théologie* 14 (October 1983): 259-72.

———. "The Levitical Origins of Deuteronomy Reconsidered." *BR* 28 (1983): 27-36.

Horner, Thomas M. "Changing Concepts of the 'Stranger' in the Old Testament." *ATR* 42 (January 1960): 49-53.

Horsley, Richard A., and Norman K. Gottwald, eds. *The Bible and Liberation.* Maryknoll, N.Y.: Orbis, 1993.

Houten, Christiana van. *The Alien in Israelite Law.* Sheffield: JSOT Press, 1991.

Hutchinson, Allan. *Critical Legal Studies.* Lanham, Md.: Rowman and Littlefield, 1989.

Jacobs, Harriet. *Incidents in the Life of a Slave Girl.* Oxford: Oxford University Press, 1988.

Jagersma, H. "Tithes in the Old Testament." In *Remembering All the Way,* edited by B. Albrektson, pp. 116-28. Leiden: E. J. Brill, 1981.

Jenks, A. W. *The Elohist and North Israelite Traditions.* Missoula: Scholars, 1977.

Jenni, Ernst, and Claus Westermann. *Theologisches Handwörterbuch zum Alten Testament.* 2 vols. Munich: Chr. Kaiser Verlag, 1971.

Jepsen, A. "Israel und Damascus." *AfO* 14 (1941-44): 153-72.

Josephus, Flavius. *Antiquities of the Jews.* Translated by William Whiston. Grand Rapids: Kregel Publications, 1985.

Joshi, P. L. "Religion, Class Conflict, and Emancipation Movements: Some Reflections." *Social Action* 39 (April-June 1989): 162-78.

Kaufmann, Stephen. "The Structure of the Deuteronomic Law." *Maarav* 1, no. 2 (1978): 105-58.

———. "A Reconstruction of the Social Welfare Systems of Ancient Israel." In

Shelter of Elyon: Essays on Ancient Palestinian Life and Literature in Honor of G. W. Ahlström, edited by W. Boyd Barrick and John R. Spencer, pp. 277-86. JSOTSup 31. Sheffield: Journal for the Study of the Old Testament, 1984.

Kaufmann, Y. *The Religion of Israel from Its Beginnings to the Babylonian Exile.* Translated by M. Greenberg. New York: Schocken Books, [1960] 1972.

Kellermann, Diether. "גּוּר." *TDOT* 2:439-49. Grand Rapids: Wm. B. Eerdmans, 1977.

King, P. J. *Amos, Hosea, Micah: An Archaeological Commentary.* Philadelphia: Fortress, 1988.

Kirkpatrick, Frank. *Community: A Trinity of Models.* Washington, D.C.: Georgetown University Press, 1986.

Knierim, R. P. "The Problem of Ancient Israel's Prescriptive Legal Traditions." In *Thinking Biblical Law,* edited by Dale Patrick, pp. 7-25. Semeia 45. Atlanta: Scholars, 1989.

Knight, Douglas A. "The Understanding of 'Sitz-im-Leben' in Form Criticism." In SBLSP 1, edited by George MacRae, pp. 105-25. Cambridge, Mass.: Society of Biblical Literature, 1974.

————. "Jeremiah and the Dimensions of the Moral Life." In *The Divine Helmsman: Studies on God's Control of Human Events,* edited by James L. Crenshaw and S. Sandmel, pp. 87-105. New York: Ktav, 1980.

————. "O.T. Ethics." *Christian Century* 99 (1982): 55-59.

————. "The Pentateuch." In *The Hebrew Bible and Its Modern Interpreters,* edited by Douglas A. Knight and Gene Tucker, pp. 263-96. Philadelphia: Fortress, 1985.

————. "Political Rights and Powers in Monarchic Israel." In *Ethics and Politics in the Hebrew Bible,* pp. 93-117. Semeia 66. Atlanta: Scholars, 1994.

————. "The Social Basis of Morality and Religion in Ancient Israel." In *Language, Theology, and the Bible,* edited by Samuel Balentine and John Barton, pp. 151-67. Oxford: Clarendon, 1994.

————. "Deuteronomy and the Deuteronomists." In *Old Testament Interpretation: Past, Present, and Future,* edited by James L. Mayes et al., pp. 61-79. Nashville: Abingdon, 1995.

————, ed. *Julius Wellhausen and His Prolegomena to the History of Ancient Israel.* Semeia 25. Atlanta: Scholars, 1982.

Kramer, Matthew. *Critical Legal Theory and the Challenge of Feminism.* Lanham, Md.: Rowman and Littlefield, 1995.

Krapf, Thomas. "Traditionsgeschichtliches zum Deuteronomischen Fremdling-Waise-Witwe-Gebot." *VT* 34 (January 1984): 87-91.

Kutsch, Ernst. "Erwägungen zur Geschichte der Passafeier und des Massotfestes." *ZTK* 55 (1958): 1-35.

————. "Am Ende des Jahres: Zur Datierung des Israelitischen Herbstfestes in Ex 23:16." *ZAW* 83 (1971): 15-21.

Lang, Bernhard. *Monotheism and the Prophetic Minority*. Sheffield: Almond Press, 1983.

————. "Anthropology as a Model for Biblical Studies." In *Anthropological Approaches to the Old Testament*, edited by Bernhard Lang, pp. 1-20. Philadelphia: Fortress, 1985.

————. "The Social Organization of Peasant Poverty in Biblical Israel." In *Anthropological Approaches to the Old Testament*, edited by Bernhard Lang, pp. 83-99. Philadelphia: Fortress, 1985.

Larsen, M. T., ed. *Power and Propaganda: A Symposium on Ancient Empires*. Winona Lake, Ind.: Eisenbrauns, 1996.

Lebacqz, Karen. *Six Theories of Justice*. Minneapolis: Augsburg, 1986.

Lemche, Niels Peter. *Ancient Israel: A New History of Israelite Society*. Sheffield: JSOT Press, 1990.

————. "On the Use of System Theory, Macro-Theories, and Evolutionist Thinking in Modern O.T. Research and Biblical Archaeology." *SJOT* 2 (1990): 73-88.

————. *The Israelites in History and in Tradition*. Library of Ancient Israel. Louisville: Westminster/John Knox, 1998.

Lenski, Gerhard. *Power and Privilege: A Theory of Social Stratification*. Chapel Hill: University of North Carolina Press, 1984.

Lerner, Gerda. *The Creation of Patriarchy*. Oxford: University Press, 1986.

Lerner, Melvin. *New Directions in the Study of Justice, Law, and Social Control*. New York and London: Plenum Press, 1990.

Levenson, Jon D. *The Hebrew Bible, the Old Testament, and Historical Criticism*. Louisville: Westminster/John Knox, 1993.

Levi, Thomas E., ed. *The Archaeology of Society in the Holy Land*. New York: Facts on File, 1995.

Levine, Donald N. "Simmel at a Distance: On the History and Systematics of the Sociology of the Stranger." In *Strangers in African Societies*, edited by William A. Shack and Elliot P. Skinner, pp. 21-36. Berkeley: University of California Press, 1979.

Levinson, Bernard. *Deuteronomy and the Hermeneutics of Legal Innovation*. New York and Oxford: Oxford University Press, 1997.

Lohfink, Norbert. "Das Deuteronomische Gesetz in der Endgestalt — Entwurf einer Gesellschaft ohne marginale Gruppen." *BN* 51 (1990): 25-40.

————. "Poverty in the Laws of the Ancient Near East and of the Bible." *TS* 52 (March 1991): 34-50.

Machinist, P. "Literature as Politics: The Tukulti-Ninurta Epic and the Bible." *CBQ* 38 (1976): 455-82.

Maine, Sir Henry Summer. *Ancient Law: Its Connection with the Early History of Society and Its Relation to Modern Ideas.* Tucson: University of Arizona Press, 1986.

Malchow, Bruce V. "Social Justice in the Israelite Law Codes." *WW* 4 (summer 1984): 299-306.

————. *Social Justice in the Hebrew Bible.* Collegeville, Minn.: Liturgical Press, 1996.

Malina, Bruce J. "The Social Sciences and Biblical Interpretation." *Int* 37, no. 3 (1982): 229-42.

————. "Why Interpret the Bible with the Social Sciences?" *American Baptist Quarterly* 2 (June 1983): 119-33.

Mann, Michael. *The Sources of Social Power.* Cambridge: Cambridge University Press, 1986-1993.

Martin, J. D. "Israel as a Tribal Society." In *The World of Ancient Israel: Sociological, Anthropological, and Political Approaches,* edited by R. E. Clements, pp. 95-117. Cambridge: Cambridge University Press, 1989.

Mathias, Dietmar. "Levitische Predigt und Deuteronomismus." *ZAW* (1984): 23-49.

Matsuda, Mari. "Looking to the Bottom: Critical Legal Studies and Reparations." In *Critical Race Theory,* edited by Kimberlé Crenshaw et al., pp. 63-79. New York: New Press, 1995.

Mayes, A. D. H. "The Rise of the Israelite Monarchy." *ZAW* 90 (1978): 1-19.

————. *Deuteronomy.* Grand Rapids: Eerdmans, [1979] 1991.

————. *The Old Testament in Sociological Perspective.* London: Marshall Pickering, 1989.

————. "On Describing the Purpose of Deuteronomy." *JSOT* 58 (1993): 13-33.

————. "Deuteronomy 14 and the Deuteronomic World View." In *Studies in Deuteronomy,* edited by F. García Martínez et al., pp. 165-81. Leiden: E. J. Brill, 1994.

Mazar, Amihai. *Archaeology of the Land of the Bible, 10,000-586 B.C.E.* New York: Doubleday, 1990.

Mazar, B. "The Aramean Empire and Its Relations with Israel." *BA* 25 (1962): 97-120.

McBride, S. Dean. "Polity of the Covenant People: The Book of Deuteronomy." *Int* 41 (July 1987): 229-44.

McCarter, P. Kyle, Jr. *1 Samuel.* Anchor Bible Commentary Series. Garden City, N.Y.: Doubleday, 1980.

McCarthy, Dennis J. "The Inauguration of Monarchy in Israel." *Int* 27 (1973): 401-12.

McConville, J. G. *Law and Theology in Deuteronomy.* Sheffield: JSOT Press, 1984.

McCurley, Foster R. "The Home of Deuteronomy Revisited: A Methodological

Analysis of Northern Theory." In *A Light unto My Path,* edited by H. Bream, pp. 295-317. Philadelphia: Temple University Press, 1974.

McEvenue, S. E. "The Elohist at Work." *ZAW* 96 (1984): 315-32.

McKay, John. *Religion in Judah under the Assyrians.* Naperville, Ill.: Alec R. Allenson Press, 1973.

McKeating, Henry. "Sanctions against Adultery in Ancient Israelite Society with Some Reflections on Methodology in the Study of Old Testament Ethics." *JSOT* 11 (1979): 57-73.

McKenzie, John L. "The Elders in the Old Testament." *Bib* 40 (1959): 522-40.

McNutt, Paula M. *The Forging of Israel: Iron Technology, Symbolism, and Tradition in Ancient Society.* Decatur: Almond Press, 1990.

Mendenhall, George E. "Covenant Forms in Israelite Tradition." *BA* 17, no. 3 (1954): 50-76.

Menes, Abram. *Die Vorexilischen Gesetze Israels.* BZAW 50. Giessen: Alfred Topelmann, 1928.

Merendino, Rosario P. *Das Deuteronomische Gesetz.* Bonn: Peter Hanstein, 1969.

Mettinger, Tryggve N. D. *Solomonic State Officials: A Study of the Civil Government Officials of the Israelite Monarchy.* Lund: C. W. K. Gleerup, 1971.

Meyers, Carol. "Procreation, Production, and Protection: Male-Female Balance in Early Israel." *JAAR* 51 (1983): 569-93.

————. *Discovering Eve.* Oxford: Oxford University Press, 1988.

Milgrom, Jacob. *Studies in Cultic Theology and Terminology.* Leiden: E. J. Brill, 1983.

Miller, J. M. "The Elisha-Cycle and the Accounts of the Omride Wars." *JBL* 85 (1966): 441-54.

————. "The Fall of the House of Ahab." *VT* 17 (1967): 307-24.

————. "So Tibni Died, (1 Kgs 16:22)." *VT* 18 (1968): 392-94.

Miller, J. Maxwell, and John H. Hayes. *A History of Ancient Israel and Judah.* Philadelphia: Westminster, 1986.

Miranda, José. *Marx and the Bible: A Critique of the Philosophy of Oppression.* Maryknoll, N.Y.: Orbis, 1974.

Mitchell, Christopher W. *The Meaning of BRK "to Bless" in the Old Testament.* SBLDS 95. Atlanta: Scholars, 1987.

Moore, Rick D. *God Saves: Lessons from the Elisha Stories.* Sheffield: JSOT Press, 1990.

Morrow, William S. *Scribing the Center: Organization and Redaction in Deuteronomy 14:1–17:13.* Atlanta: Scholars, 1995.

Mouw, Richard J. *The God Who Commands: A Study in Divine Command Ethics.* Notre Dame, Ind.: University of Notre Dame Press, 1990.

Mowinckel, Sigmund. "Cult and Prophecy." In *Prophecy in Israel,* edited by David L. Petersen, pp. 74-98. Philadelphia: Fortress, 1987.

————. *The Psalms in Israelite Worship.* Vol. 2. Oxford: Basil Blackwell, 1962. Reprint, Sheffield: JSOT Press, 1991.

Nakanose, Shigeyuki. *Josiah's Passover.* Maryknoll, N.Y.: Orbis, 1993.

Nash, Ronald. "The Economics of Justice." In *Economic Justice and the State,* edited by J. Bernbaum, pp. 9-23. Grand Rapids: Baker, 1986.

Nelson, Richard D. *The Double Redaction of the Deuteronomistic History.* JSOTSup 18. Sheffield: JSOT Press, 1981.

Nicholson, E. W. *Deuteronomy and Tradition.* Philadelphia: Fortress, 1967.

Niditch, Susan. *War in the Hebrew Bible: A Study in the Ethics of Violence.* Oxford: Oxford University Press, 1993.

————. *Oral World and Written Word.* Louisville: Westminster/John Knox, 1996.

Nielsen, Eduard. "Moses and the Law." *VT* 32 (1982): 87-98.

North, Robert J. "עָשַׁר, מַעֲשֵׂר." *TDOT* 11:404-9. Grand Rapids: Wm. B. Eerdmans, 2001.

Noth, Martin. *The History of Israel.* San Francisco: Harper and Row, 1958.

————. *The Laws in the Pentateuch and Other Essays.* Translated by D. R. Ap-Thomas. Philadelphia: Fortress, 1967.

Nozick, Robert. *Anarchy, State, and Utopia.* New York: Basic Books, 1974.

Olson, Dennis T. *Deuteronomy and the Death of Moses.* OBT. Minneapolis: Fortress, 1994.

Olyan, Saul. *Asherah and the Cult of Yahweh in Israel.* Atlanta: Scholars, 1988.

Otto, Eckart. "Sozialgeschichte Israels. Probleme und Perspektiven. Ein Diskussionpapier." *BN* 15 (1981): 87-92.

————. "Stellung der Frau in den ältesten Rechtstexten des AT (Ex. 20:14; 22:15f) — Wider die hermeneutische Naivität im Umgang mit dem AT." *ZEE* 26 (July-September 1982): 279-305.

————. *Theologische Ethik des Alten Testaments.* Stuttgart: W. Kohlhammer, 1994.

Oyen, Hendrik van. *Ethik des Alten Testaments.* Gütersloh: Gütersloh Verlagshaus G. Mohn, 1967.

Pals, Daniel. *Seven Theories of Religion.* Oxford: Oxford University Press, 1996.

Parkin, Robert. *Kinship: An Introduction to the Basic Concepts.* Malden, Mass.: Blackwell, 1997.

Patrick, Dale. *Old Testament Law.* Atlanta: John Knox, 1985.

————. "Studying Biblical Law as a Humanities." In *Thinking Biblical Law,* edited by Dale Patrick, pp. 27-47. Semeia 45. Atlanta: Scholars, 1989.

Patterson, Richard D. "The Widow, the Orphan, and the Poor in the Old Testament and the Extra-Biblical Literature." *BSac* 130 (1973): 223-34.

Paul, Shalom. *Amos.* Philadelphia: Fortress, 1991.

Pedersen, Johannes. *Ancient Israel: Its Life and Culture.* Vol. 1. London: Oxford University Press, [1927] 1973.

Perdue, Leo G., et al. *Families in Ancient Israel.* Louisville: Westminster/John Knox, 1997.

Phillips, A. C. J. "The Laws of Slavery: Exodus 21:2-11." *JSOT* 30 (1984): 51-66.

Pienaar, D. N. "The Role of Fortified Cities in the Northern Kingdom during the Reign of the Omride Dynasty." *JNWSL* 9 (1981): 151-57.

Piven, Frances F., and Richard A. Cloward, eds. *Regulating the Poor: The Functions of Public Welfare.* New York: Vintage Books, 1993.

Pixley, Jorge. *Biblical Israel: A People's History.* Minneapolis: Fortress, 1992.

Pleins, J. David. "Poor, Poverty." In *ABD*, 5:402-14. New York: Doubleday, 1995.

Podgorecki, Adam, et al. *Legal Systems and Social Systems.* Dover, N.H.: Croom Helm, 1985.

Pospisil, Leopold. *Anthropology of Law: A Comparative Approach.* New York: Harper and Row, 1971.

Preuss, Horst D. *Old Testament Theology.* Vols. 1-2. Translated by Leo Perdue. OTL. Louisville: Westminster/John Knox, 1996.

Pritchard, James B., ed. *Ancient Near Eastern Texts Relating to the Old Testament.* Princeton: Princeton University Press, 1969.

Provan, I. W. *Lamentations.* Grand Rapids: Eerdmans, 1991.

Quinney, Richard. *The Social Reality of Crime.* Boston: Little, Brown, 1970.

————. "The Ideology of Law: Notes for a Radical Alternative to Legal Oppression." In *The Sociology of Law: A Conflict Perspective,* edited by Charles Reasons and Robert M. Rich, pp. 39-71. Toronto: Butterworth and Co., 1978.

Raboteau, Albert J. *Slave Religion.* New York: Oxford University Press, 1980.

Rad, Gerhard von. *Studies in Deuteronomy.* Translated by D. Stalker. London: SCM Press, 1953.

————. *Holy War in Ancient Israel.* Translated by Marva J. Dawn. Grand Rapids: Eerdmans, 1958.

————. *Old Testament Theology.* Vol. 1. Translated by D. Stalker. New York: Harper and Row, 1962.

————. *Deuteronomy.* Translated by Doretha Barton. OTL. Philadelphia: Westminster, 1966.

————. *The Problem of the Hexateuch and Other Essays.* Translated by E. W. Trueman Dicken. London: SCM Press, 1966.

————. *Genesis.* Translated by John H. Marks. OTL. Philadelphia: Westminster, 1972.

Rattray, S., and J. Milgrom. "ראשית." *TWAT* 7:291-94. Stuttgart: W. Kohlhammer, 1990.

Rawls, John. *A Theory of Justice.* Cambridge: Harvard University Press, Belknap Press, 1971.

————. *Liberty, Equality, and Law.* Salt Lake City: University of Utah Press, 1987.

Rendsburg, G. A. "David and His Circle in Genesis XXXVIII." *VT* 36 (1986): 439-46.

Renkema, J. "Does Hebrew *YTWM* Really Mean 'Fatherless'?" *VT* 45, no. 1 (1995): 119-22.

Reviv, Hanoch. "The Traditions concerning the Inception of the Legal System in Israel: Significance and Dating." *ZAW* 94, no. 4 (1982): 566-75.

Rhode, Deborah. "Feminist Critical Theories." In *Feminist Legal Theory*, edited by Katherine Bartlett and Rosanne Kennedy, pp. 333-50. Boulder, Colo.: Westview Press, 1991.

Rich, Robert M. "Sociological Paradigms and the Sociology of Law: A Historical Analysis." In *The Sociology of Law: A Conflict Perspective*, edited by Charles Reasons and Robert M. Rich, pp. 147-79. Toronto: Buttersworth and Co., 1978.

————. *The Sociology of Law*. Washington, D.C.: UPA, 1978.

Ringgren, Helmer. "יתום." *TDOT* 6:477-81. Grand Rapids: Wm. B. Eerdmans, 1991.

Robertson-Smith, William. *Lectures on the Religion of the Semites*. London: A. & C. Black, 1927.

Rodd, Cyril S. "On Applying a Sociological Theory to Biblical Studies." *JSOT* 19 (1981): 95-106.

Rodes, Robert E. *Law and Liberation*. Notre Dame, Ind.: University of Notre Dame Press, 1986.

Rofé, Alexander. "The Arrangement of the Laws in Deuteronomy." *ETL* 64, no. 4 (1988): 265-87.

————. "The Vineyard of Naboth: The Origin and Message of the Story." *ZAW* 38 (1988): 89-104.

Rogerson, J. W. "The Use of Sociology in Old Testament Studies." In *Congress Volume: Salamanca*. VTSup 36. Leiden: E. J. Brill, 1985.

————. "Anthropology and the Old Testament." In *The World of Ancient Israel: Sociological, Anthropological, and Political Approaches*, edited by R. E. Clements, pp. 17-37. Cambridge: Cambridge University Press, 1989.

Rokumoto, Kahei, ed. *Sociological Theories of Law*. New York: New York University Press, 1994.

Roth, Martha T. *Law Collections from Mesopotamia and Asia Minor*. Atlanta: Scholars, 1995.

Sampford, Charles. *The Disorder of Law: A Critique of Critical Legal Theory*. Oxford: Oxford University Press, 1989.

Sarna, Nahum M. "The Biblical Sources for the History of the Monarchy." In *The World History of the Jewish People*, edited by A. Malamat, pp. 3-19. Jerusalem: Massada Press, 1979.

Scheppele, Kim Lane. "Legal Theory and Social Theory." *Annual Review of Sociology, Annual* 20 (1994): 383-407.

Schulte, Hannelis. "The End of the Omride Dynasty: Social-Ethical Observations on the Subject of Power and Violence." In *Ethics and Politics in the Hebrew Bible*, translated by Carl Ehrlich, pp. 133-48. Semeia 66. Atlanta: Scholars, 1994.

Scott, Jack B. "אלמנה." In *Theological Wordbook of the Old Testament*. Chicago: Moody, 1980.

Sernett, Milton C., ed. *Afro-American Religious History: A Documentary History*. Durham, N.C.: Duke University Press, 1989.

Shack, William A., and Elliot P. Skinner. eds. *Strangers in African Societies*. Berkeley: University of California Press, 1979.

Shanks, Hershel, et al. *The Rise of Ancient Israel*. Washington, D.C.: Biblical Archaeology Society, 1992.

————. *Ancient Israel*. Washington, D.C.: Biblical Archaeology Society, 1995.

Silver, Morris. *Prophets and Markets: The Political Economy of Ancient Israel*. Boston: Kluwer-Nijhoff, 1983.

————. *Economic Structures of the Ancient Near East*. Totowa, N.J.: Barnes and Noble, 1985.

Simmel, Georg. *Soziologie*. Munich: Duncker & Humblot, 1923.

Simpson, Evan. "The Subject of Justice." *Ethics* 90 (July 1980): 490-501.

Sinha, Surya P. *Jurisprudence: Legal Philosophy*. Saint Paul: West Publishing Co., 1993.

Smith, Daniel L. *The Religion of the Landless*. Bloomington, Ind.: Meyer Stone Books, 1989.

Smith, Mark S. *The Early History of God: Yahweh and the Other Deities in Ancient Israel*. San Francisco: Harper and Row, 1990.

Smith, Morton. *Palestinian Parties and Politics That Shaped the Old Testament*. London: SCM Press, 1987.

Soden, Wolfram von, ed. *Akkadisches Handwörterbuch*. Wiesbaden: Otto Harrassowitz, 1965.

Soggin, J. Alberto. "Compulsory Labor under David and Solomon." In *Studies in the Period of David and Solomon and Other Essays*, edited by Tomoo Ishida, pp. 259-67. Winona Lake, Ind.: Eisenbrauns, 1982.

————. *An Introduction to the History of Israel and Judah*. Translated by John Bowden. Valley Forge, Pa.: Trinity Press International, 1993.

Spina, Frank A. "Israelites as *gērîm*, 'Sojourners,' in Social and Historical Context." In *The Word of the Lord Shall Go Forth*, edited by Carol L. Meyers and M. O'Connor, pp. 321-35. Winona Lake, Ind.: Eisenbrauns, 1983.

Sprinkle, Joe M. "Literary Approaches to the Old Testament: A Survey of Recent Scholarship." *JETS* 32 (spring 1989): 299-310.

Stager, L. E. "The Archaeology of the Family in Ancient Israel." *BASOR* 260 (1985): 1-35.

Stahl, Nanette. *Law and Liminality in the Bible*. Ithaca, N.Y.: CUP Services, 1995.

Stampp, Kenneth M. *The Peculiar Institution: Slavery in the Ante-bellum South.* New York: Vintage Books, 1956.

Stavenhagen, Rodolfo. *Social Classes in Agrarian Societies.* Garden City, N.Y.: Anchor Press/Doubleday, 1975.

Steinberg, Naomi. "The Deuteronomic Law Code and the Politics of State Centralization." In *The Bible and the Politics of Exegesis,* edited by D. Jobling et al., pp. 161-70. Cleveland: Pilgrim Press, 1991.

Stendahl, Krister. "Biblical Theology, Contemporary." In *IDB,* vol. 1. Nashville: Abingdon, 1982.

Steuernagel, Carl. *Die Entstehung des deuteronomischen Gesetzes.* Halle: J. Krause, 1896.

Strange, J. "Joram, King of Israel and Judah." *VT* 25 (1975): 191-201.

Stuckey, Sterling. *Slave Culture.* New York: Oxford University Press, 1987.

Stulman, Louis. "Encroachment in Deuteronomy: An Analysis of the Social World of the Deuteronomic Code." *JBL* 109 (winter 1990): 613-32.

Sweeney, Marvin. "The Critique of Solomon in the Josianic Edition of the Deuteronomistic History." *JBL* 114, no. 4 (winter 1995): 607-22.

Tadmor, Hayim. "Assyria and the West: The Ninth Century and Its Aftermath." In *Unity and Diversity,* edited by H. Goedicke and J. J. M. Roberts, pp. 36-45. Baltimore: Johns Hopkins University Press, 1975.

———. "Traditional Institutions and the Monarchy: Social and Political Tensions in the Time of David and Solomon." In *Studies in the Period of David and Solomon and Other Essays,* edited by Tomoo Ishida, pp. 239-57. Winona Lake, Ind.: Eisenbrauns, 1982.

Talmon, Shemaryahu. *King, Cult, and Calendar in Ancient Israel.* Jerusalem: Magnes Press, 1986.

Tamez, Elsa. *Bible of the Oppressed.* Maryknoll, N.Y.: Orbis, 1982.

Taylor, Charles. "The Nature and Scope of Distributive Justice." In his *Philosophy and the Human Sciences,* pp. 289-317. Cambridge: Cambridge University Press, 1985.

Taylor, Walter. "Sociological Exegesis: Introduction to a New Way to Study the Bible: Pt. 1: History and Theory." *Trinity Seminary Review* 11 (fall 1989): 99-110.

Therborn, Göran. "Critical Theory and the Legacy of Twentieth-Century Marxism." In *The Blackwell Companion to Social Theory,* edited by Bryan S. Turner, pp. 53-82. Cambridge, Mass.: Blackwell, 1996.

Thompson, D., and T. Thompson. "Some Legal Problems in the Book of Ruth." *VT* 18 (1968): 79-99.

Thompson, J. A. *Deuteronomy.* Downers Grove, Ill.: InterVarsity, 1975.

Thompson, R. J. *Moses and the Law in a Century of Criticism Since Graf.* Leiden: E. J. Brill, 1970.

Tigay, Jeffrey H. *Deuteronomy.* Philadelphia: Jewish Publication Society, 1996.

Tillessee, Minette de. "Sections 'tu' et Sections 'vous' dans le Deutéronome." *VT* 12 (1962): 29-87.

Timm, S. *Die Dynastie Omri, Quellen und Untersuchungen zur Geschichte Israels im 9 Jahrhundert vor Christus.* Göttingen: Vandenhoeck & Ruprecht, 1982.

Tiruchelvam, Neelan. "The Ideology of Popular Justice." In *The Sociology of Law: A Conflict Perspective,* edited by Charles Reasons and Robert M. Rich, pp. 263-80. Toronto: Buttersworth and Co., 1978.

Torres, Gerald, and Kathryn Milun. "Translating 'Yonnondio' by Precedent and Evidence: The Mashpee Indian Case." In *Critical Race Theory,* edited by Kimberlé Crenshaw et al., pp. 177-90. New York: New Press, 1995.

Tov, Emanuel. *Textual Criticism of the Hebrew Bible.* Minneapolis: Fortress, 1992.

Trubek, David. "Where the Action Is: CLS and Empiricism." *Stanford Law Review* 36, nos. 1-2 (January 1984): 575-622.

Tullio, Caputo, et al. *Law and Society: A Critical Perspective.* Toronto: Harcourt Brace Jovanovich Canada, 1989.

Turabian, Kate L. *A Manual for Writers of Term Papers, Theses, and Dissertations.* 6th ed. Chicago: University of Chicago Press, 1996.

Turk, Austin T. "Law as a Weapon in Social Conflict." *Social Problems* 23 (1976): 276-91.

Unger, Roberto M. "The Critical Legal Studies Movement." *Harvard Law Review* 96, no. 3 (January 1983): 561-675.

Uys, P. H. "The Term *'almānâ* in the Book of Proverbs." In *Studies in Wisdom Literature,* edited by W. C. Wyk, pp. 74-81. Hercules, South Africa: NHW Press, 1981.

———. "The Term *yātôm* in the Book of Proverbs." In *Studies in Wisdom Literature,* edited by W. C. Wyk, pp. 82-88. Hercules, South Africa: NHW Press, 1981.

Vaux, Roland de. *Ancient Israel: Social and Religious Institutions.* Vols. 1 and 2. New York: McGraw-Hill, 1961.

Waldow, H. Eberhard von. "Social Responsibility and Social Structure in Early Israel." *CBQ* 32 (1970): 182-204.

Walton, John H. "Deuteronomy: An Exposition of the Spirit of the Law." *GTJ* 8, no. 2 (1987): 213-25.

Wartenberg, Thomas E. *The Forms of Power.* Philadelphia: Temple University Press, 1990.

Weber, Max. *The Theory of Social and Economic Organization.* Translated by A. M. Henderson and Talcott Parsons. New York: Free Press, 1947.

———. *Ancient Judaism.* Translated by Hans H. Gerth and Don Martindale. New York: Free Press, 1952.

Weems, Renita J. "Reading *Her Way* through the Struggle: African American Women and the Bible." In *Stony the Road We Trod: African American Biblical Interpretation,* edited by Cain H. Felder, pp. 57-77. Minneapolis: Fortress, 1991.

————. *Battered Love: Marriage, Sex, and Violence in the Hebrew Prophets.* Minneapolis: Fortress, 1995.

Weinberg, Joel. "The *'Am Hā'āreṣ* of the Sixth to Fourth Centuries BCE." In *The Citizen-Temple Community,* translated by Daniel L. Smith-Christopher, pp. 62-74. Sheffield: JSOT Press, 1992.

————. "The *Bêt 'Abôt* in the Sixth to Fourth Centuries BCE." In *The Citizen-Temple Community,* translated by Daniel L. Smith-Christopher, pp. 49-61. Sheffield: JSOT Press, 1992.

Weinfeld, Moshe. "The Origin of Humanism in Deuteronomy." *JBL* 80 (1961): 241-47.

————. "Deuteronomy: The Present State of Inquiry." *JBL* 86 (1967): 249-62.

————. "Tithes." In *EncJud* (1971), pp. 1156-62.

————. "The Emergence of the Deuteronomic Movement: The Historical Antecedents." In *Das Deuteronomium,* edited by N. Lohfink, pp. 76-98. Leuven: Leuven University Press, 1985.

————. *Deuteronomy 1–11.* Anchor Bible Commentary Series. New York and Toronto: Doubleday, 1991.

————. *Deuteronomy and the Deuteronomic School.* Winona Lake, Ind.: Eisenbrauns, [1972] 1992.

————. *Social Justice in Ancient Israel.* Minneapolis: Fortress, 1995.

Welch, A. C. *The Code of Deuteronomy: A New Theory of Its Origin.* London: James Clarke and Co., 1924.

Welch, D. Don, ed. *Law and Morality.* Philadelphia: Fortress, 1987.

Wellek, René, and Austin Warren. *Theory of Literature.* New York: Harcourt Brace Jovanovich, [1942] 1977.

Wenham, G. "Deuteronomy and the Central Sanctuary." *TynBul* 22 (1971): 103-18.

West, Cornel. *Keeping Faith: Race and Philosophy in America.* New York: Routledge, 1994.

Westbrook, Raymond. *Property and Family in Biblical Law.* Sheffield: JSOT Press, 1991.

Westermann, Claus. *Die Klagelieder: Forschungsgeschichte und Auslegung.* Neukirchen-Vluyn: Neukirchener, 1990.

Whitelam, Keith. "The Defense of David." *JSOT* 29 (1984): 61-87.

————. "Israelite Kingship: The Royal Ideology and Its Opponents." In *The World of Ancient Israel: Sociological, Anthropological, and Political Approaches,* edited by R. E. Clements, pp. 119-39. Cambridge: Cambridge University Press, 1989.

Whitley, C. F. "The Deuteronomic Presentation of the House of Omri." *VT* 2 (1952): 137-50.

Williams, Delores S. *Sisters in the Wilderness.* Maryknoll, N.Y.: Orbis, 1996.

Williams, Patricia J. *The Alchemy of Race and Rights.* Cambridge: Harvard University Press, 1991.

Williams, Ronald J. *Hebrew Syntax: An Outline*. 2nd ed. Toronto: University of Toronto Press, 1992.

Williamson, H. G. M. "The Old Testament and the Material World." *EvQ* 57 (January 1985): 5-22.

Wilmore, Gayraud S. *Black Religion and Black Radicalism*. Maryknoll, N.Y.: Orbis, 1986.

Wilson, Robert R. *Prophecy and Society in Ancient Israel*. Philadelphia: Fortress, 1984.

————. "The Role of Law in Early Israelite Society." In *Law, Politics, and Society in the Ancient Mediterranean World*, edited by Baruch Halpern and Deborah W. Hobson, pp. 90-99. Sheffield: Sheffield Academic Press, 1993.

Wolf, Eric R. *Peasants*. Englewood Cliffs, N.J.: Prentice-Hall, 1966.

Wolff, Hans W. *Joel and Amos*. Philadelphia: Fortress, 1977.

Wolff, K. H., ed. *The Sociology of Georg Simmel*. New York: Free Press, 1964.

Wright, Christopher. *God's People in God's Land*. Grand Rapids: Eerdmans, 1990.

Würthwein, Ernst. "Die Josianische Reform und das Deuteronomium." *Studien zum deuteronomistischen Geschichtswerk*. BZAW 227. Berlin: Walter de Gruyter, 1994.

Yadin, Yigael. *Hazor, with a Chapter on Israelite Megiddo*. London: Oxford University Press, 1972.

Yeivin, S. "Social, Religious, and Cultural Trends in Jerusalem under the Davidic Dynasty." *VT* 3 (1953): 149-66.

Young, Iris M. "Self-Determination as a Principle of Justice." *Philosophical Forum* 11 (fall 1979): 172-82.

————. *Justice and the Politics of Difference*. Princeton: Princeton University Press, 1990.

Zajonc, Robert. "Aggressive Attitudes of the 'Stranger' as a Function of Conformity Pressures." *Human Relations* 5, no. 2 (1952): 205-16.

Zobel, Hans J. "Das Recht der Witwen und Waisen." In *Gottes Recht als Lebensraum*, edited by Peter Mommer et al., pp. 33-38. Neukirchen-Vluyn: Neukirchener Verlag, 1993.

INDEX OF AUTHORS

INDEX OF SUBJECTS

INDEX OF SCRIPTURE REFERENCES

DATE DUE

11/4/13			